FASTNESS OF FRANCE

'Those tawny terraced hills which rise as if there were a circumflex over the A in France.' So Bryan Morgan describes the Massif Central, the heart-shaped highland mass of that many-faced country.

It is a region of great mountains and young rivers, of ruined castles and romanesque churches enshrining black Virgins, of sunlight and of storms. Little known even to the French, it offers the leisurely unlimited fields for exploration and those hurrying south the temptation to a hundred lovely detours.

No book in English has yet described the whole area. *Fastness of France*—which has been written for fireside reading as well as on-the-spot reference and is meticulously equipped with maps and index —should meet that need for many years to come.

Y'a un long voyage à faire

Rodez (Aveyron): Cathedral tower, 16th century.

Fastness of France

A BOOK ABOUT
THE MASSIF CENTRAL

BRYAN MORGAN

CLEAVER-HUME PRESS LTD
LONDON

Some other books by Bryan Morgan

NOVELS

Vain Citadels—Heinemann
Rosa—Hodder & Stoughton
The Sacred Nursery—Hodder & Stoughton
The Business at Blanche Capel—Hamish Hamilton

NON FICTION

Men and Discoveries in Electricity—John Murray
The End of the Line—Cleaver-Hume

COMPANY HISTORIES

Total to Date—Newman Neame
Golden Milestone (Ed)—Newman Neame
Apothecary's Venture—Newman Neame

FORTHCOMING

Men and Discoveries in Chemistry—John Murray
The Railway Lover's Companion (Ed)—Eyre & Spottiswoode

CLEAVER-HUME PRESS LIMITED
31 *Wright's Lane, London W*8

© BRYAN MORGAN 1962

Demy 8vo, xvi + 279 *pages*
14 *maps,* 24 *pages plates*

Printed in Great Britain by
WESTERN PRINTING SERVICES LTD, BRISTOL

Contents

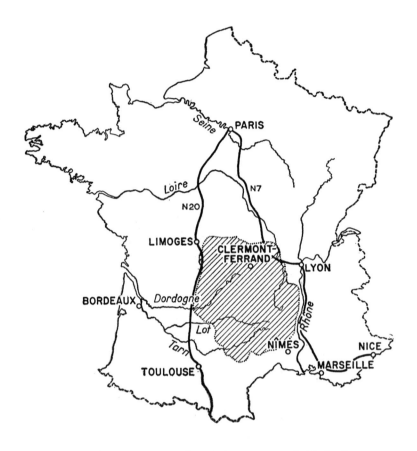

The shaded area represents the country of this book

Illustrations

Page by page the reader's attention is drawn, by footnote references, to any subjects which are illustrated.

vii

Illustrations

Bibliography and Acknowledgments

So far as my publishers and I know, there has never before been a book published in English (or, for that matter, in French) and designed to be read consecutively as well as used for reference, covering the whole of the central plateau of France. That is the *raison-d'être* of this one. But there is a mass of literature which deals with the region in whole or in part and from one aspect or another, if almost invariably in French.

First come the standard guides, written in note form and mentioning every obscure ruin and mountain track, which have lain on my desk beside eight or nine Michelin maps throughout the compilation of this book. The most comprehensive was the Baedeker *Central France*; but this was last edited in 1893, is now a collectors' piece, and is not likely to be revised and reprinted. Its descendant, the Guide Bleu *Auvergne et Centre*, though a mine of facts, is poorly provided with maps and very badly printed: furthermore, it covers only about two-thirds of the plateau (as well as a lot of Berry and so on) and leaves you to search through three or four other costly companion volumes such as *Cévennes* and *Hérault* for the extreme south and west. A similar objection applies to the green Michelin series, pleasantly portable and well-arranged (if sometimes over-glamourised) as they are: *Auvergne* covers only the north, and the absurdly titled *Gorges du Tarn* makes rather a jigsaw of some of the rest.

These latter are available only in French, and the current English-language guide-books to France, with the possible exception of a Blue Guide to the whole of the south, mention the plateau only marginally or sketchily. But you can at least obtain them all in this country. If you want to burrow more deeply, you will find in the bookshops of the Auvergne tourist-centres (if little else) numerous highly-coloured and highly-priced volumes of photographs or lithos

ix

of the region with a romantic linking text: these are tempting but rather unsatisfying and narcissistic, the *confiserie* of guide-books. At the other extreme, there may be a foully-produced but scholarly local monograph by some learned *abbé*. And finally, of course, every *syndicat* is stocked with informative folders and brochures, sometimes in rather inventive English: the former will usually be free and the latter sold at a subsidized price.

Of more literary discursions on the history, topography and sociology of the area, anything written by Ajalbert, Arbos, Artières, Balme, Balsan, Benech, Besson, Bossuat, Buracora, Charlier, Chamson, Cerel, Cortat, Farges, Gerbe, Girou, Jacoupy, Meraville, Murat, Nolhac, Pourrat, Raux, Raynal, the Réclus, Soleillant or Vilette is likely to be worth-while—though not up-to-date since most of these are, either through nostalgic choice or because they are long dead, 'period' writers. And this group in turn merges, through the poems of Vermenouze, to the imaginative works of Dumazet, Lucien Gachon (*Maria*), Paul Bourget (*Le Démon du Midi*, almost a *Lorna Doone* for the tourist trade here), Ferdinando Falve for the Cévennes, and—again—Henri Pourrat (*Gaspard des Montagnes*). All of these give vivid accounts of the old Auvergnat life. But the only fiction which deals with the Auvergne even *en passant* and which is available in English was (so far as my knowledge goes) written by George Sand or Maupassant.

Some of these remarks, however, apply only to the Auvergne proper; and its southern region—perhaps because between fifty and a hundred years ago it was more romantically off the beaten track *than* the Auvergne proper—has the distinction of having thrown up the only classic travel-books originally published in English which deal with any parts of the plateau. These are Stevenson's *Travels with a Donkey*, and two or three works—compromises between the comprehensive description and the cursory collection of essays— by Sabine Baring-Gould—whose other travel-books, significantly enough, were on Wales, Cornwall and Brittany.

Intermediate in time between these stands M. Bentham Edwards, a delightfully Victorian exploreress who carried her own teapot, taught Rhone boatmen and Caussenards how to use it, fortified herself with salt tablets and a rubber tub, and conducted a running war with Thos. Cook and the PLM: her *The Roof of France*, published at a time when the *Guide Joanne* did not even recognize the existence of the Causses, is in this same tradition. And finally, on its western rim, the plateau impinges on the Dordogne country of prehistoric grottoes and reputed gastronomic delights which has inspired more recent English writers such as Freda White (*Three Rivers of France*) and Philip Oyler (*The Generous Earth*).

There is hence no lack of documentation *as such* to the central plateau (the Guide Bleu alone quotes over a hundred sources); and this book would doubtless be a more thorough one if I had read more than a tenth of the above *op. cit.* Certainly any merits it has, though none of its faults, derive largely from the good offices of my personal friends in England and France who have advised on it: my greatest debt is, once again, to the acute eye and encyclopaedic knowledge of Mr J. H. Price. In addition, my publishers' colleagues Maurice Zarb, Jeanne Meuriot and Gavin Brown have devoted many hours to reading the proofs.

To the staffs of the *syndicats* of Clermont, Limoges, Brive and dozens of smaller towns, to hoteliers, railwaymen, commercial travellers, priests and other informants, and to the typists and cartographers who have battled with the orthographical and other difficulties inherent in a book of this kind, go my thanks too. But the greatest benefactor of all has been Mr Paul Edmonds, Managing Director of the Cleaver-Hume Press Ltd, who has put into every stage of this book far more passionate love and meticulous attention than any author has the right to expect from any publisher.

B.M.
London, 1961

The Photographs

Acknowledgment is gratefully made to the following sources, quoting where known the original photographers. Unless stated, their offices are in Paris.

Tournier, Rodez (1); P. J. Edmonds, London (2, 3, 5, 6, 26, 29, 39, 44, 46, 48, 51, 52, 53); Feher* (4, 7, 8, 15, 22, 30, 35, 36, 41, 42, 43, 45, 47); Abbé Malapert, Le Moutier d'Ahun (9); Georges Martin (Rapho) (10); Landau (Rapho) (11); Roubier (Rapho) (17); Gamet,

Lyon* (12); Marcano* (13); Goursat (14, 23); Viguier* (19); Karquel* (16); Touring Club de France* (20, 24); Commissariat Général aur Tourisme* (18, 21, 38); Barbara Riley, London (25); Les Artistes Paysagistes, Aigueperse (27); Ina Bandy* (28); Roubier* (37); Hélène Adant* (31, 40); Matchatscheck* (32); Mappus, le Puy (33, 34); André Gamat (Rapho) (49); Denise Bellon* (50).

Prints from the sources asterisked were kindly lent by the Photographic Archives of the Commissariat Général au Tourisme, and it is a particular pleasure to acknowledge the help extended to the publishers by Madame Cloutier de Mannoury and her colleagues in Paris and London.

The Maps

The key map on the following pages expands the sketch facing the illustrations list. It shows the principal towns of the Massif, its major roads, and its through-route railways. Departmental frontiers are also included, the Roman numbers show the approximate centres of the various chapter areas, and the grid of the relevant Michelin map-sheets is overlaid on the whole.

After the first page or two of every chapter (except the first) there appears a map of the region described in it. On these, the department-lines have been sacrificed to make room for physical features: in particular, the shaded zones roughly represent the ground more than 2,000 ft. (or some 600 metres) above sea-level. All the railways open to passengers are shown by ticked lines, and roads numbered up to N 199 in general by heavy ones. Other roads have been selected on the grounds of the access they provide to the localities shown rather than of their intrinsic importance or motorability. Similarly, the style of lettering of the town names suggests their regional importance rather than their absolute size. It should perhaps be mentioned here that one or two names that have an accepted English form are anglicized in the text but not on the maps.

These chapter maps have been compiled on the principle that they should show every place and feature mentioned in the section of the book to which they apply—and nothing else, except for a minimum of links to bordering areas. This has inevitably made for some curious shapes and unequal scales. But consistency seemed more important than beauty, and in any case it should be stressed that all these maps have been prepared to help the fireside reader to appreciate the lie of the land, *not* for guidance on the spot. For this latter purpose, the Michelin is essential.

The maps were prepared by P. J. Edmonds in collaboration with the author, and were drawn by P. J. Evans.

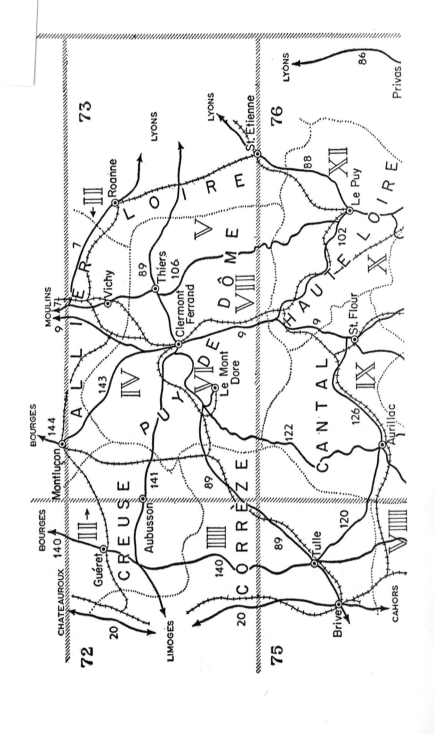

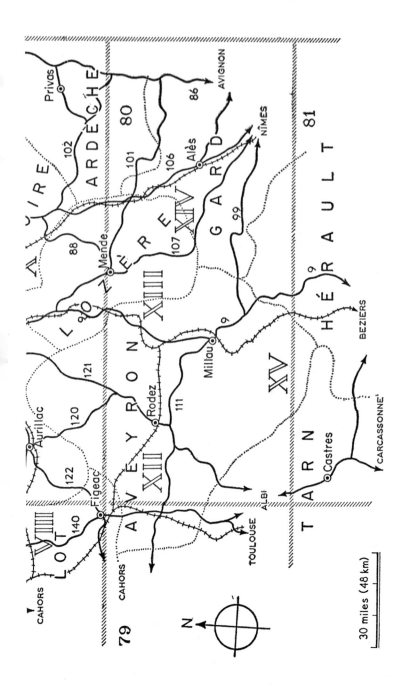

30 miles (48 km)

Introduction

The French hold, amongst other curious beliefs, that the British eat bananas with the skins on. We too have our misapprehensions. England and France have, indeed, long acted like lovers who cannot live apart or together. They have fenced and flirted, embraced and squabbled, but they have never quite understood one another. 'They order these matters better in France': '*Très snob, presque cad*': *le rosbif*: '*Oo-là-là, les nues parisiennes*': the cloud-cuckoo-lands of André Maurois and Nancy Mitford: at many levels and on both sides of the Channel the record is one of insecure grasps on the wrong ends of imaginary sticks.

Perhaps at last, though, both parties are beginning to pass from that adolescence in which the boy or girl next door seemed an ideal complement and have begun to recognize that in this long affair they have to live with *actual* qualities. Those qualities, however, are rarely expressible in a neatly-turned phrase; for Britain and France are neither identicals nor opposites. They are suggestively similar and devastatingly different; and almost every easy attempt to simplify their relationship breaks down at the crucial point.

But the time-worn image of male and female, lover and mistress, does, I think, have a certain validity. And it begins with the basic anatomy and physiology of the lands.

*

Take, then, the map of France. Scaled down, and maybe inverted, it resembles that of England-and-Wales at least as much as a short fat woman resembles a tall thin man. Brittany is Cornwall: Normandy Wessex: Maine the parklands of Somerset: the Loire valley that of the Thames. The north coast is our south coast, Picardy

Kent. ... And then one realizes that the French industrial north is in the wrong place, and it all will not quite work.

Furthermore, on moving south one passes through another distorting mirror and must exchange east for west so that the Landes may be equated to Lincolnshire, the Alps to the Cambrian mountains, and Cannes find in Blackpool the equivalent it deserves. Only at the end does a range stretching from sea to sea divide France (like England) from a land-neighbour.

Far-fetched, then, this parallel appears. But it points two morals. One is that in comparing the structure of the two lands many adjustments of scale and orientation are called for. And the other is that —county for county, in hills and rivers and cities—some kind of analogy *can* generally be drawn.

The analogy to our Pennines is that mountainous upheaval which lies below the waist of France, about as far south of London as London is south of John o'Groats; that upheaval which they call the central *massif* or plateau.

*

The Pennines have been termed the spine of England. Their counterpart is anatomically more akin to the womb or stomach of a land of which the Nord is the brain, the Ile de France the pretty face and Paris the mouth—a land which stretches arms from the Jura to Finistère and dabbles its toes in the Mediterranean and the Atlantic, whose breasts are Burgundy and the Beauce and whose heart Touraine. But the parallel is *only* structural, for these south-central uplands are not a womb in the sense that anything vitally French has ever come from them nor a stomach in the sense that they play any great metabolic part in French life (nor even, for that matter, in the sense that they are interested in good food).

This plateau has indeed been dubbed the least characteristic part of France. This is an exaggeration: culturally, as geographically, it is little more remote from Paris than are Brittany or Alsace and nearer than High Savoy or the Pays Basque. But it is certainly less travelled-over than any of these regions—and less written-over too.

Such is the justification for this book appearing at a time when the travel-guide in all its varieties is as much a staple of British publishing as the wine-guide. For our presses seem to hum with news from foreign parts. One recent season, for instance, a title appeared every fortnight on Iberia alone; and most of the intervening days must have been filled by a collection of hints on how to do Luxembourg on the cheap, a new series bobbing in Baedeker's wake, or the diary of the latest poet to travel from the Indies to the Andes in his undies. But there is hardly one book on the plateau to be found amid the dozens on Burgundy or Touraine or Provence, and on the travel shelves of our libraries there is too often a space where a survey of France's most central province ought to be.

I cannot claim to be elect to fill that gap: I am far too conscious of my limitations. I know, for instance, little of geology, ecology or even such obvious subjects as French history. I have not travelled every mile of my terrain on a bicycle, as did those parsons who produced the guides of more leisured and scholarly times. All I have tried to do here is to complement the formal guides by bringing together the facts which are common knowledge and by glossing them with impressions—brief, human, fallible impressions scribbled on the backs of hotel bills and second-class tickets—from those few months-in-years when I have lost myself in this purple centre and utter fastness of France.

*

For here a man *does* lose himself. Our Europe has uplands on every scale where the contours run parallel, the watersheds and valleys are sharply-ruled, the passes come neat and narrow, and one is always aware of which horizon will see the sun set or the Pole Star shine. Of such a type are the Chilterns or the Apennines. But there are also hills which form less an escarpment than a countryside. And to this class—which includes the Rhenish ranges, Connemara and the Alps themselves—belongs the great plateau which touches all the trodden lands from Touraine to Provence and from Beaujolais to Gascony yet which is itself so very little known.

On its heights boundaries double back on themselves, rivers box the compass before finding their last direction, hills indefinably steepen to mountains and ease away to upland plains again. Crossing it a hundred minor modifications obscure the greater changes which occur down meridians and along parallels: natural frontiers seem as unreliable as political ones are unrealistic: and one is tempted only to walk on and on, perhaps to find a sudden valley where one expected yet another *ascente pénible, peu pratique aux camions* or perhaps to cross the ridge and discover that this is the end—that half France and beyond lies below you arched with an infinite sky, that one has walked (as a friend of mine expressed it, a friend who once marched with rucksack on back from Nevers to the Rhone) off the face of this small planet.

Amongst the more perplexing features of such lawless lands is that it is too easy to sense where they begin and too hard to abandon them whilst some hint of their character remains. One smells the Wessex downs at Basingstoke, for instance; and one is reluctant to leave them even when the Severn promises delights beyond. But a book is a book, and a countryside is a countryside, and it is always a good idea to start by saying what one is talking about.

*

From Brive to Valence it is 175 miles; from Montluçon to the hills above Montpellier it is further yet; and most things included within a rough circle drawn on these diameters (as well as a few things without it) could be classified as belonging to the central plateau. In its largest sense, indeed, this covers some 35,000 square miles and fills a fifth of France (which is an area not far short of that of all England) with a single rock formation generally 2,000 feet or more above the sea and climbing above 6,000 at the highest of all wholly-Gallic peaks.

And it is—geologically speaking, if not always to the eye—one mass of land, created about five hundred million years ago from that herculean fold of granite which creased Europe like a bed-sheet and tossed up highlands from Cornwall to the Ardennes. It is hence one of the oldest parts of the whole continent, ten times older than the Pyrenees and gouged by the grindstones of time aeons before they arose. Of that pristine, dinosaur-stalked and palm-afforested form it could today be said that 'The wind and the rain have undone it again'. But this is only partially true, and the plateau remains a unique and recognizable table.

That table, however, is far from homogeneous. Vast areas of it to the south are not of granite but of limestone (and you know which kind of country you are in each time you wash your hands) in memory of those long millennia, some hundred million years ago, when it lay below the sea; and there are a dozen alien outcrops of sandstone and coal, of metal- or jewel-bearing strata, to confuse the land. On top of this it was, particularly in its north, the scene of an intense and basalt-making volcanic activity in the tertiary period which began about fifty million years ago with the rising of the Alps and which continued until men walked the smoking slopes, only a few tens of thousands of generations back. And on top of everything—literally on top—the usual migrations of surface soil have generated such local variations in the look and life of this great and ancient mound as to befog those who claim that geology holds any simple clue to topography.

For this reason, the plateau is a difficult area to define. No two Frenchmen, no two guide-books, have yet agreed on the matter; and I cannot hope to do more than inflame more outcries, particularly from those who know one part of the area well and will dispute the right of any other part to take its place here. In political terms perhaps five departments are wholly, exclusively and (as the tax-men say) necessarily of the plateau as commonly understood; but half a dozen more are mainly of it, and another half a dozen partially so. In geographical terms . . . Well, who can say whether the Berkshire and Hampshire downs are a single range or two, whether Salisbury Plain is one with them, or what truly divides them from the South Downs or the Chilterns?

In fact, I can give only two trivial hints to help a man to decide when he is in the Massif. One is to note the local paper most in vogue: this is always a significant guide to the regions of France, and I fancy that the terrain of this book corresponds closely to the circulation-area of *La Montagne*. The other clue is to listen to public clocks, or even some indoor ones. For everywhere in the plateau (but nowhere else in France save in the most Germanic of the Alps or Spanish of the Pyrenees) these sound first on the hour and then again a minute or two later. It is in two senses a striking fact, though none of the books I have read and none of the men I have talked to can explain this continental-upland tradition which can be only a few centuries old. Yet if I were writing a 'tec set in these heights, I would use the gimmick of the land where the clocks chime twice.

*

Since I am not writing a detective story but a descriptive book, though, I have not only to delimit my land but to divide it into regions. And that poses its only problems. For the component parts of the plateau are even harder to particularize than the plateau itself, and there is a vast confusion of terms and an entanglement of natural borders with ancient and modern political ones.

What, in the first place, *is* the 'Massif Central?' The term comes easier to the tongue than 'central plateau', and is certainly more evocative of the look of the land: one is almost willing to forget the inconvenient fact that the highlands fall much more to the south than to the north of the waist of France. But many purists would confine this term to the northern hills alone—to the Dômes, the Dore, and perhaps the Forez and its associates. Others would let it run down to the Cantals and even the Margeride, and others again all the way to Hérault. A fine example of this kind of arbitrariness is afforded by the otherwise well-thought-out Michelin guides, which call everything north of Rodez 'Auvergne'—but give to the south the indefensible regional name of 'Gorges du Tarn'.

To equate 'Massif' with 'southern Puy-de-Dôme' is certainly too pedantic. Perhaps my own interpretation is too loose. But it seemed to me that nothing should be allowed to obscure the fact that only on a geological map can one distinguish the purist's Massif from the surrounding massifs. It is all—with its dozens of ranges and hundreds of rivers and thousands of local names—all *massive*.

*

A later land-exploding force remains. For if the heredity of geology was the first factor to shape the plateau, the environment of climate has played at least an equal part. The wind and rain *are* angry elements here; and so the mountain-face has been split by many cataclysms, scoured and strewn by repeated ice and boulder-wrack, creased by the pressure of neighbouring mountains, gouged by water escaping into swift rivers, pock-marked and eroded by all the interactions of earth and air. Even in its present form it has been exposed for fifty thousand centuries to the expiring gasps of rain-laden Atlantic gales, to the hard dry breath of Africa, to the baking summers of a semi-southern land and the half-year-round snows of its peaks. Eastward it has recently had the young Alps for shelter: but to the south there is no range as high until one comes to the Atlas, to the west none until the Appalachians, and to the north nothing—nothing at all, up to the Pole.

This shared experience, though disrupting on the topographical scale, has imposed a larger discipline and unity on the wider Auvergne, even where the changes were so radical that the valleys were exalted and the mountains laid low. And so in this book (if only to avoid unbearable repetitions of one term) I have taken 'plateau' and 'massif' as almost synonomous and have drawn no arbitrary frontiers until the land has fallen away beneath me and the habits of men proclaimed that they were of Hérault or Berry or Perigord rather than of the uplands.

I only wish that there were an adjective or two to cover this region of which every part is more like its other parts than like the rest of France. But I will not be cavalier enough to call the Vivarais or Lacaunes 'Auvergnat'; and we will have to skate round *that* one.

*

'Auvergne'—the very word is like a bell. It is a school-bell, ringing the break from the geography to the history class. For though it strictly stands only for a medieval province now roughly represented by two departments, it has a dark ring which *ought* to cover all this high country which divides north from south, Langue d'oc from Langue d'oil.

The history, like the geography, is harsh and stormy. For the affairs of the men of the mountains have mirrored, if on a scale small in comparison with humanity's more recent disasters and trivial when measured against the cataclysms of nature, the tempests which are never far from Auvergnat skies. It must be confessed that these affairs are, in the wide view, only a tidy island for thesis-hungry research students to roost upon: Europe would probably not look much different today had the whole range quietly sunk in historical times and become an inland sea once more. Indeed, great hills tend to be more culturally barren even than great oceans. Men *have* to cross water; but any range less strategic than the Alps can be by-passed by traders and invaders alike—and, if its resources are fairly thin and its inhabitants demand only to be left alone, it commonly is. This is not to say that the Auvergnats are not proud of their rough island story. They are. So are the Welsh. But in the long run the stories don't matter that much.

If the history of man in the plateau is not vastly important, however, it is of some interest and considerable length. It has, indeed, been characterized as 'rich—but mostly tragic'. The western foothills, of course, contain the cave scribbles of those who died 30,000 years ago; and even the standing stones of the marginal mountains were lifted up in the dawn of the neolithic period, sixty centuries past. Some time in the ensuing millennia (and probably about the sixth century BC) the whole upland area was taken over from its primitive Iberians by invaders no less small, dark and strange—the once all-conquering Celts, the Gaels who named Gaul, here called Arvenes. They beat back some later colonizers described as Cimbrians. They had two kings with recorded names, Luern and Bertuit. and *enfin*, of course, *César vint*.

Even if he did so rather half-heartedly, even if the mountains were only loosely under the lictor's rod and only remotely responsible to the eagles of the *senatus populusque*, Rome drew up as its antagonist the one towering figure of Auvergnat history. This was Vercingetorix. His distinction is Boadicea's or Caradoc's—that of a hero who fought against impossible odds and lost. His symbolic importance is that of the secretive man of earth or sea driven back to a mountain fortress, wave after wave, by the invaders of the sun. His memory is green, for they still christen factories after him. And one fact emerges from his story—that in the first century before Christ the scattered clans of the northern part of the plateau had knit themselves into a tribal community whose capital was named Gergovia.

The legions imposed their own order, planted their wheat and vines, fought the faith (as represented by such disciples of St Denis as the mysterious, male St Mary) and burned the Auvergne's first martyrs. They bowed to the cross, and then bowed to the Franks. And after their departure, after the Indian summer epitomized by the great fifth-century bishop Apollinaris whose throne stood in the new capital of Clermont, the whole dark ages could show few darker parts than this which was repeatedly ravaged by Goths and Visigoths, Almains and even Saracens.

The south was dubiously held by the kings of Aquitaine or the Languedoc or bound in thin fiefage to the Spanish-affiliated dukes of

Perigord and Uzès: the north—always the archetype of the plateau—was autonomous (and virtually anarchistic) Auvergne: and all was largely given over to interminable tribal squabbles like that between Pepin le Bref and Duke Waif, border raids, and rebellions against Carolingian central authority and the tax-masters of the Holy Empire. Yet plodding even through this darkness there went—as in all such lands—the scholar-saints and the saintly prelates. They set up their hermitages on lake-islands or in subterranean cells, they shed a little light on a little space for a little while, they battled against obscure heresies, and then they died and left behind only Celtic legends and a litany of names feted in no calendar. But it was through them that the plateau joined so many of Europe's highlands as holy ground.

*

There was a tremoring of the leaves as men awaited world's end in AD 1000, with the first king of all France on the throne: the pilgrim routes were thronged, the Normans were marching south and driving sanity as far as Clermont, and little Aurillac itself had given birth to the ruling Pope. But full daylight did not break until the close of the eleventh century.

Then, suddenly, churches arose about the capital in that peculiar idiom of the romanesque which was born in Burgundy or the Saintonge but whose perfection is the one great contribution of south-central France to our culture—churches such as one could not ask better to visit or to pray in. Then dedicated men carved madonnas in wood as well as storied capitals in stone. And then in Clermont—Le Puy being deemed too small—pope and hermit together in the narrow streets proclaimed the first crusade.

Politically, most of the plateau now belonged to Aquitaine—the province, whose name is cognate with 'Basque', which was known in other times as Gascony-and-Guienne. And it was this affiliation which gave it that little hour of grace and *courtoisie* recorded in *Roland*, and which contrasts so wildly with the bloodthirstiness of its barons who killed for killing's sake. Even the Black Prince, even the Lion-Heart, even à Becket, even Henry V himself, were hardly gentlemen when they ranged the western foothills of the Auvergne.

There was at this time the possibility that France might become a united kingdom; but when the whorish Eleanor became free of her

9

imbecile Louis VII and in the middle of the thirteenth century married Henry II it passed to the devil-spawned house of Plantaganet—and so to the throne of England. The event rocked France; for it meant that London was to rule just twice as much of the *terre majeure* as did Paris. And even today it is a strange memory, lending an extra dimension to these battles long ago, that for that brittle hundred years or so in which the British took to drinking wine the whole western seaboard of France, from Flanders to the Pyrenees, was linked back by liege law to Westminster.

The next century saw the commencement of the Hundred Years' War. In fact this was not a war at all but only the angriest part of three centuries of blind brigandage, pointless pillage and tedious treacheries—the unhappy years of France; and was itself broken into two phases, at least so far as the Auvergne was concerned. Officially, however, it *was* a territorial squabble between England and her maritime colonies and the rest of France; and for long years after 1345 the castles fell to the west, loss upon loss from Crécy to Poitiers and Agincourt, until even Rodez was an English city.

In 1369 du Guesclin began the returning wave, and with his men beat back Sir Nigel and studded with quarrels the English gateways. But the great chance was lost, and it all did not end until the 1430's when Joan rode out of Lorraine to be greeted by a Clermont drunk with joy—nor perhaps until the final end of English rule in 1473, after which poor Mary Tudor had not even Calais to write on her wounded heart. And for that hundred years more the ravaged Auvergne was a rabbit-warren of plagues as well as of the looters, free-booters, professional brigands and carpet-baggers from England, Gascony, Flanders and Brittany who are lumped together under such names as *routiers*, *pillards* and *côtereaux*—blasphemous black-massers the lot, who drunk themselves vomiting out of chalices and dressed nuns in chasubles before ravishing them. Their captains— 'friends of God and foes of all men', like Cerrole the self-styled archpriest of the Society For Profit who sacked Avignon itself, had a certain grim nobility. But their men were the roughest of mercenaries. Fittingly, they called the Auvergne a *terre brûlée* in those days when even the cave-refuges were put to the fire and all war was civil war.

By 1550 a Paris-centred nation was at last emerging, the outcome as much of territorial barter as of conquest. But it was not until the Valois kings who began amid the splendour of Henri Quatre had tottered their last weary course, and not until after the confusing affair of the treachery of the constable of Bourbon, that the Auvergne was united for the last time to the crown of what is today called France. The people's first demand then was for the throne to rid them of the tyranny of such robber-barons as the one who levied two rates of taxes—both equally steep—on those who ate meat and those who did not. Louis XIV (a well-esteemed monarch hereabouts) did his best; for like the Louis before him and the great Henri himself he deemed the Auvergne castles 'nests for birds of prey'. But the lords proved harder to catch than mountain hares, and only one was actually executed. During these 'Grands Jours de Clermont', certainly, a good time was had by all, with barons being beheaded thirty at a time—in effigy. But the folk still had to pay their taxes.

*

After so many upheavals, which stunted the development of a gothic architecture and set the plateau centuries behind most of Europe, peace might have been expected to fall upon it and men be left free to enjoy a last *flamboyant* fling, the amenities now grafted on to their rude castles, and the vernacular verse of Gaudilhon, *Gens d'Armes*. If such peace did not come, if the renaissance here (as nowhere else in France) destroyed as much as it produced, that was largely due to the universal genius of the Celt for getting himself into theological trouble.

Four hundred years before, the south had been torn by the Albigensian revolt against Rome (miscalled a heresy, since it was not *about* anything) whose echoes still mutter through the curia and proscriptions of Holy Church. Now a deeper but equally witless schism was to rack the central mountains, and in its first twenty-seven years alone work more damage than all the Hundred Years' War. The battles which began in Geneva and St Andrew's and Wittenberg, insensate as they became, had an intellectual content: the protagonists on both sides had a clear belief, however far their emotions betrayed their faith. But the battles which raged throughout the southern plateau throughout the sixteenth, seventeenth and even middle-eighteenth centuries—no peaceful ones anywhere in Europe—had the curious quality that for the most part the neutrals alone understood the issues involved. And *they* soon lost their jobs, their manhood or their lives on orders from red Richelieu and his prelates of Paris.

For the lay historian there are two recognizable stages in this horror, as in the preceding one—from the St Bartholomew's Eve massacre of 1572 (which sounds like a gangster slaughter and unleashed the first phase which lasted nearly sixty years) until the Peace of Alès, and then from the revocation of the Edict of Nantes in 1695 until almost the Revolution. The first is associated with Merle and the Auvergne proper, the second with Cavalier and the Cevennes. But for the most part there was only a rabble of Jansenists (or Huguenots) and catholics, of black and white mantles, of conforming or protesting princes sacred or profane, who bashed at each other's skulls with unpleasant blunt instruments or demonstrated the equal futility of passive resistance to fanatics.

In general, the further the religious battlefields were from Paris the greater were the atrocities and the greater the confusion between ideological and territorial claims. In the southern Auvergne, for instance, the nobles looked to the protestants to help them sack the monasteries. And by the time they had all done, artillery had shot the tops off most of the five hundred and more strongholds which earlier contretemps had spared.

Truce came at last towards the close of the eighteenth century; and after five hundred years of guerrilla warfare times became comparatively peaceful—except for the soldiers of the crack Auvergne regiment, who marched in their violet uniforms to great glory in small wars. Even the Revolution (whose manifestoes as to the need to smash regional individualism could sell second serial rights to the Kremlin today) made little difference to peasant life, beyond the desecration of images—though less severely here than in much of France—and the division of the old provinces, principalities and dukedoms into tidy departments. D'Aussy's *Voyage en Auvergne* of 1788 suggests an only-just-awakening land, and indeed the most striking act of the last Bourbons and of Napoleon was a steady, unspectacular programme of draining marshes and improving roads. But the castles were still too far off the beaten track for anyone to class them as *monuments historiques*, the natural sites and sights were unremarked, and indeed it was little over a hundred years ago that the greatest change of all began, when the railways first steamed out of St Etienne.

*

The main lines did not conquer this terrible land, but they ended its deeper isolation. It could never be an easy journey from St Flour to Paris, any more than from Inverness to London; but from the middle-nineteenth century onwards it was at least not a matter of Sterneian tortures. Furthermore, branch-lines built at fabulous expense—and straggling roadside tramways too—allowed men to move beyond the confines of their *commune* more than once a year: these implied viaducts which are still the greatest in France and among the greatest in the world, though their present function is more as tourist-sights and to provide centres for fishermen and washer-women than as means of access. Even at the zenith of the railway age the Massif stood out on the map as a patch of white emptiness; but under the Third Republic there were new ways from here to there, though often such devious and ill-patronized ones that they have since been abandoned.

Still more important than the changes which passenger traffic brought to men's leisure were the patches of industrialism which the railways let in on their work. Timber and stone, everywhere for the asking, became industries rather than trades on the more accessible slopes: agriculture expanded: seams of coal and ironstone were opened up: and the plateau no longer lived by village crafts alone.

This railway-change was making its effects felt when Stevenson travelled the Cevennes. By the time Baring-Gould followed him a further development had begun, implying the addition to the industries of the Auvergne of a vast, invisible one. The air smelt now of dynamite and tar as the roads were straightened and surfaced: half a dozen touring clubs agitated for flea-bitten inns to give up the four-posters in the common bedroom, air their sheets, pave their latrines and prepare for a princess to rest her head in Le Lioran: and Martel (the founder not only of speleology but of all the modern cult of academic adventuring) and his colleagues had put the caverns and the stone forests of the south on the map of every Grand Tour.

13

The tourist age, with all its amenities and horrors, was making inland: one of its odder effects was the convenient discovery by local leeches of specifics in the well of every village panting to add *-les-Bains* to its name.

Before the Franco-Prussian war, the railways: before the Great War, the roads: and before the Little Great War (during which, of course, unscarred France-South-of-the-Loire was a scene of shame and heroism) a last change was under way. Water, falling thousands of feet from its sheds to the sea, had ever been plentiful in the middle hills—even at the seasons of late autumn and early spring when Alpine streams were frozen. But it had been put to no more use than the driving of random mills. Now it became another great industry, as the western rivers were blocked back into staircases by barrage above barrage, dam above dam, power-house above power-house until a fifth of all the energy of France was captured. For the third time in its history the plateau rang with nitro-cellulose, for the fifth or sixth with explosive smoke, for the ninth with the violence of change.

This last change is still upon it. It may be that, with all this skill with water, an age will dawn when large towns and starred hotels do not regard taps dry for all but a few hours a day as a summer necessity. It may even be that a quite new age of exploitation will come, for men are beginning to smell oil deep in the tangled strata. And so this intolerably compressed history of a countryside ends in the middle of . . .

*

. . . a sentence. And now one must render some account of the plateau today—of the plateau as a whole.

It is, of course, what nature and man, geology and history, have made it. The former has been, touristically, all to its advantage, for this is a land of stupendous scenic clashes. Rocks are cracked into chasms like mud under the sun, trees swarm up cliffs a quarter of a mile high and end abruptly as limestone deserts take over, white peaks of snow stand fairy-sharp above the purple plains, valleys sleep under a wind-domed sky which stretches out like a converse of the cosmologist's space, infinite but bounded. After this great legacy of nature it is almost an anticlimax (and, in the age of tourism, not

14

even more economically important) to note the other gifts of geology
—building-stone galore, enough coal and ore to supply a few valleys-
full of heavy industry, and the mineral waters which support the
spas.

The effects of the history of the plateau on its present state are
more complex. It has not made for material richness, but it has left
all the overlaid strata of man's past to be sensed if not seen. These
begin with prehistoric remains which are rather surprisingly localized, and move on to a smattering of Rome and its long Gallic
twilight: the coming of the Faith, in particular, is represented more
by legends than by artefacts. Then there followed that romanesque
recrudescence which shines through a dozen basilicas without peers
in Christendom and adds to the charm of many village churches
too: the tourist information here is that Auvergnat churches usually
stand open to worshipper and (*soyez decoreuse*) visitor, but that in
a few cases you must apply to the *curé* and that to view their special
treasures you usually have to pay quite an entrance fee.

Equally characteristic are the fortresses which accompanied them
so closely that often the church *was* the stronghold. A few of these
castles stand today little removed from their first starkness: more are
embellished with renaissance comforts: but most are ruined in
various degrees. A number are officially-owned (entrance costs rather
more than you would pay for an English stately home, plus a tip to
the guide), and a few remain inhabited (*on ne visite pas*). And if
their attraction is in general romantic rather than strictly architectural, if after the first two or three they become monotonous, there
is still something to be gained from the scaling of the conical crests
on which they stand which the more publicized chateaux of more
accessible lands do not give.

I cannot really dispute the general view that the later ecclesiastical
architecture of the plateau is disappointing, though one Ambierle
can atone for much gothic which is derivative, decadent or dim.
Domestic building followed even further behind; and despite the
manors built by the Polignacs and Ventadours, the Estaings and
Urfés, it never found a distinctive idiom until the days of the Charles-
Addams-like *art nouveau* of Victorian villas. But even this is not
without interest. There are half a dozen walled towns of the plateau
as perfectly complete in their late-medieval or renaissance form as

15

any in France; and those are not scraped museum-pieces but places as living from their ruins as the loosestrife sprouting from crumbling finials or from broken pediments more broken *que jamais*. In almost every village, too, one may turn a corner to find something small and charming—a seventeenth-century lava-stone doorway, an ancient madonna in a niche—which has been quietly there down difficult centuries.

*

If this were all it could still be argued that only in the romanesque age was Auvergnat art of European interest. But when 'art' is extended to include engineering, a new and modern period comes in with a thunder like pile-drivers. For it is equally arguable that the central plateau of France is one of the few parts of our world whose looks have been generally improved by the materials and methods of technology.

To say this is not to forget the horrors of Decazeville and the industrial valleys. But (and there is something very French in this), the Michelin stars Victorian railway viaducts indifferently with neolithic dolmens, and I think it is right to do so. The great bridges of the Massif—the bars of steel fingertip-touching their colossal piers of brick or basalt or granite, the lovely curving arches of stone—are not merely breathtaking (and, I think, beautiful) in themselves. They give scale to rivers and cliffs and gorges which might otherwise be too large to be seen: they frame a landscape too huge for human eyes: and they attest that men can not merely love this land but master it.

Britain did such great things a century ago; but France is still doing their like, with hydro-electric dams which are almost classed as *monuments historiques* before the cement is set. It is easy to make fun of this power-worship, but the barrages do most marvellously provide a modern-romanesque equivalent to the modern-gothic of the viaducts. The latter are impossible confections of stress and space: the former have the absoluteness, the patient Pharonic amassment, of a pyramid. They are just cubes of concrete piled one upon the other until the whole weighs perhaps half a million tons. But it is not merely that the schemes of which they form a part have changed the shape of a score of valleys and rendered half a dozen map sheets

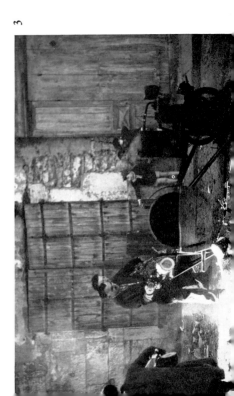

Much of the labour of the Massif remains as primitive as the shoeing of an ox or the cutting of wood (*left*) Marvejols. But a new age of technology is moving in (*right*) St Étienne Cantalès.

5

Saturday afternoon in the mountains: (*Above*), *boule* in the market-place, Le Cheylard and (*below*) the school train setting down its travellers, Eyrieux Valley.

6

out-of-date. They are themselves—whatever the word quite means—
architectonic.

*

It is, however, false to judge such things by aesthetic standards alone,
for they exist to give new life to France in general and to the plateau
in particular. And that new life is most desperately needed.

The existence of the peasant on his windy *montagne* was always
bitter, and for long years before the railways came it was his custom
to migrate in winter to valleys of higher wages and easier living.
(A letter of introduction proving exceptional hardship to the lowland
mayor's satisfaction was sometimes called for; but a wily Auvergnat
who could not afford the forty sous for a pedlar's forgery could
always put half a dozen snails in an old sabot, abandon the lot, and
then swear he had lost a habitation and six horned beasts.) But
with better communication these seasonal wanderers began not to
return, and so for a century or more the population of the Massif
has been steadily falling. The inland isle, like a true isle, has sent
forth its emigrants. And its people, like its waters, have flowed across
all France.

Today's labourer—and even more his wife—feels himself too old
at thirty to till the upland soil; and even if it means abandoning his
steading to winds which whistle as sadly over slateless roofs and
grass-grown thresholds as in Snowdonia he drifts away to the valleys,
the cities of the south, or Paris. There, working at some menial trade
itself traditional to the emigrés from his valley, he may keep up his
associations with the fervour of a London Yorkshireman. But (except
in the soft Cevennes) he returns only to die. The Auvergne's total
population today is just what it was five hundred years ago, and the
rural population is considerably lower: even the fertile Limagne, for
instance, has lost half its peasantry in the last hundred years.

Some French John Gunther of a demographer has calculated that
the greatest city of the Auvergne is Paris; and if his estimate that
one Parisian in ten was born on the high plateau is correct, then
there are three times as many Auvergnats in the capital as in
Clermont itself. It may be that the industries brought in by elec-
trification will do something to reverse this trend, but that is specu-
lation. And what is certain is that, since a region exists in terms of

not merely its landscape and buildings but its people, it is time to say something of this mountain-peasant-Frenchman-Celt of an Auvergnat.

*

A people marries and begets and dies, however: it changes down the generations as a church does not, and is always harder to characterize than a church. Nowadays too—even in backwoods parts—it changes fast. The traditional Auvergnat has been described in many different phrases, depending on whether one likes or loathes him, whether one is writing a come-hither travel-book or an objective survey. The general consensus, though, would seem to be that he is a Cornishman rather than a Welshman—a Celt of a dour, unlyrical and almost inarticulate kind, with his Celtishness much attenuated by intermarriage and standardized compulsory education. Despite the romanticism of George Sand, for instance, she found him 'meagre, gloomy, rough and angular'.

Regional guide-books love to generalize about populations; but for myself I have had to get way off the beaten track to find the Auvergnat noticeably different from any other Frenchman living a comparable life—and even then he was not *very* noticeably different. His patois, for instance, is intrinsically quite comprehensible, and when he is difficult to understand it is not because one word in a hundred may be regional but because he is either shouting his head off like any mountain-man and Frenchman or—on some solemn occasion like showing you the way—keening in the chant of a minor poet or a *Comédie* actress.

It is true that there are moments in the central plateau where you feel that men are living a life as primitive as an Irish or Spanish peasant's (which is to say as primitive as any in Western Europe), with all the virtues and vices that that implies. High on the misty rocks a fur-coated woman watches her cows, as immobile and slow-thinking as they. Through a wayside window one glimpses an interior like those gutted by the antique-dealers' sly tricks and now reconstructed in local museums—a single large room where a family is eating, breeding on straw mattresses in curtained bed-recesses (and notably interbreeding, for incest is rife hereabouts) and generally living amid the swine and the fowl, the smell of woodsmoke and cauliflower. But though these blue-smocked and black-sombreroed people may *live* medieval they rarely *think* medieval: the moustachioed neatherd probably reads *Paris-Match*, his widowed sister is dressed in professional black but his daughter wears big-city clothes, and under that smoky wooden ceiling, beside the great hearth, there may stand a refrigerator or even a television set.

Except in one respect—that of diet—the middle ages are over in even the highest of the high Auvergne. They began to die nearly a hundred years ago, with the advent of modern transport and communications. Their last throw came just before the last war, when the Auvergnat realized that his local costumes had become only a tourist gimmick and laid them aside, saying with dignity '*N'est bien porté que ce qui n'est habituellement porté.*' And now they have ended utterly. Thirty years ago Henri Pourrat blasted against the sickly popping-up of dead customs for tourists to gloat over, and today the amateur ethnologist on the hunt should be warned that he will not find folk on the high plateau, but only people.

*

There are, however, still certain relics of an independent way of life as characteristic as those humble work-clothes of denim and broad-brimmed straw hat which have outlived the festive costumes. Some are sincere if dusty local habits, largely connected with marriage and death, such as nuptial maypoles (these were supposed to remain in place until the birth of a child, but nowadays they often fall down first, and perhaps with encouragement), thistles pinned to widowed doors, and small greenhouses in graveyards. Others are less genuine, but rather more colourful.

For instance, the tourist agencies would have you believe that the land is forever lit by the flambeaux of the quasi-religious celebrations which go by such local names as *vagues, votas, baladoires* and *frairies*. Even allowing for my genius for missing great events by a day one way or the other, I cannot agree. There *are* a dozen or so outstanding festivals which survive and whose dates you can check from any handout, and colourful affairs they are in both their spiritual and their secular aspects. But they have nothing of the note of an Andalusian fiesta, and one senses behind them the local chamber of commerce and the desperate, ill-conceived French attempts to bolster up tourism. These bunfights, a bit more spontaneous than the Lord Mayor's Show and a bit less so than Guy Fawkes' Night, are chunks of folksiness which usually take the form of an enormous and platitudinous harangue from some visiting bishop, followed by the bearing of a figure of the Virgin up a mountain and down again, followed by a day or two of fireworks, drinking and immoderate dancing.

The latter will probably be to the best band the village can afford, or at least to an accordionist billed as a *grande vedette de Paris* and hired out by the travelling showmen who play their one-night stands all over France. The traditional music of the plateau—the plaintive-gay mountain strains of the lute-like *vielle*, the *cabrette* horn and the *musette* bagpipes (which 'have only one drone and are squeezed out but not blown') are still supposed to be heard in lonely villages of a Saturday night; but I have been to quite a few such places and heard nothing but Radio Luxembourg. Indeed, my only contact with these instruments—or with the sexy *bourrée* country-dance which goes with them—has been through an old man playing for money in the waiting-room of the bus station at Clermont-Ferrand.

I am afraid you will hear more spontaneous wood-notes in the pubs off the Irish end of the Edgware Road than in Besse-en-Chandesse—or, for that matter, in Galway. For the Celt is still losing, and men now keep up their ancient customs most fervently when in exile. The really exciting Auvergnat event today is the arrival of a circus sponsored by an aperitif company.

*

There *is* a local quality to the more everyday religious life of the plateau. For this is, possibly more than any other part of France, Our Lady's land: She has two hundred shrines here, and has held them for a thousand years. But here too the accent has changed. The black Virgins, with their legends of subterranean discovery which express so perfectly that *buried* quality of the plateau which reflects its peaks, are still held in some veneration. But the veneration is less, I think, than is accorded to the tawdry grottoes imitating Lourdes. Perhaps the Massif thirstily awaits its own apparition, as Ireland awaited one until that dubious business at Knock.

So too it is with the local saints of the plateau. Very few are represented in the official calendar, and for only a minority is there much evidence that they lived at all. Often enough even the reason for their unofficial elevation is obscure: they simply escaped martyrdom by Vespasian's legions, or defied gravity as Celtic saints did so universally. But great churches were raised above their relics, cities were christened from them, and their legends were entered in many local litanies.

Today their reputed bones still lie in deep unlighted crypts and their grisly remains are enshrined in monstrances of curious device which yearly grow greener in obscure sacristies. But few candles burn to them, and the votive plaques erected since 1900 surround a mass-produced iconography which does not differ much from Tourcoing to Toulon—Joan of Arc flag-wagging, Little St Theresa and the Curé of Ars simpering smugly at each other, and (*why?*) St Anthony of Padua.

Yet the Faith in the central plateau remains not quite the Faith elsewhere. In the first place, the proportion of protestants in those lands south of Clermont which took the reformation most bitterly is still the highest in France. It never approaches parity; but in many small towns the evangelical kirk challenges the catholic church in size and there is a streak of passionate puritanism everywhere. This rivalry does not result in any rallying to the colours as in Alsace, however, and in fact observance anywhere in the plateau is rather indifferent.

Perhaps men are worn out by the ancient struggles, for even the village atheist seems to have quietened down in the last seventy years. But I *have* detected a curious and vernacular note in the Masses said in these parts. Students of liturgy, fascinated by the way in which the same strict canon can be given totally different accents in Athlone, Granada, Rheine and the Brompton Oratory, might well care to look in on Mauriac one Sunday morning.

*

And what do they do after Mass? The work of the plateau-men is obvious enough—husbandry (mostly dairy-farming) to the extent of ninety per cent in some departments, timber and stone-cutting, the usual service trades such as clearing roads or snow, heavy industry in a few pockets, light industries where they have been planted. But what, for instance, does a peasant's life include except watching cows and urinating?

One's first impression is that the only answer to these idiotic questions is—'Sleep'. Nowhere, even in France, do shutters go up so early as in the Massif. Except in major cities the cafés start emptying at eight-thirty and are deserted by nine—when the French family on holiday is itself ready to call it a day and the *patron* begins to lock up. It takes a brash personality to demand a drink much after that, and a dogged walker to find even a packet of Gauloises. Often enough—even in provincial capitals—I have been driven to bed like a child while there was still light in the summer sky though none in any window; and I have loved England then for those licensing laws which ensure that there is life in the remotest village at the scandalous hour of ten-thirty p.m. But in fairness, of course, this is a country ruled by the cockerel and the milch-cow, a country which wakes at five in the morning and where '8' would look outrageous on a commercial hotel's call-board.

You can forget at the start about art and conversation and politics and all that sort of rubbish. But the men of the plateau *do* have some leisure and killtimes. There is nothing remarkable about their indoor or café sports: they comprise, as everywhere in France, playing violent and incomprehensible card games, dicing for drinks, pin-tabling, watching men ride bicycles in circles, shouting down a radio which is playing the ten-year-old numbers from that American musical which you missed in London five years ago, and arguing loud and long about the time of the train (which must be either 8.30 or 4.30), the distance to the next town (which you know to be fifty kilometres even without the map: it always is) or how many beans they had for dinner—with all these arguments punctuated by schoolboy raspberries.

Organized outdoor recreation is curious in that it centres all the year round on the elliptical football, whether handled by thirteen or fifteen amateurs or professionals: there should surely be a statue to Dr Arnold (or to that reverend gentleman whose name I forget but who is buried in Menton) in every town square between Moulins and Narbonne. And on the individual level there are—in addition to *le tennis* and *le golfing* for the tourists—three very French pastimes even more popular in the plateau than elsewhere. These are shootin', fishin', and bowlin'.

*

The opening of the *chasse* in September is a very great day, and as ritual as an Aubusson tapestry. For despite the fact that Auvergnats have a Teddy-boy fondness for knives too, guns are their great love. There is, after all, a general association between mountain-folk and firearms, and it is not for nothing that (since its own county regiments no longer exist) the Auvergne contributes generously to the *Chasseurs Alpins*.

The monomania of this annual slaughter, indeed, recalls the American hunter rather than the *sporting milord anglais*. Suddenly every bus is invaded by men with guns, optimistic canvas bags and huge snuffling shaggy dogs. Cartridges are sold across tobacconists counters, and for the seven months through to April the double blast of the 12-bore rings loud down the valleys and the boasts of the sportsmen (there is no real English equivalent to *chasseur*, of course: not huntsman or marksman or shootsman or even gunman) almost as loud in the pubs. To an outsider, the results rarely look worth this expenditure of cordite—for it is mostly pretty rough stuff, rabbit and rook with hare and pigeon as big game. Still, his shot-gun is commonly the most valuable possession of the Auvergnat farmer, and there *are* pheasant and partridge for the bagging across huge afforested areas of common land.

If shooting is coarse, fishing can be fine in two senses. The Sioule, the Vézère and a dozen others are among the great trout rivers of the world, with crayfish ('easy and amusing to catch . . .'), gudgeon and other game as well: even salmon are not rare in the Allier. It seems odd that the products of this cold-blood-sport come to the restaurant table so rarely and so expensively, but some say the rivers are being fished-out. Meanwhile, most of their vast mileage is free or available at a florin or so a day, and the *pêche* alone might provide a good enough reason for an English enthusiast to spend his holiday hereabouts—when he would also see the rare phenomenon of Frenchmen keeping quiet. But this book is not the place to set out all the local rules of season and size—nor even to classify the centres, for that is done in every pocket tourist-guide.

As to bowling, this naturally bears only a cartoon-like resemblance to the plimsolled game played on cathedral-close lawns under the elms of England. The whole point in France is that one chooses as rink the dustiest, flintiest, bumpiest bit of the village square, and the general technique is more akin to that of skittles or ninepins—local variants of which, in some Auvergnat villages, eclipse *boule* itself in popularity. But there is skill in the game for all that; it is a genuinely vernacular one, played by children in their school breaks as well as by greybeards in the cool of the day; and it has its beauty too.

The sound of cricket bat on ball brings back my strawberry summers. And the clash of *boule* on steel cannon-*boule*, though heard perhaps in the wastes behind the quays of Calais, recalls to me many June nights when I have sat under planes festooned with naked electric bulbs and swooping martins and have heard, behind those thuds and clanks and cheers, all the sounds of summer in the Low Auvergne.

*

These last pages have spoken of the private life of the hills. But they have inevitably spoken of it as understood through a stranger's senses, and in any case this book will be read mainly by those thinking of *visiting* the area, probably for the first time. For them, the three time-worn questions are: 'How do I travel about?'; 'How do I eat and sleep?'; and 'What's the weather like?'

In answer to the first, one could crack back that one can travel by any method one chooses from helicopter to camel-back. But it is a reasonable supposition that most explorers (*must* one keep saying 'tourists'?) aiming to cover more land than can be done by taking a single town as a centre will own some private mechanically-propelled vehicle—and most likely what *I've* never owned, a car.

It is hence not for me to give motoring tips; but of course one should remember when approaching these heights that the flat, straight, poplar-lined roads beloved of the English motorist are just not there. Whether yours is a Jag, a dearly-loved antique picked up for £25 from the scrap-yards and done-it-yourselfed, or a cosy family Austin, it is as well to be ready for the fact that the N20 is *not* the A40. The Malverns are mere bumps in the road from St Flour to St Etienne: the Cat-and-Fiddle divides every trivial village from the next in the Forez: and you must pass through Glencoe ten times between Clermont and the sea. She may be a good little bus, but if you try to take it in top the radiator cap will go higher than the cap of the Puy de Dôme. Don't include agoraphobics or sooth-seekers in your party. Don't be put to shame by the nun off to do a bit of district-nursing on her power-assisted bicycle: her habit isn't as heavy as it looks. And don't try to copy the local bus-driver either: he knows every twist.

Look to your tyres and brake-drums then: don't think the Monte Carlo rally is a kind of French driving-test: and light a candle to St Christopher if you will. But for the competent driver (and he *must* be competent, for caution is no substitute) who is aware of his own and his car's limitations, the Massif holds no special terrors. The roads are inevitably twisted and twisted again to climb terrible slopes and follow pinched defiles: inevitably too they are sometimes so narrow that if another car approaches you must stop and if a lorry approaches you must retreat. But even the tertiary routes are adequately metalled (they are far better, for instance, than their Highland-Scottish equivalents) and engineered with an ever-revised balance of utility and economy.

In any case, you will have the 1/200,000 Michelin maps in the dashboard pocket to warn you what is coming. *Pas de piston, pas de pot de vin,* they say: I have certainly received neither from the company, and have increasing reservations about their red hotel-guide. But I must here insert an unpaid puff to the effect that these are the best motoring-tourist maps I know. The 1/1,000,000 *grandes routes* sheets are fairly useless except for the commercial travellers and overlanders for whom they were designed. But the larger scale gives the sightseer-driver better-selected detail than our own quarter-inch ordnance survey. It still costs only 2s a *carte*—and since this is the first price I have mentioned, it is worth noting that when this book was finally revised French prices, even of tourists' needs, seemed to have achieved some stability and the heavy franc stood at about 14 to the pound. And to my mind it represents the best bargain in France.

As to the general conduct of your *auto*, ask the British motoring organizations. It is a good two guineas' worth.

*

But we do not all have cars, nor even motor-bikes, nor even one of the pony-breed of scooters and mopeds. (These, incidentally, are perfectly practicable in the plateau and in fact form the inhabitants' standard means of communication, since the ordinary push-bike is as much trouble as it is worth except for the Tour de France athlete or the ingenious traveller willing to start every excursion with a train trip to the top of a mountain.) We may dream of following Stevenson on his donkey, or even of hiring a caravan, but that is the kind of thing which never quite comes off. And so much of my own travelling of the plateau has been done by local bus and train.

This has usually been achieved in the face of discouragement from tourist and transport offices which believe that once you get off the few major railway lines you are at the mercy of the market bus taking the *gens du pays* to the nearest big town at 6.30 a.m. and back at 4.30 p.m. The picture is not, however, quite as dark as the French mania for pulling up branch-lines and 'co-ordinating' buses has tried to make it—nor as official sources pretend that it is.

First, as to how to get there. Two main lines out of Paris skirt the Massif—to the west through Limoges to Toulouse, to the east down the Rhone from Dijon to Marseilles. Each takes a day and night express (and maybe a midday one in summer) which will get you down from Paris to a kicking-off point in about six hours. They loosely connect with the London boat-trains, of course, giving a total transit time of about eighteen hours at a single adult fare of some £8 second, £12 first. There are also the directer but rather slower lines to the Clermont area which continue—even more slowly—right through the heart of the plateau. On all these routes there are through cars and sleeping-carriages which are interknit with such ingenuity that, however far off the beaten track your destination station is, you can get there from Paris in less than twelve hours— and probably sleep undisturbed all the way, if you have the temperament and the £2 or so *couchette* supplement.

There are a few long-distance coach services, but they are infrequent and more expensive than the railway. Air travel too is not particularly practicable unless you happen to be starting from North Africa, though a British private operator runs direct flights to Vichy. And so it will probably come back to the SNCF, in which context it is worth remembering that there are several cross-country *directs*—

from Toulouse or Bordeaux or Limoges to Lyons or Geneva or Marseilles—which give the plateau a semi-express service off the Paris routes and which pass through spectacular country where every maddening cutting is followed by a fine embankment.

*

Once you have got to the region you will be mostly at the mercy of branch railways and forever consulting your hotel's *Indicateur Chaix*. Those lines which remain have a passable service (though one anathematized in the nineteenth century, when it was better than today) of about three railcars daily—though the plateau is one of the last hide-outs of the unbelievably slow goods-cum-passenger train. It is only on a few surviving light railways that you will be driven mad by the nonsense of 'Fridays-only-also-on-market-days-as-far-as-Villefranche-except-the-third-of-the-month-and-may-be-cancelled-without-notice-anyway'. Worth investigation, if you are concentrating on one small area, is the possibility of a holiday-runabout type of ticket.

The rural bus service (which works out rather more expensive than second-class trains, especially if you have children) is less bright, and seems to exist mainly for the benefit of housewives, garage mechanics, priests and (*why?*) sailors. Nowhere is there anything approaching a fixed-interval service, and only too often there *is* only that one bus a day, perhaps starting (since it has a 150-mile journey to make) at an hour when no holidaymaker is anxious to be on the road. Yet somehow or other—maybe deviously, maybe at inconvenient times and after a long wait, but rarely retracing my steps—I have managed to get almost everywhere I wanted by little buses piled high with cheeses and cauliflowers and mail, buses with bicycles or easy chairs on the roof, buses with a new-born lamb in the boot, a stack of cartridges on the hot engine-housing and two kegs of wine kicking round the gangway, buses in which I (bound from terminus to terminus) have been the only passenger going more than a couple of stops, buses with the drive on the wrong side because of the gorges, but buses which were still *correspondances* SNCF and which connected up very neatly all across a lonely land.

You will have to inquire locally about them, hunting from café to café, for only an arbitrary selection appears in the official timetables. You will have to ascertain the stop by hearsay, taking the average of three opinions '*A l'ancienne gare*': '*Non-non-non. Pour Decazeville? Pour Decazeville c'est en face de la Poste*': '*Pas les samedis*': '*Ah, d'accord. Café des Sports, alors*': '*Café Guillaume.*' '*Hotel Lion d'Or....*' But it is a vernacular way of getting about, affording many refreshment stops and charged with that ritual significance which mountain country always lends to its means of communication—to the telephone, the post, the taxi.

*

Walking in (or over) the plateau may be done for two reasons—perforce to reach an objective which cannot otherwise be attained, or for pure pleasure. Either way the locals will think you are mad to attempt it, just as you will think *they* are mad to spend all day watching a goat which is tied up anyway. You will both have to get used to that.

Those walking from necessity may be doing so for several subpurposes. There are the tourist attractions—notably, of course, the great mountain-views—which can *only* be reached after a last few miles on foot: it can be a gruelling climb, especially for us portly ones, but never dangerous where the well-known peaks are concerned. Again, there are the times when the explorer trusting to public transport has to cover five or fifteen miles on foot to take in some castle perched between one bus-route and another: this is mere road-work, with not much to be said about it except that (*pro*) there is usually a view coming up and (*con*) there are a lot of twists and turns and it can be a long way between drinks. Finally, of course, the car may have broken down.

If the walker-for-pleasure is a valetudinarian taking a little stroll before dinner in Châtel-Guyon he will find posted paths with litter-baskets all the way. But the hobnailed tramper will have to go largely by guess and by God, by his compass and his bump of locality. The Massif is not colonized Alpine country: providing tough untidy scrambles rather than formal climbs, it has few defined and blazoned tracks and once one leaves metalled roads one is in a wilderness of every horror known to the hiker. Pasture turning to bog-land: streams just too wide to jump, just too deep to ford, and with no bridge for miles: shapeless forests: barbed-wire estates full of gunmen and (one suspects) mantraps: these are everywhere. It would not matter so much if there were universally good walking-maps of the area. But in their absence one must pick off the Michelin something as attractive-looking as those tracks along the Cantals which run almost level for fifteen marvellous miles above the 2,000-ft contour—and then trust to the sun in the sky, the moss on the trees, and the hope that the mist will not fall with as little warning as rain in April.

*

If there is only this to say about walking in the plateau, there is even less to note concerning boating there. One guide publishes a map of navigable waterways in the Auvergne, from which it is quite clear that there are no navigable waterways in the Auvergne. Not even the French ever drove a canal through these parts; and the rivers, though often providing an *entry* for the canoeist, become impracticable except for the most dedicated as soon as the great hills begin. Shallows, rapids, waterfalls, weirs and millraces and (now) hydro-electric dams make the upper Dordogne—for instance—one long portage, as unrewarding to those who like a boat to keep afloat as its lower reaches are attractive.

There are small craft of all types for hire (though not cheaply) on many lakes and reaches, including all the famous ones like Lac Pavin and the Tarn Gorges. There are grottoes and so on which can *only* be seen from organized boat-tours. And, in this context, it is worth recording that in high summer the waters of these parts (so warm-cool and bright, with clean gravel shores) can provide entrancing bathing. One will not perish for lack of water—though, three times further from the sea than it is possible to get in Britain, one may suddenly contract a midnight nostalgia for the sound of gulls and sirens. But a connected aquatic progress is *peu pratique*, and to attempt one is best left to the fanatical canoeing schoolmaster.

*

I have devoted a good deal of space to the individual travellers who believe in finding their own way about, and still not mentioned either hitch-hiking (which may be indulged in with reasonable chances of success by both the young who favour this kind of begging and by those who find it thrust upon them) or taxis (which can be found in almost every village and cost about 3s a mile). Such enterprising people particularly need to know what they are in for. But it would not be fair to close the subject without mentioning that there are in summer a vast number of conducted tours arranged round the accepted attractions of the plateau.

Of course there are: you will find such things in any holiday area. The office with its blackboard announcing day and half-day trips in pastel chalks (Monday afternoon the Puy-de-Dôme: Tuesday the Tarn: Wednesday the spa-circuit: Thursday evening a bit of *son-et-lumière*): the sharrer (one always thinks of the things as 'sharrers', even when they are equipped with vista-domes and chromium ashtrays and music while you watch): the gabbling guide ('Don't look left, the view's *this side*'): the discreet stops for natural needs: these are not much different from Ramsgate to the Rhine, except that the French like to set out at seven a.m. and spend four hours over lunch and that their trips tend more to shade-off into regular bus services. It is hard not to squirm; but these tours do open up the country to the nervous or sedate, and even for the individualist they provide the best way of seeing some celebrated spots miles from public transport and not easy of access even by private car. They operate not only from the plateau's own tourist towns but from such outlying centres as Tours and Limoges and Montpellier; and working from only a couple of cities, I think, one could with their help see in a fortnight all the three-star (and most of the two-star) sights of the Massif. It is only the Massif itself which would, somehow, slip away.

For it is not wholly for the bad that public transport in the plateau is so infrequent. This is not a land to be skimmed over so much as delved into as deeply as time and resources permit. And, having said that, it remains to consider how one will fare when *not* on the move.

*

Unless you live at millionaire level on an expense account—and even if you do but have interests beyond lunch and dinner—eating in the plateau is a matter of refuelling rather than of gastronomy. It would be possible to plan a whole trip—perhaps guided by the Trust-House-like *Logis de France-Logis d'Auvergne* sign—in which you could spend thirty shillings a night on overfeeding as well as you could anywhere; but you would have to dedicate yourself exclusively to this object. On tour with any other interests you must take the ordin-

ary level of Auvergnat cooking—and all that can be said of that is
that it is rather worse than the ordinary level of cooking in French
rural hotels, and decidedly worse than the ordinary level of cooking
in English country inns. No matter how cultured your palate, how
deep your pocket, how apparently objective and trustworthy your
guide-books, or how remorseless your effrontery, it will make little
difference above the 1,500-foot contour except in a few selected hotels
in a few sophisticated centres at the height of the season. Forget the
nostalgic nonsense about that vine-hung inn by the river where old
Madame X serves her unforgettable regional specialities for a song.
This is what you will most probably get in the plateau, as in much
of backwoods France, if you are there sharp on 7.30. . . .

Menu à 7f.
Potage
(Potato soup: no salt. Auvergnats regard cabbage soup as a real treat)
Jambon d'Auvergne
(Dry, uncooked, semi-smoked bacon. It may be tinned)
ou Tripoux
(stuffed sheep's feet)
Biftek—Pommes Frites ou Légumes en saison

(The northern Auvergne being beef country, you would have thought
they could have cooked the steaks which come up as remorselessly in
Aigueperse as in Alice Springs. They sometimes try; but the gristle
usually defeats them, for all the best cuts are exported. In any case,
it usually comes to the table mooing. The French, like the Americans, have yet to learn that *cooking* is one of civilization's achieve-
ments and that meat tastes better than blood.)

Salade
(Grass soggy with vinegar)
Fromage ou
Corbeille de Fruits
(Grapes)
Suppléments et Spécialités
Truite—4f.

(If they are in season, at the right size and all that, these may be worth the 7s. Otherwise, though notices proclaiming their merits are posted all over town, they will be such cast-offs that the kitchen has not even taken the trouble to gut them.)

The brighter side of this picture is that now and then the chef will throw in something he does quite well, like a good terrine, a *coq au vin*, or *pâtisserie*. There may also be the *friture* of the local river, well worth the labour of eating. But this does not add up to a picture of a land of plenty, and the cold fact is that the cooking of the plateau—tied as it is to a peasant diet of bread and potatoes—is always unimaginative and often bad. Do not be misled by all those enamel *panneaux* outside the door: half the recommending clubs— too numerous anyway—have been framed, and the other half have to suggest *something*. For here a hotel which does boiled potatoes in addition to fried ones is a *relais des gourmets*, unripe walnuts are a *spécialité du pays*, and a town with two restaurants offering a slight choice is a *vrai centre gastronomique*.

*

To be more positive there is one commendable thing—the plateau's *plat de fromages*. Sheep and goats as well as presentable cows abound, with the result that all kinds of cheeses are made on the heights. Some are imitations of Gruyère, Touraine *chèvres* or the like: even fondu is prepared in this quasi-Alpine region. But in its own right the Massif can claim one classic (Roquefort, of course), and several flavoursome vernacular cheeses which find their way to the more eclectic restaurants of Paris—and sometimes to the grocers of Soho too.

There is the rubbery-textured but characteristic *bleu d'Auvergne*, for instance—the subtlest of its breed, punctured with little holes, veined as thinly as a Victorian belle and as mildly blue as a March sky or a family-panto joke. There is Ste Nectaire, which pleasantly recalls Port-du-Salut, and—blue again—the strong-tasting Ambert (watch for wild life in this one). And there is Cantal, which to my mind is one of the great cheeses of Europe. It is a dense thing, of which the patrician breed is marked by long striations like those of our own splendid Leicestershire: even the coarser, mousetrapped varieties have a characteristic tang, not unlike that of the glorious Caerphillys.

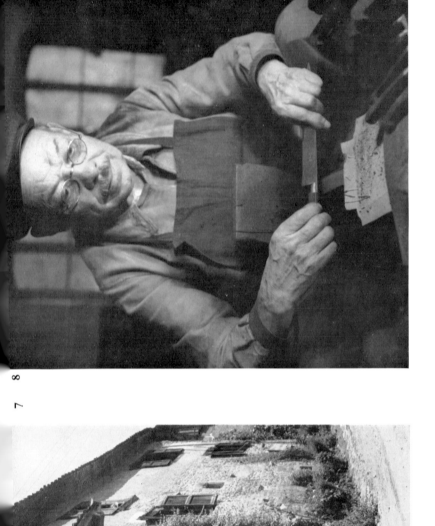

7

8

The caption of the photograph (*left*) reads *Ambert: Fabrication du Papier*: it is not a busy trade; but the knife-grinder of Thiers has still a useful job to do (*right*).

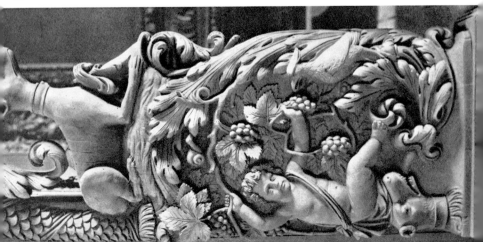

A detail from the carvings of le Moutier d'Ahun (*left*). Not far away in Aubusson tapestries woven with a comparable skill are designed by the great

That is all I want to say about the food of the central plateau—except to add the odd bit of information that *un auvergne* is French for Yorkshire pudding. There are various purported specialities—chocolates, almond rock and so on—which measure up to English mass-production standards. But when they mention them I just smile into the camera, remember the patient labours with *tome* and *forme*, and say 'cheese'.

*

As regards wine, the situation is at least interesting. You can drink, as in France in general, on three levels. The highest comprises the standard international bottles, priced at only a little less than you would pay in equivalent English establishments. The middle range embraces the named, semi-local vintages which mostly come in from the edges of the plateau—from the Limagne or the Limousin, the Languedoc or the Roannais: these will cost at the table about 7s a bottle, the price an English grocer would charge did he stock them, and some provide noteworthy experiences. And at the bottom of the scale there are the *ordinaires* which—let us face it—we all have to drink for most of these hard times. When they are real *vins du pays* and not Algerian imports, these have their own plebeian hierarchy. The *rosé*, at 4s in a restaurant, is the best risk, for it is always innocuous and often charming: sometimes it has a tawny colour and a nutty, muscatel-type flavour which recalls a light sherry and lasts well all through a meal. The *blanc*, at 3s can be decidedly rough; and as for the 2s 6d *rouge* . . . Well, as I have said, wine is always *interesting*. . . .

In addition to these rude potations, befitting a land whose speciality is water rather than wine, the plateau throws up its *boissons diverses*. The only ones specific to the area are aperitifs made from the bitter *gentiane* of Puy-de-Dôme and Cantal, which is a kind of sunflower which looks like flax and is no relation to the Alpine gentian: these medicaments are unlikely to appeal to the non-French palate. But in the Velay and elsewhere they brew their own Chartreuse-like liqueurs, notably those flavoured with verbena—pleasant enough tipples, these, but rather sticky and not among the great boozes of the world.

*

This, then, is no country for those who cherish the illusion that French *haute cuisine* is to be found in every farmhouse—or that, when found, it is really worth the effort. But the above distressing account is only true in general, and I know of a dozen or two reasonably-priced tables in the plateau memorable for one quality or another.

My publishers have asked me to indicate them. Reluctantly, I must say 'No'—at least *en principe*, which is what the French say when they are about to break a rule. In the first place, everybody has different ideas of value-for-money. In the second, I want to duck away from angry come-backs from dissatisfied clients. And in the third, old Mme Leblanc of the *Grand Cerf* dies and bequeathes her hotel to an unimaginative chain, while across the square the grim-looking *Commerce* changes its ideas and takes to gingham and gastronomy. It is the job of the annuals to keep tourists primed of such things; and even *they* often make a dewy-eyed mess of it.

All that I can try to do throughout this book, then, is to indicate certain centres where the visiting fireman may dine not too disastrously. They come up rather arbitrarily, these townships where the two hotels decide to become rivals rather than form a cartel. But when they do you will get a better meal a whole franc cheaper than elsewhere. For it is a dire fallacy to believe that French eating is better value off the beaten track than on it—or, indeed, that any enterprise can thrive without competition.

*

There is one more blast which must be delivered against contemporary catering in France and the Auvergne. It concerns a subject which I would like to see given far more publicity in travel-books and travel-columns. For I do not think the English traveller is as yet quite aware how far the so-called 'American' custom of demanding that you eat your evening meal in the hotel where you sleep has spread in recent years.

You arrive in Villeneuve, for example, and on your way into town you pass a restaurant (*sans chambres*) where the local populace is licking its lips in pleasant surroundings over what—as you can see from the card outside—is a delicious menu. You make a mental note, and then find the one classified hotel of the place—which, as a hotel, looks reasonable enough. Maybe you check in your Michelin or other guide as to whether this *exige le dîner* or not; but the books are not at all reliable on this score. Then you ask *madame* if she has a room.

'*Souper?*' she snaps without looking up, '*manger?*' And now you are in an intolerable situation. Maybe there was a yellowing menu outside announcing a wretched meal for 10f: more likely you just see through to the dining-room—to the peeling yellow distemper, the greasy table-cloths and the one miserable resident shivering in the corner under the one dim light, with on his left a chipped plate on to which has been flung a mess of concrete artichoke, bloody brains and weeping camembert, and on his right a glass of chemical beer because he knows better than to attempt the wine.

Shall you then lie that you have already eaten and hope madame will relent? That hope appears faint, for she looks far more likely to fix you with the eye of a college dean telling off a freshman for cutting too many meals in Hall and to shrug, '*Pas de souper, pas de coucher, c'est ma règle.*' Shall you plead a gut-ache and ask for an omelette? Or shall you tell her to keep the lot? And if you do so, will there be another acceptable hotel? Will it go in for the same *vilain* practice—for nearly half of them do, after all? Or, most humiliating of all, will it prove to be merely an annexe of the first one, with a *patron* who frog-marches you back across the square to the yellow distemper and the artichoke? Even this has happened to me.

This vicious system is, of course, both an outcome of and a factor in the recent decline of the French *cuisine bourgeoise*. It is proving the death of many excellent independent restaurants. It has already proved the death of such traditional holiday pleasures as strolling leisurely round a town looking at menus after your room is assured, or stopping for dinner at an attractive wayside inn and then driving twenty more miles before sleep. Cheat the slovenly *patrons* who adopt it by every means you can—best, by choosing a hotel *sans restaurant* in the places (usually, alas, only large cities) which have one. But do not expect help from any touring club, for here is Bibendum's philosophy . . . '*Vous ferez toujours plaisir aux hôteliers en dînant à leur restaurant, toute-fois certains vous logeront même si vous ne prenez pas de repas . . . Soutenez-le dans son effort en dînant chez lui chaque fois que possible.*'

I regret that I feel unable to alter my course in the slightest to sustain and give pleasure to the French hoteliers who fall so low to haul you to their tables.

*

If the legend of fine French cooking is twenty-five years out of date, however, the traveller can at least console himself with the knowledge that the devilment of French filth ended seventy five years back. Even in an unclassified hotel in a lonely mountain-village your comfort may be spoiled by a blaring juke-box—but not by fleas. And almost every village mentioned in this book (except *en passant*) boasts a reasonable place to sleep.

From the thousand-and-one nights I have spent in middle-to-lower-level French hotels I remember only a handful of outstanding, reasonably-priced meals—and few of those were in the Auvergne, for it is significant that the sign of the latter-day *routiers* is rare in these parts. But I recall only two which bore the star of national homologization (and they were not the most unprepossessing from the outside) in which the beds were damp, dirty or verminous. That, I think, is a better average than England can offer.

You will sleep well enough off the beaten tracks of the Auvergne, then, once you have adjusted your neck to the bolster. You can even excrete quite comfortably, for the Touring Club de France began telling French *mesdames* how English ladies worked around 1900. Would that the Michelin still carried that particular flag as high as does the AA, for most backwoods hotels only installed one real wc in order to get accepted and were still a bit worried about VD and (dirty word) seats. The rest of the conveniences may be inconvenient enough. But if there is nothing attractive on your own landing, try the situation one floor below. If it looks as bad there—well, how low can you get?

*

Inefficient sanitation is one of the terrors of the English tourist abroad. Bad weather is another, and one less easily disposed of so far as the plateau is concerned. For there is no insurance against it, and little guidance to be obtained from meteorological records.

Auvergnat summers tend to be either rainy (which is disastrous for tourism) or sunny (which starts forest-fires), and either way the farmers curse. As would be expected, the average annual precipitation is heavy, being of the order of forty inches. As would be expected, mountain mists drift down in autumn and winter snows arrive so deeply as to block many roads and make parts of the Massif a minor ski-country. And, as would be expected, nightfall comes like a glacier and the sun of day is a mountain and semi-southern one, sometimes cutting down like a ray-lamp from the crystalline sky and sometimes (one feels) hidden behind ninety million miles of mist. But more than that it is dangerous to say.

There is some truth in such generalizations as that the plateau's seasons are retarded a month behind the plain's (blackthorn is in bloom in June, for instance, strawberries are in season in August and autumn crocus blossoms in late October); that storms are commonest about the autumn equinox; and—of course—that the northwest is wettest and the south warmest. But all these rules are as unreliable as rules for English weather; and in fact the Massif, though technically having a 'continental' climate, can exhibit the wildest changes from hour to hour and from town to town at any season. In one historic twenty-four hours in Clermont, for instance, the thermometer reeled from below freezing to ninety-in-the-shade and back again. And I have myself picnicked on a day which was followed by a night in which the steam of the Paris express froze down its coaches.

It is not for nothing that the Auvergne is riddled with old local weather-saws—which, perhaps, give a better guide than any met. forecasts. Certainly this is no country for sun-baskers, and the tourist must either take an assortment of clothes or put up with some discomfort to compensate for the marvels of triple rainbows, of clouds whose undersides drip like stalactites, and of the sunsets which come after storms—pink and green, terrible and serene, like picture-postcards sent from Paradise. For this is a land of gales so frequent that (they say) there is not a single windmill in Puy-de-Dôme, of hurricanes so violent that (as with the hailstones in Touraine) they must be endured to be credited, and of twenty inches of rain in one day.

*

Yet if nature has imposed little seasonal discipline on the Auvergne, men have invented a ruthless one. Most of the tourist attractions of the region—floodlit chateaux and boat-trips, hotel and transport services above the minimum demanded by local travellers, information-offices and even museums—are geared, less to the climate itself, than to the *congés annuels*. And outside those months, apart from a revival around Christmas in the spas and ski-centres, everything is rather quiet and difficult.

High season begins some time between Easter and May Morning. Its end is less sharply defined, in tune with the slow death of autumn rather than the sudden upsurge of a revived earth. But early in September the first flurries of snow come down from the peaks and the restaurants drop their *repas touristiques*. By the middle of the month it is advisable to check in advance that the hotel where you are planning to spend the night has not put up its shutters. Before the first of October the winter timetables come into force (slashing out all the tourist circuits and buses not essential to the life of the country), the cows are driven down from the hills, floodlights are turned off, and *expositions permanentes* prove less permanent than that. One has the impression that the *chasse* opens with the shooting of the few surviving tourists (as sometimes, to judge from Dominici-like manslaughter cases, it does.) And even if one escapes that fate, one will dine in deserted rooms in commercial hotels and one's steps will ring ghostly through cities silent but for the sound of sneezing.

*

There is another reason for not essaying those slopes other than when the tourist industry wants you to. You may well get better weather outside the season than during it; but the nights at least will be cold, and a French hotel is a rotten place on a bitter night. All that makes winter supportable, cosy and even exhilarating in Nordic inns—hot spiced wine, open fires in hallways, comfortable lounges, the little coke stoves of Austria or the throbbing central heating of Switzerland or the great porcelain ovens of Germany—is unknown here. Auvergnat innkeepers have gasped at the marvels of science when I have told them of the shilling-in-the-slot meters of the ordinary British hotel: even so obvious a device as the double-window is rare in this frosty land: and though the plateau is rebuilding many of its tourist caravanserais to a bogus-Swiss standard of architecture, they remain below even English standards of warmth

38

and comfort. Who cares about dendrophilia and varnished pine—or even about good food and wine—when his shoes are damp and his teeth chattering? A friend of mine had to pile clothes on his bed in the best hotel in La Bourboule one August, and cursed himself for not following the official recommendation to take a heavy overcoat in high summer.

The Michelin could do something about this, perhaps by a picture of a glowing grate. But one has to conclude that the French are not so much indifferent to creature comforts (for they are always *telling* each other how cold it is) as cheese-paring about them. One fire in one public room would cost little enough in this timber-rich country —assuming a hotel sophisticated enough to have any public rooms except the bar-restaurant. For this reason amongst others, one cannot really recommend the plateau to ski-men. Scotland is nearer, Austria cheaper, Switzerland better organized, Norway more exotic —and even in France the Alps and the Pyrenees provide better sport.

*

Of the intermediate seasons in the Auvergne, spring is beautiful enough. It comes late and briefly; but when it comes the western valleys blossom bountifully, Cevenol apple-orchards swell with a loveliness the more tender for its contrast with the mountains above, and on the more fertile slopes there are Alpine flowers such as scabias and aconite. But more lovely still is autumn, when the October stains of the cliff-forests—complemented by the fodder-maize and vines of the villages—set one beating hopelessly about for all the tint-words between red and gold. Amber and umber, saffron and scarlet, garnet and grenadine: how few of them there are, when one *coup d'oeil* can encompass a hundred thousand individual trees and every one has its individual colouration. And above them are the gorse and heather flaming like fire and smoke, while all the meadows are lilac with crocus.

There are people who may think these glories worth the bad transport, the risk of cold or shuttered hotels, and the generally reduced facilities of the plateau *hors de saison*. Indeed, spring and autumn are the *recommended* tourist seasons for the more meridional valleys. But those who choose more conventional months need not fear that they will find the Massif a Blackpool beach. The more accessible tourist towns in July and August can be crowded with the French on family holidays, and that is no prettier a sight than the British on family holidays. But except in the major spas you will not even then find much English spoken—or, for that matter, understood. Prices are very little higher. And at no time of the year—except possibly in late July and early August, when a phone call or an arrival before six is a sound precaution—need the tourist arriving unannounced late in the evening fear much difficulty in finding a room.

*

This is perhaps more than enough talk of the weather, for Auvergnats regard it with a pagan dread (*'Parler du temps et du gouvernement'* they say, *'sera tojours pour se mettre dedans.'*) And indeed, after so lengthy a preamble, there is little to be added about the general technique of exploring. The central plateau is, after all, a part of the homogeneous life of France and all the standard tourist facilities are there—such as a *syndicat d'initiatives* in every small town avid to give more detailed information than this book can. (It is, however, wise to brush up your French if necessary, to carry a larger float of ready francs than in an area where bank-towns are closer together, and to invest 3s in a bath while the going is good.) Prices, too, are much the same as anywhere away from Paris, the industrial north or the ports; and though there is the usual disproportionate discrepancy between commercial and tourist inns, in the *hôtels simples assez confortables* which most of us patronize single rooms run at about 8f and double at 12f. Your dinner, with an aperitif, a half-bottle of *ordinaire*, coffee and a cognac, will finish at around 9f. (If a menu promises much less, look up the complaints section of your phrase-book.) And so a meal, bed and breakfast for two (check the *addition*: without malice, Auvergnats tot up even worse than other continentals) works out at about £3, *service compris*. Adding a pound for petrol or fares, and another pound or so for etceteras (including a scratch picnic or at most workman's-café lunch), a couple can potter not uncomfortably round the country on £6 a day and have something in hand for beanos or disasters.

Taking one place as a centre, this figure could of course be substantially reduced by residential terms. I am aware that a large number of holidaymakers—even of those who call themselves 'tourists'—

dislike moving on, especially if there are children and enormous bags. But the plateau is not geared to long stays on more than a boarding-house level, and I know of few inns where one would not be driven mad after three or four days by the same burnt soup and the same snivelling brat, by the half-drunk bottles of wine cravated with napkins and by the Vichy laid out on the same long table. Still, maybe it is just the gypsy in me which makes me shudder at the very word *pension*—though I could be tempted by a villa hired through an English magazine or the Agence Havas.

At the other extreme of enterprise, of course, the itinerant student roughing and cadging it (camping sites are plentiful, farmers will mostly welcome the individual tenter if he looks like being sensible about fire precautions, and there are also over 200 youth hostels) can live on practically nothing—especially in the fruit season.

*

I thought of including a final section in these notes subtitled 'the medicine chest'; but I know of no peculiar pharmaceuticals demanding to be packed, and even if you do not know the French for your affliction you have only to point to the disorganized organ to get some international brand-product at twice the English price. The busiest worriers, I suppose, are the mosquitoes: in summer you are *bound* to be bitten and driven to histamine creams, but a preventative as well as a cure is a good investment and the new anti-'skeeter preparations work on most of us. There is also that beastly anonymous disease, mild-dysentery-*cum*-food-poisoning, which implies twenty-four hours of a vomiting and diarrhoea which—since wc's are hard to come by—may hold you to your hotel.

This thing inexplicably hits even the most hardened continental travellers. The French attribute it to good food, and the British to bad water, but as I have found neither common overseas I remain agnostic. The local apothecary (who has an almost Scandinavian splendour in the high plateau) will serve you something for it, if only china-clay or those little charcoal sticks which an artist friend of mine uses for sketching when his bowels are bound again; or you may prefer one of the rather pricey specifics like 'Entero-Vioform' now available in London. As late as 1931, Baedeker recommended "castor oil . . . the use of a body-belt, rest and a strict diet: opium is to be avoided'. But I have found the best palliative a *grog à rhum*. In any case, this 'gyppo tum' or whatever is soon over.

And in any case, too, I do not want to dwell on horrors. For something has got away. Trying to correct old and disillusion-making legends, I have probably concentrated too much on the tourist inadequacies of France and of the central plateau. This was not from duplicity, for I detest that attitude of 'The delicious-little-place-which-only-I-know-about-and-I'm-not-telling', which is not only selfish and snobbish but rubbish too. (If the little place is more than a flea-pit, every travel-agent will nowadays have a hand-out on it.) The good places should be proclaimed so that they may be filled with men and women who will love them. And it is the job of this book to proclaim the Massif.

*

But still I have not said why I think people should go there. It is not for the waters: those are a joke. It is not for eating or ski-ing, sunlight or any easy living; for the towns can be hostile and the country witless. It is not even (except for ecclesiologists) for the churches, nor (except for monomaniacs) for the fishing. It is not just for the castles, nor yet perhaps for the scenic splendours of mountains, great rivers and small lakes: the Alps are higher, the Rhine wider and deeper, and the Sahara more solitudinous. Botanists should find some upland specimens, but there is little for the zoologist except *felis domesticus* in lean, cross-bred profusion. I have not been squared by any *syndicat,* and indeed the only people apart from speleologists to whom I can confidently say that the Massif is a *must* are entomologists. For there are beetle-like things which stalk the Causses on six or eight legs which look as if God had made them up in a jocular mood and let them find their own gossamer way out of heaven, while in Puy de Dôme even earthworms seem to come by the foot.

But I *am* writing a book about this land—a land which all must respect if not all can love. And even if I have little right to do so, I must have my reasons.

I have; and I wish they could be expressed in one neat sentiment. But the fascination of the plateau is in its contrasts and paradoxes, in its unity and variety within the unity and variety of all France. The mountain heart, for example, can remind one successively of Dartmoor, the Cairngorms, the High Peak or the marches of the Severn: the bordering valleys can seem Kent or Somerset: here and there the Rhondda steams and smokes: and all this is knit together on a scale ten times anything that our small land knows. It may be space—but inhabited space, space still within man's grasp—that is the great gift of the central plateau.

Yet other lovers will have other definitions of the fascination of those tawny, terraced hills which rise under cannon-puff skies like a towering circumflex accent over the 'A' in 'FRANCE'. Perhaps all that matters is that the Massif is a land which over years becomes part of a man and enriches him, so that he cannot cross Bodmin Moor through looming mists without recalling the Causse Méjean, see any satanic Fitzpatrick sunset which is not in part the blood of day streaming across the Limousin foothills, watch a fall moon rise which does not remember the moons of Puy-de-Dôme, or even stand in the shade of a church porch, beside a sunlit deserted square whose shadow fails to reach, across the narrow seas, to Villefranche-de-Rouergue.

*

So finally I must confess the boundaries which I have imposed on this land and explain how I have largely disregarded the accepted through-routes, how I have moulded my country as on an army sand-table, how I have modified political confines as merrily as a diplomatic draughtsman, and how I have generally taken liberties in order to produce a series of chapters of which each covers a reasonably 'natural' region.

After this introduction I have begun by writing of the foothills into which the plateau ebbs away on its uncertain northern edge, from the Limousin right round to Roanne; and I have continued by following the western edge down to Tulle. Then in the fourth chapter I have entered the plateau itself by the route so many have used—southward from Montluçon into the welcoming funnel of the Limagne; and after that have turned to the granite hills, such as the Madeleine and Forez, which flank it to the east. Two more chapters complete this account of the northern half which contains most of the Auvergne proper, one dealing with the volcanic heart of

Puy-de-Dôme south of Clermont and the other—though still in that many-sided department—with the sleepy land of the Livradois.

In the southern half which is watered by the Gironde rivers rather than the Loire system—and which has its own history, geology and outlook—there are still stronger contrasts; but it is at least more amenable to division into lateral belts running from west to east. And so the eighth chapter looks at the south-western guardian arc of all the Massif, the land of the Atlantic rivers; and it is only in the next that one ascends the high and lonely Cantals and re-enters the last of the true Auvergne. The subject of the tenth chapter is the very heartland of all France, which includes the Margeride but has as a whole no accepted name: that of the eleventh has too many names, for it is the complex of hills (not of the old Auvergne, though as volcanic as any which are) which lead from the Velay to the Vivarais and so to the great barrier of the Rhone.

This corridor ends in sight of the Alps. A more southern one begins in the red-rock country of the Rouergue and then finds itself in those calcite deserts which form the loneliest—though not the least-known—region of the plateau. Still better known, though, is the subject of the fourteenth chapter—a range which is also of the highlands but not of the Auvergne, the green Cevennes. And this book closes with a glimpse of the Massif's last, southern rim—the undercliff which looks at last upon the Mediterranean from Toulouse to Nimes.

Such is the shape of the land. Or such, at least, is the shape of this book.

2

Northern Approaches

The two most obvious characteristics of the Massif are that it is large and that it is near to the middle of France. For these reasons, it might have been expected to become a well-worn area for tourists and travellers of all types.

It has not done so, of course. The plateau is one of the least-known areas of France to those French who are not its special devotees, and probably the least known of all outside its borders. Tourism there takes several forms—water-cures, *villégiatures* and *estivants* (terms for which we have no equivalent: they mean spending your August fortnight in a car-horn-loud place called a *station de repos* with no attractions except its height), hasty raids in coaches, ski-stays, and so on; but all are essentially local matters, designed for Provençals escaping their stupefying midsummer heat while the British rush towards it. The commerce of the area is not such as to attract much attention from the outside world. And for the birds-of-passage —whether men moving turbine parts on horrible great transporters or Australian students driving ancient taxis—the Massif is as strictly avoidable as it was for Caesar or Napoleon.

The plateau is not, of course, comparable to (say) the Scottish highlands; for there is something important beyond it. The whole Languedoc coast of ports for oil and wine, of manufacturing cities and residential towns, of Narbonne, Béziers, Sète, Montpellier and Nimes, lies in its shadow; and the most direct route to this from Paris runs through Clermont. But direct as it may be it is a terrible journey, and men in a hurry have immemorially preferred to skirt round the edges and make their itineraries through the Rhone valley or the western foothills. Still today it is quicker to get from Paris to Béziers by road or rail via Toulouse (or to Nimes via Avignon) than to attempt a comparative beeline.

45

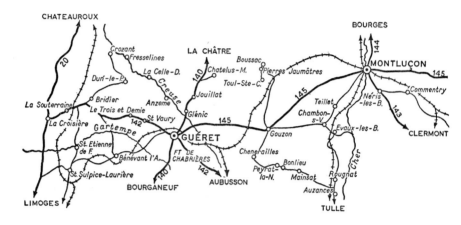

Laterally the detours become relatively greater, so that the plateau's commercial traffic is largely orientated from east to west. But the British tourist is far more likely to be thinking in terms of north-and-south, and traversing (for the kiddiz *do* love the sea) the country on his way to more colonized tourist lands such as the Riviera or Costa Brava. Theoretically one could just as well traverse it on the way *back*; but there never seem enough francs or time or patience on the homeward run, and so it is long odds that when the northern traveller comes upon the plateau for the first time it will be standing black against the midday sun.

He could not choose a vaguer frontier.

*

From north-east clockwise almost to due south the contours of the Massif curve like a scimitar: from south to north-west they at least climb like a stairway: but along the northern edge they are as vague as a cloud. In a sense the great plateau begins with the names painted on signboards at the Porte d'Orléans or plates of expresses at the Gare d'Austerlitz; and for me, at least, it empurples all the familiar

46

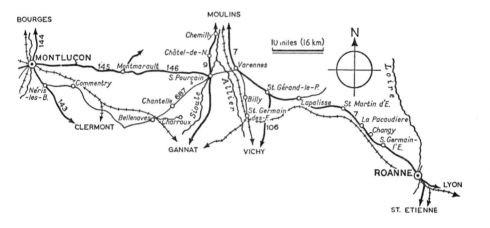

country for 200 miles south. The forests of the Ile de France, the Beauce below Chartres, the dim Orléannais, the Morvan and Beaujolais edges of Burgundy, the silver country of the Loire with Touraine and half Poitou, the Bourbon lands and Nivernais and the whole plain of the Centre ringing with its redder roofs the bourgeois splendours of Bourges—all these roll up like a sea to wash the hither foothills of the plateau with tide-lines as dubious as lines on the shifting sands of Somme.

Along no road from Paris is it possible to say 'Here the Massif commences'; and even if it were there are many roads to consider. But in this chapter, covering the northern foothills from west to east, I have chosen as starting-point the junctions for Lyons on the Paris-Toulouse artery—for motorists a crossroads called la Croisière, and for railfarers the near-by embranchment of St Sulpice-Laurière.

Neither place is of much intrinsic importance, though St Sulpice is so proud of its position that it has built a contemporary railwaymen's church—dedicated not to St Christopher but to its own creation, Notre-Dame des Voies. But together they will serve as the north-western origin for the graph of this book.

By the 20 road or the Toulouse express you will have come here fast—down through Arpajon and the long grey memorable town of Étampes, down through Angerville and Toury and Orleans itself at the Loire bridge where the south begins. Then comes the Sologne, with its mere-studded forests smelling of mists and wood-smoke, its wild boars (still, they say) and its little towns in the clearings—La Ferté and La Motte, Nouan and Salbris—leading down to the sweet wilderness about Vierzon and the Cher. Beyond this the 20 sweeps on to Vatan and the railway to the better town of Issoudun in the grey wine country, for here the ways bow a little apart. But they rejoin at Chateauroux—recently a bright brash tarty garrisoned town where Arab girls camp-followed coloured USAF corporals, Pierre from Marseilles kept a nitery under the name of Pete from Mississippi, and Main Street and the Casbah met in the heart of France, but today, since the troops have thinned out, almost respectable. And after that there is only the pretty cantonment of Argenton before the cross-country route turns left to Lyons out of a maze of heather and foxglove and granite.

That route runs for nearly 200 miles to Roanne with only one significent dip into plain-country. It leads east and a little south for further than it is from la Croisière to the Atlantic, further than from Roanne to Switzerland, further than from either to Paris. And though it has perhaps less of a homogeneous personality than one would wish, it must form the axis of this chapter.

*

La Croisière stands, if only just, in the department of Creuse—which takes its name from a smallish river which runs north on its way to the Vienne and then the Loire. If some ghastly party of Francophiles were asked to make a list of departments from memory, I fancy that Creuse would slip away; but if it lacks great distinction (it has, for instance, few churches of any note and almost none of those natural curiosities which tourists are supposed to long for) it is still no bad place to be. The dimness of its long non-history endures, but though Creuse is still a coldbed of rural radicalism its traditional poverty is past. Today this is a gentle, intermediary department of sweet rivers, clean prosperous townships, cowbells, a strengthening smell of garlic, and the prettiest girls you will eye south-west of the Jura. Its rural richness lends it an almost English air (its inns can *sometimes* be as cosy as saloon bars, for instance), and it is not as surprising as it might be to remember that the department, as part of the ancient county of the Marche, was quietly *sold* to Henry II for over twenty years. But here the drystone and bougainvillea begin, the station toilets are carved out of living granite, and there are gorge-shaped hints of the plateau which lies ahead.

In a land so lonely (it is one of the most sparsely populated of all France, although its fingers touch those of Touraine's last outstretched hand, and now that they have pulled up most of its railways it is intolerably difficult to explore too), it seems artificial to string a description along a chain of towns. But men travel from habitation to habitation, skimming past the figures bent in the fields or plodding home behind red cows; and they define a country by its townships; and at least there is a place of note within hailing distance of la Croisière.

*

This is la Souterraine, which stands on both the north-south railway and the east-west road. Many people hence pass through it, as I did myself five times before descending. But I never did so without brooding on its name, so darkly evocative of saints' cells and truffles, of stalagmitic caverns measureless to man and of buried images. And at last, after a conversation with some sort of a farmer from Amsterdam, I got out at The Underground where the big trains stop.

This is no city of eyeless troglodytes: it is rather a hilltop one, and its name seems to be derived only from an ancient holy place now part of the crypt of the church of Notre-Dame. But this church is itself immensely impressive. The interior is rich enough; but it is the outside which lingers in the mind, with the great battered buttresses which retain it against the slope of the market-place, the four-square tower, and above all the west door whose orders have that strange and saracenic note which entered, God knows whence, into so many romanesque churches of south-western France.

Nothing else in la Souterraine, not even the old gateway, challenges this near-masterpiece. But it is a fine enough township (with over 5,000 inhabitants it is the third largest in Creuse) and worthy of more renown. There are streets with ancient names, and a few

ancient houses too: in the cemetery there is a *lanterne des morts*
which again reminds you that you are on the western side of the
land: and nearby there are all the right appurtenances of a French
town—a small lake, a fine creeper-hung castle-keep at Bridier, and
bits of romanry. Yet it is within the trace of its walls, and especially
in its market-square, that la Souterraine convinces you that it is a
fit place to pause (remembering, perhaps, that its altitude is nearly
1,250 ft) before turning eyes over St Etienne de Fursac and its pretty
twin (which are all that is left of a great city which the normans
sacked) and the pure twelfth-century church and precincts of Bénévent
l'Abbaye, to the vastness of the south-east.

*

But it is nearer due east that the Lyons road—here the 142—first
runs, climbing a few hundred feet through brushwoody woods or
sweeping down across those small tributaries of the Gartempe which,
with their look peculiar to all the no-man's-land between the Loire
and the great hills, are glimpsed beyond the hedgerows. Away to the
north of this, past a crossroad nicely christened '3½', lie some of the
best towns in Creuse—or so their repute runs, for the peculiar bloody-
mindedness of the department's public transport means that I have
explored few of them and they are poorly linked even for *autos*.

There is towered Crozant on its lovely promontory, for instance,
once a castled stronghold but now a holiday village; Fresselines at the
confluence of two arms of the eponymal river which wanders below
castle-walls through all this land; Dun-le-Palestel, once the centre of
a quite important county, and La Celle-Dunoise; Anzème, where
the recurrent legend of a devil's bridge has a French twist with sex
interest (Old Nick was promised the miller's daughter if he could
build the span before cock-crow, but as he was laying the last stone
the virgin woke the cockerel, thereby winning a bridge for the village
whilst retaining her honour); and many more. But for all the tree-clad
gorges about these places, for all that they stand well above the 1,000-ft
contour, they belong only to the foothills of foothill country.

Beyond the village of St Vaury—which is worth stopping at for
a drink—comes the next portal-city, the capital of Creuse (and
anciently of the Marche) and the only place in it of over 10,000 inhabitants, Guéret. There is not much, however, to say of this; for if

50

not the smallest *préfecture* in France it is certainly the dimmest. Its most famous child, for instance, was the first wife of Ingres, and the *syndicat* had to dig hard for that one. Its food is as unimaginative as the worst in France, and it has not a single building of real note. The guide-books make the best of it, referring to its Hôtel des Monney-roux, its versatile museum, its few eighteenth-century houses, the ancient virgin in nearby Glénic's high and fortified little church, the charms of Jouillat on the 140 road and of Chatelus-Malvaleix further to the north, and the forest of Chabrières spreading over the rocky hills to its south. But for me its only interesting feature is that even in this scattered and centreless place a sense of the frontier persists. For the Café du Berry and the Café du Massif Central face each other here across a grey street.

If you want to ask the way to Guéret, it is worth remembering that the 'G' is hard and the 'u' silent. But I, at least, would be more interested in asking the way out of it.

*

The 142 peels off to the south, and on its generally eastward route runs on for forty miles or so before it meets another considerable city. The railway is equally uneventful; and even on the main highway— the 145—Gouzon is, despite its two-storey church, a dull place. A little to the north, however, on by-roads and an abandoned railway, there is a small town of great interest called Boussac.

For Boussac forms as memorable a gateway to the Massif as any place along its colder confines. Its castle (which housed the Lady of the Unicorn tapestry until Paris filched it) is hardly more orna-mented than a prison on the outer face, and rises as starkly as the cliffs which here face the Marche above ancient and modern bridges: norman in origin, it was rebuilt by a companion of Joan of Arc. But on its town side the building is symbolically more ornate: it is civil-ized, like all this town of steep stepped streets, a handsome market square, and an inn which caters for everyone from the visiting mi-lord to three railwaymen without a railway sharing a bed in the attic.

*

A granite-glittering road climbs south from Boussac to two places starred on every tourist itinerary. These are the Pierres Jaumâtres

51

and Toulx-Ste-Croix. The former stones are found on a crest in the
heart of a country of bracken and heather, foxgloves and thickets of
lichened trees, and appear as mysterious in their form and function
as all such monuments. What the Pierres Jaumâtres are is a collection of a dozen or more rounded stones perhaps fifteen feet in
average diameter: what they mean, no man knows. It may have been
the elements which formed them into those shapes resembling mushrooms or cheeses or pumpkins or ribbed sea-urchins; but it is more
than possible that it was by human hands that these 1,000-ton
boulders were poised on their points. Whatever the method and moti-
vation of this madness, '*Elles se tiennent*' (wrote George Sand, the
presiding spirit of this region) '*depuis une trentaine de siècles dans
un équilibre inaltérable.*'

To see the hanging stones of Jaumâtres against a thunder-loaded
sky (a phenomenon for which one need rarely wait long in these
parts) is an experience which reminds one of the darkness out of
which we came. The roman station of Toulx-Ste-Croix, well over
2,000 feet up on the next crest, may have had prehistoric origins
but speaks of more comprehensible things. The village itself centres
about a church which looks as lone and tempested as a sea-chapel
without, but which inside is bright with painted twelfth-century
columns. Detached from it stands the bell-tower, buttressed and
fortified and surrounded by three granite lions: these are the lions
of England, set up long ago to celebrate the sack of the stronghold.
And further away still there rises a lonely, rebuilt castle-keep.

It is itself visible from Boussac and beyond, and from its top one
can (even if still o'er-topped by a television mast) sweep the horizon
of eight departments—the plains of Berry rolling in a single arc past
Sainte-Sévère in Indre from east through north to west, then the hills
of the Limousin as for another quarter they lead over to the mysterious seaboard of Aquitaine, and finally—south-eastward, to the left of
Gouzon, over the head of Chenerailles where there was one of the
typical 'vitrified' castles of Creuse whose walls were mortared by
fusion from within, and through the gaps revealed—the darker and
more distant mountains of the Auvergne.

*

But these are not yet to be approached. Heading still eastward, on secondary roads now, there are more long bounds to be beaten.

Past the longitude of Boussac, and of Gouzon where the 145 itself turns north, the country becomes greener with the sense of a major river nearby. This is the Cher; and here, as it leaves the hills through a narrowing valley on its way to lands more closely associated with its name, every winding road within a five-mile radius is picturesque to a degree. There are, however, two towns over 1,500 ft up and separated by a railway viaduct more than 300 ft high which serve as special centres. One is Chambon-sur-Voueize, distinguished by its church of Ste Valérie—noble in itself, and rich in metal and wood and stone. The other is Evaux—'les Bains', and 'station de radium' too.

Evaux itself is basically a good enough market town of 2,000 inhabitants (including, when I was there, a rather colourful village drunkard) and a number of attractive houses. There is also the church of SS Peter and Paul which still preserves all kinds of noble or remarkable features, such as the octagonal lantern of Burgundian architecture set on a circular drum—even though the Evauxois, whose IQ runs at a pretty low level, allowed it to be gutted by fire a few years back. But 'les bains' are, of course, just nonsense.

Half a mile out of town, at the bottom of a deep combe, warm water which smells faintly of sulphur, tastes of nothing in particular, and hardly affects a geiger-counter, gloops up into open-air sitz-baths. Its official description is 'sulfatée, chloruée-sodiguée, brome-iodurée, bicarbonatée-mixte, manganésienné, ferrugineuse et lithinée.' From the municipal cure-house and several hotels redolent of damp-caked salt and Worcester sauce, 'Euphoryl Infantile' and bridge and boredom, the hypochondriacs potter out to wallow like hippopotami as the slow sad rain drips down on their ailments and the water-boatmen slither above the much-advertised *boue verdâtre et onctueuse* to bump their bellies. It is all supposed to cure gynaecology, if I translate rightly; and maybe it does. . . .

*

Upstream the country climbs lonely towards the market-town of Auzances in the forest with only one other place-with-a-church to note in Rougnat and a few villages like Peyrat-la-Nonière, Bonlieu and Mainsat away to the west. Down the Cher (which has just accepted two tributaries to become the frontier out of Creuse) there are several things of interest—like the disaffected church of Teillet, a hilltop pilgrimage chapel, gold-mines and some castle-ruins too—before you come to the considerable city of Montluçon, a *sous-préfecture* of the neighbouring department of Allier.

I like Montluçon, with its tidy circles of building. Its bull's-eye is the rather scraped and artificial-looking castle, but round this runs an inner ring of crumbling churches and fifteenth-century houses where chickens peck at the moss: it is highly, tightly picturesque, if rather insanitary for such an important place. There is a strong contrast when one leaves this mound for the magpie-ring of Montluçon, which is all stylish boulevards and neon signs. And beyond that again lies a shaggy outer country of industry, leading off the target into hills and forests.

With all this, Montluçon is as typical a middling-large town as you will find in all France. But it is more than that: at the end of the 144 road which has come down from Bourges by way of the strange, open city of St Amand-Montrond, it too is a frontier. It is almost the southernmost town linked to the great canal system of the Centre. But one of its neighbours is rheumatic and nervous Néris-les-Bains, where—they say, with the odd superstition of spas—blood once spurted from the springs which are now supposed to contain helium and renowned for their scum, and the earth opened at the Lisbon earthquake. For Néris, with its generous roman ruins and a quite good church, is the northernmost (except, perhaps, for the sad shrine of Bourbon-l'Archambault) of all the Auvergnat water-works.

*

Northward, for those who seek France's obscurer corners, lies the topmost bulge of Allier which contains many little-known things. But these really belong to the Bourbonnais. And in its bordering of the Massif it is eastward still that the 145 runs on from Montluçon, mercifully missing the unspeakable industrial town of Commentry —whence came the Keir Hardie of France and whence today come such unexpected products as liquid oxygen and artificial gems. Then at Montmarault it changes hats and becomes the 146, gives a shudder as it crosses a stream, and passes not far north of a delightful place called Chantelle.

This is well worth the detour, for its centre is filled with a mixture of church, convent and castle whose history is an epitome of that of the Faith in France: after countless sieges and revolutions, the monks are back and the pilgrimage of the Ascension takes place again. There are other good churches nearby at Bellenaves and walled Charroux. The main road is a dull one, but another twenty or so miles along it delivers you in St Pourçain. And there another great way from the north will also deliver you.

For St Pourçain above the rather stagnant Sioule has more claim to fame than that it possesses a passable if somewhat ragtime church, has some gastronomic importance as a centre of the white beef country, and feeds the land for miles around with a wine not *quite* as good as it ought to be. Here the medial highway to the plateau comes in; and again beside the road there has been a railway almost all the way. Fontainebleau: the Loire side towns of Gien and Briare: the necklace of easy-living villages of marvellous wine like Cosne, Sancerre, Pouilly and La Charité following as the river curves ever truer south: these are the landmarks as the artery flows on down to Nevers (where the Loire's great tributary of the Allier breaks away) and so to Moulins.

At Moulins—that subtle, gentle, comfortable Bourbon capital—the 7 road which is the *route bleue* to the Riviera heads a shade east. Its southward continuation towards Clermont and Béziers is numbered the 9. And it is this, with the old PLM line dithering beside it, which wanders gracefully down the last of the easy miles south, past the romanesque churches of Chemilly and Châtel-de-Neuvre, and so comes to St Pourçain.

*

Thus, at this central entry to the Auvergne, St Pourçain stands as a crossroads—or as part of a crossroads, one which extends across the Allier to where the 7 itself scalds through to St Gérand-le-Puy and the ivy-covered watch-towers of Billy and its sisters guard the great railway junction of St Germain-des-Fossés. With all this hullabaloo of people going left, right and centre, in a little turntable-country called the Forterre whose capital is Varennes, it is pleasant to find so clear-cut a town as Lapalisse, anciently spelt La Palice.

Out of so many names (for this is a populous quarter) that of

Lapalisse sounds like that of a place one feels one *ought* to know about. But in fact its main claim to fame is an indirect one, and its own contribution to *la belle France* is only a much-restored pink château of the fifteenth century which looks little more mysterious when floodlit: the contents are better than the building itself, though still not quite worth the entrance fee. Still, Lapalisse is what an eminent travel-writer would informatively describe as a pleasant town with a nice hotel—and with, as so often, its pleasantest quarter down by the bridge and the malodorous little river.

*

Not far beyond the Allier gap begins the last of the three depart-ments of the northern frontier, the one called Loire. There is a sense of a new countryside trembling to the right as one enters it—of considerable hills which do not belong to this ambiguous belt—while to the left the castle-crowned undulations are gentler as they spread north to the marshes of the Bourbon Sologne. The corridor is nar-rowing to a single line as the 7 runs on, about 1,500 feet up, by the chapel of St Martin d'Estreaux to the old houses of La Pacaudiere and on to Changy, St Germain-l'Espinasse, and at last Roanne and the Loire river itself.

And Roanne, still on a highroad from Paris to the Alps and the sea, is its end. It is a railhead and canal-head of thought, a full-stop to this exploration which began with a query at la Souterraine.

Let Roanne, then stand for itself. It is, after all, well equipped to hold the north-eastern portal of the Massif; for in addition to its 50,000 inhabitants and its distinction of a *sous-préfecture* it is a garri-son town, has an arsenal, and holds the *légion d'honneur* for its de-fence against the Austrians. (It was also—and this is the kind of science with which I like blinding people—the fourteenth largest port in all France on a 1930 census.) There is something about this cardinal approach-city of the plateau which I do not quite under-stand: maybe it is just what makes Roanne tick, for its industries all seem satellites of Lyons and there is no predominating feel to the place, acceptable as it is. But the northern bounds have at last been beaten, and it is time to retrace one's steps to la Souterraine and the yet more tantalizing corridor which leads southward from there.

The Sunset Marches

Vienne, Vézère, Corrèze, Dordogne, Lot, Avéyron, Tarn—
these are the Atlantic rivers which one must cross on that
journey south from La Souterraine almost to Toulouse which
defines the western edge of the plateau. Whether you take the 20
road—the so-called *route mauve* of heather and wild violets, with all
its hairpins between valley and valley—or whether you speed down
on the electric *rapides* which skim from crest to crest as a pebble
skims a pond and takes people from Paris 150 miles nearer Spain,
these are still the landmarks.

Vienne, Vézère, Corrèze and all the rest . . . the names sing themselves, the seven rivers like seven Pleiades shine. Without exception
they rise in the Massif itself: with the exception of the first only they
form a system shaped like a comet, whose head is in the great estuary
of Bordeaux and whose broadening tail curves to the east, south and
then north for over 300 miles, until it fades amid the huge hills. The
Paris-Toulouse artery, running down the shoulder of the plateau
at an average altitude of 1,000 feet, slices them all—the major ones
not far from their mid-points—and each bridge-town marks a deepening stratum of the south, though one is far more conscious all
the way of the east-west contrast between the stern mountains and
the rolling foothills than of the slipping latitudes. Although only the
northernmost province met on this journey was once called the
Marche, this is in fact one great strip of march-country as surely as
that between Chester and Chepstow (Creuse can look *very* like Here-
fordshire) or between Newcastle and Carlisle. Hold to the landmarks
and remember the names again: Vienne, Vézère, Corrèze, Dordogne, Lot, Avéyron, Tarn. . . .

But though the western foothills form a far more unified land-

57

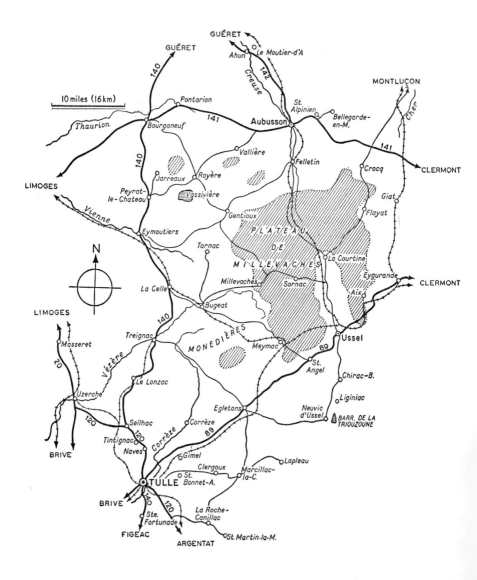

scape than the northern ones they reach far out of this book, and it is only the countryside of the first three or four rivers which belongs in this chapter. Furthermore, there is a stroll southwards to be made from la Souterraine through the last of Creuse before one meets even the Thaurion—officially a tributary of the Vienne, though in fact, above Limoges, quite as important a river.

If one is exploring the edge of the plateau this is a stroll which should not be taken along the 20 itself, for though the hills through which the road runs rise to 1,500 feet or more they are still Limousin hills where the villages have cream walls and brown roofs. The railway, a few miles inland, takes one nearer to the western undercliff: but it is the departmental border itself which here affords the best guide. And, making a decision of the 'cats is dogs but tortoises is insects' type, I hereby announce that Creuse is of the Massif and Haute-Vienne—of the former high Limousin—is not.

*

Down the 140 from Guéret over a 2,000-ft ridge and past some anthracite mines and dubious megaliths, one comes to Bourganeuf. This is a substantial town, and a pleasant one too. 'Newtown' often means the oldest spot for miles around, and Bourganeuf of the crumbling towers with their unexpected names and reputed memories of the Crusades keeps past and present in happy balance—as well as having a good inn and a church dedicated to St Jean which, if it lacks much other distinction, was part of a grand priory of the Auvergne. South of it, on the edge of Haute-Vienne, a waterfall marks the oldest hydro-electric site in France—Jarreaux, which first made its juice in 1888. South-west is the town of Royère, surrounded by a Breton landscape of strewn granite and dolmens broken by parklands and reservoirs. But more important than any of these places— as well as being nearer to the Massif proper—are those inland of the 140.

First comes Pontarion, east from Bourganeuf on the 141 road which comes in from Limoges by the fascinating town of St Léonard. You will not find much mention of Pontarion in any guide-book, though they say that artists use the place; but it has not only a magnificently-sited château above the brown Thaurion and a Victorian church with a vastly impressive exterior, but a richly south-western look imparted by its sun-baked, timbered hills. One feels that, elsewhere than in this dim belt of France between Limoges and Clermont, Pontarion would have had some greatness thrust upon it.

Greatness *has* been thrust upon le Moutier-d'Ahun—twenty miles north-east, surrounded by several good little churches and chateaux, and near a railway junction above a viaduct from which a branch off the Limoges-Lyons line trails dozily south. There is a town nearby called simply Ahun (and Ahun is a *very* simple thing to call a town); this is a grassy spot on the 142, well sheltered from the little mines of the area, where you will find a very decent tenth-to-twelfth-century church, dedicated to the Creusian St Silvain, which contains half the skull of St Giles and some good renaissance woodwork too. But this is only a mild introduction to the splendours of its neighbour.

For le Moutier—cosily nestling under a hill which looks down on a norman bridge and the hundred-tributaried Creuse—preserves the remains of what was the finest church in all the department. Even the remnant is a noble one. A garden marks where the gothic nave was, for all that is left of this is a splendid west front with six or seven orders to the tympanum and some dispersed romanesque carving. But the basically norman choir contains a wealth, famed throughout France, of seventeenth-century *boiseries*. Religious and secular, medieval and renaissance motifs are piled on each other in baroque profusion: mermaids, dolphins, angels with trumpets, putti, bacchanalian figures entwined with grapes, serpents, snails, flambeaux, flowers, grenades, twisted columns, broken pediments, a hunting-dog supporting the lectern, caryatids, saints and above all hawks and stags and pheasants—these came alike to the hands of the carvers of le Moutier-d'Ahun.

Carry this lively forest in your mind and eye: bless the modern priest who spent fifty years in repairing the ravages of the age of reason: and do not despair that men no longer take such joy in making things. For less than fifteen miles away, a gentle drive south-east down the 142 and the valley of the upper Creuse, stands a town whose name has sounded loud to lovers of the visual arts for three quarters of a millennium but never louder than today—the little town of Aubusson.

*

Illustration 9

The Glory of Aubusson

It is no job of this book to act as a guide to contemporary French art. All over the country—and not least in the backwaters of the plateau—you will find individual painters and groups barely known in Bond Street working out their visions, running their local exhibitions, meriting their half-columns in the regional press. Time will winnow them. But what has happened at Aubusson since the war is a *fait accompli*; and since it has received in England nothing of the publicity it deserves it should have at least a mention here. It would have more than a mention were Aubusson nearer to the heart of the Massif.

The brief history, then, is that the tapestry industry which eclipses all Aubusson's other claims to fame began with the clear colours and haunting stylizations of the later middle ages. When tapestry was one of the queens of art its own queen-city was Aubusson: half the great houses of France and beyond boasted its products until the Musée de Cluny stole them. The renaissance, to my mind, marks a sudden collapse: tapestries became woven pictures, and I see little to choose between the seventeenth century and the nineteenth, when the art-historians catch up with me in contempt for their merely technical virtues. The Lady of the Unicorn demanded only fifty colours: those Fragonard fabrics devised by painters like J. J. du Mons incorporated over 1,500.

But after the war, when this *sous-préfecture* of Creuse felt peculiarly isolated and hopeless (it had only one limping goods-cum-passenger train a day, one which still potters down through the department to amaze the diesels), came the counter-revolution associated with the name of Lurçat. Fascinated by this castle-art, Lurçat called in his painter friends (Gromaine, Dubreuil, le Doux and the great Lucien Coutaud) to break it back to its essentials: that done, he chartered Picasso, Matisse, Derain and Rouault to submit cartoons to the discipline of the loom. None of these men had local affiliations (Lurçat himself, for instance, is a Parisian who lives in a castle further down the marches and who pots in the Pyrenees); but all came to Aubusson to work on the rediscovery of the technique. And out of it all the glory of the town came riding back in flame and fire and feathery plumes.

I believe that the place for abstract and semi-abstract art is not in a frame but in a furnishing: that it is better lived with than self-

Illustration 10

consciously looked at. If this is so, then it is the secret of the triumph of modern French tapestry—as of modern French ceramics, ecclesiastical glass and even playing-cards, all of which are linked to the school of Aubusson. Certainly one of the things I would do if I were a millionaire would be to own a great stone house somewhere between Clermont and the Atlantic covered over on floors and walls (for *tapis* and *tapisseries* are almost interchangeable words) with the visions of Lurçat and his confrères.

*

So Aubusson recovered its soul; and though in the half-dozen local tapestry works you still see them putting through more imitation-renaissance stuff than living creations, its museum can show a blazon of beauty. For the rest it is an ancient narrow town, watched over by a round tower up in the woods and flowing along the quays of the Creuse with little turrets rising amid grey roofs: an ancient viscounty of about 5,000 inhabitants, tidy, picturesque, private and quietly prosperous, though with few outstanding souvenirs of former glory.

A sense of vanished splendour is in fact easier to find in Aubusson's close, older but less famed southern neighbour, Felletin. Once this rivalled the major tapestry-town; and the magnificent tower of its parish church (there is another chapel too) and the linked fragments of renaissance mansions still witness a past as splendid as that of the sunken wool-towns of East Anglia. But though Felletin still weaves its fabrics and cuts a few diamonds too, it is today almost a suburb of Aubusson. It will not wake again, though the *lanterne des morts* in its cemetery crumbles down to dust.

*

There are still three small zones of Creuse unexplored. To the east the country climbs up towards Auzances and the departmental edge with few towns to mark: Crocq (which takes its name from a king, is one of the highest resorts in the department, has a few things of note, and stands near to the sources of the Cher), St Alpinien with a passable church and Bellegarde-en-Marche with a tower are perhaps the most mark-worthy. To the west there is pretty little Vallière before you come back to Royère. But on the other hand (on the *other* hand) there is a new and different country.

South of Felletin, there spreads a heathland, perhaps a thousand square miles in area and 2,500 feet or more high. This divides the tributaries of the Sioule to the east, the Vienne and Cher to the north, and the Dordogne to the south and west, and is studded with an infinitude of sad and shallow meres—and also with a few rather more dramatic man-made reservoirs, like that which surrounds the artificial island of Vassivière and feeds the distant underground power-station of Peyrat-le-Château. It is a range all its own, linking the Massif to the Limousin so outrageously that its wooded westernmost slopes tumble sheer down into gentle Haute-Vienne from heights of over 2,000 feet. And it is called the Plateau de Millevaches.

I do not know why it is called the Millevaches plateau, for the local notary who might have told me more than that it surrounded a village called Millevaches was not around when I was; but I should not think the word has anything to do with cows. These are present, but not conspicuous.

It is a strange mixture of barrenness and fertility, this high scrub-forest where the longitude of Paris and the latitude of Clermont cross and which you approach from the west through the ancient town of Eymoutiers. There are rounded, bare or heather-covered crests already called *puys*, and there are the lush water-meadows which feed many major rivers—for before the volcanoes came the Millevaches was *the* watershed of France. Even the trees are a mixture of isolated windbreak poplars, random dwarf cypresses and hazels, and the French forest-blend of beech, birch, chestnut, ash and Commissioner's conifer. There is a mining industry of sorts, a lonely back-yard of exploitation based on a few heavy metals like lead and bismuth and half-metamorphosed things such as pitch and asphalt and soft brown lignite coal: miners' concessions are divided up in the pubs like fishing rights here, and it is all a little like the Forest of Dean—though it reminded a friend of mine more of *La Belle Dame Sans Merci*. One August recently it froze there . . .

The Millevaches is an uninhabited area, and few tread its mica-glistening roads. In the central part, belonging to Creuse, there is one small town used to strangers—la Courtine, which has an observatory and a vast artillery range. (This place has been called the French Aldershot, and indeed the whole area also has resemblances to the sandy, heathy wastes of the Surrey-Hants border.) But for the most part it is a vastly untravelled land, where in little lakeside towns you can find a norman church where some very contemporary plastering is proudly signed by the local mason, where a domestic utensil has been pressed into use as a font, and where the chickens peck and mate and dung amid it all.

I do not think anybody has ever really penetrated the Millevaches, for though they talk of roman remains the romans would have left a road. Druids are more like it, in this by-land which wanders over until the border of Puy-de-Dôme is marked by a branch-line dropping due south from Evaux and Auzances without (despite Giat's hotel and nearby Flayat) meeting even a township of any importance for mile upon lonely mile. Here, at the end of Creuse, they greet a traveller with the slow, amazed, rather embarrassed courtesy of the Irish midlands. And here, symbolically, my thumb has frotted much of the detail off the map.

*

The spot on a television tube sweeps its screen from left to right, tracing out a first strip of a picture. Then it snaps back, to a little below its starting-point, and starts to build up another dimension. Just so the vision of these marches leaps back along the southern border of Creuse, past the stone-workers' hamlet of Gentioux whose church is (just) worth visiting and a region called 'the Scotland of the Limousin' because of these new, artificial lochs which remind others of Norway, to find a new beginning at la Celle. This village, on the 140 road which has come down nearly thirty miles from Bourganeuf, is not far from the triple point of Creuse, Haute-Vienne and the department in which it stands—Corrèze.

Again, these counties insist on having more personality than such mechanically-begotten things ought to have. Corrèze, I think, is a favourite of everybody who has ever realized that it is there. 'The little Dordogne' it has been called; and one could also call it a French Dorset. But its riches are its own. It is the first truly southern department, its heart being of a latitude with Grenoble. And it has always been generous to me.

Deep beechwoods are served by unimportant but quite frequent railways with stations at the end of tree-shaded avenues; large, improbable dogs chase clucking ducks across the forecourts of deserted

Uzerche (*above*) is rightly called the pearl of Corrèze. But two hundred miles away to the East, Ambierle (*below*) has a finer church.

13

Amid the savage rocks of Puy de Dôme (*above*) men built churches as splendid as that of Royat (*below*).

14

cafés; spired towns are threaded on a winding necklace of roads; rabbits stare amiably into headlights; humble inns are surprisingly hospitable and their cooking is not bad either. A man can ask only one more thing of a region—except, of course, good weather, which even Corrèze cannot guarantee—and that is that its buildings should have a distinctive look. And this too the department affords.

For there is a particular type of ecclesiastical feature called a *clocher à peigne* which is essentially a gable pierced by openings for bells: and though it is common throughout all south-western France it is commonest in Corrèze. There you can tell the status of a place from the number of pigeon-holes almost as accurately as from the stars the Michelin gives its hotels or the SNCF to its stationmaster's hat. One for a hamlet, two for a village, three for a town, four for a real centre—that is the general rule.

*

Not all of Corrèze belongs in this book, for it is a created department only roughly representing the old Bas-Limousin and bulges far further west than Creuse. But the contours of the Massif themselves swell towards the sunset here, so that more than half of it *does* belong. And the most useful lateral scan-line with which to begin, I think, is provided by a rather surprising railway branch which runs south-east and then east out of Limoges on its way to nowhere in particular. I am sorry for all this harping on railways; but as they generally follow valleys rather than snake across hills, they provide a truer skeleton of a land than its roads.

Just beyond la Celle, then, this railway leaves the 140 and finds Bugeat, a town with good bits to its church which *needs* some finding. (Tarnac, a resort to the north, is even remoter.) And then it wanders through the loneliest part of all the Millevaches plateau and down to the green basin of Meymac.

Meymac is thirty-five miles south of Aubusson. It also has almost all that one can hope to find in a small cantonal town. There are old round towers with primitive carvings, there are even more primitive carvings on a cross of curious, Northumbrian-Celtic device, and there is a semi-fortified church (with fascinating sculpture again) which can almost be compared to the more famous one at St Angel a little to the south-east. But it has kept quiet, has Meymac under the heathlands.

Here the branch joins the important cross-country railway running east from Bordeaux to Clermont and the spas. A little further on still (surprisingly little further on for France) there is another junction— this time with the Aubusson line. The 89 road runs up on the same errand, too, here at Ussel.

I wish I were fond of Ussel and its suburb of N-D-de-la-Chabanne. I ought to be, for by the standards of these parts it is a *ville d'art et d'histoire,* as well as being a busy *sous-préfecture* of over 7,000 inhabitants and full of commercial travellers playing scabrous tricks on each other. It was from here, for instance, that there came the four troubadours who taught Dante his *terza rima.* But it is an oddly-shaped and rather grubby township with an air of forlorn isolation; and though it has a number of pleasant stone houses even the greatest —that of the Dukes of Ventadour—is hardly a stately home. Over it all, from the gravelly civic centre on the outskirts, a large roman (repeat *roman*) eagle stares forlornly as if wondering what he, Ussel or any of us is doing there.

*

Eastward, beyond the village of Aix, there is yet a third rail junction at Eygurande from Auzances; and away to the north-west there is a resort village called Sornac. But again (for one is here near to the entry of Puy-de-Dôme) the scanning spot flicks far back to the west. And this time it meets not a minor road and a branch-line but the 20 and the Toulouse artery: not a crossroads-village like Masseret but the hill-city of Uzerche.

'*Perle de la Corrèze*': '*Étoile du Limousin*': '*la pucelle*': for once the tourist phrases ring as true as a golden coin. This town has taken men's breath away from the days when they said '*Qui a maison à Uzerche a château*' to the far more recent day when it was chosen to represent to philatelists the most picturesque town in France. Climbing impregnable cliffs of granite above the black Vézère—the Dordogne's most important tributary—Uzerche is a profusion of cream-coloured towers and silver-grey-roofed turrets. Round, square, triangular, polygonal or irregular, they rise to a humped crest-line which is defined at one end by the spacious, towered norman church of St Pierre and at the other by the promontory of Ste Eulalie above a bend in the trout-river.

66

Illustration 11

On the Narrow Gauge

With its unspoiled beauty of situation, its inspiring past and its fine edge-of-Perigord cooking, Uzerche should be among *anybody's* favourite towns—though perhaps among a fisherman's most of all. But it has the added advantage of a physical accessibility which equals its spiritual remoteness. It is only five hours out of Paris as you speed down the 20 or take the morning express from the Gare d'Austerlitz: and when you get there it is itself a useful centre for communications.

But the great road skirts Uzerche, and the railway does something even stranger. Cutting across a shoulder of the Vézère valley, it refuses to enter Uzerche-ville and instead pauses at Uzerche-gare, only a mile away but as out-of-sight of the roofs of this lovely town as I—alas—am now. And it leaves railfarers to make that last fragment of journey, through a tunnel which divides two worlds, on the narrow-gauge.

*

I have elsewhere spoken in some detail of the delights of the small, half-private railways which lace the heart of Corrèze. But I have to come back to them here, for they not only provide most exciting journeys in themselves but irrigate the whole centre of the department.

From Uzerche-gare to Uzerche-ville then, and south-eastward into the steep hills, a gallant metric railway runs. And after twenty miles it comes to Tulle, a city which I would like to commend since it is the 20,000-strong *préfecture* of this lovely county and stands, ringed with wooded hills and faced with an old suburb called Laguenne, in a combe so steep that the Clermont-Bordeaux trains must reverse where the brief river Corrèze achieves manhood. But I cannot really like this place of lace.

There is a restored norman cathedral with thirteenth-century cloisters which is still an interesting example of lobed Limousin architecture even though the choir has collapsed into the river: there is the usual tangle of old houses—some of them good—and a museum: and within hailing distance are the churchly villages of Ste Fortunade, Naves and St Bonnet-Avalouze, the waterfalls of Gimel and a township up in a large, lonely but far from dull countryside which has escaped attention but is as old and charming as it ought to be

67

considering that it is called Corrèze itself. They make a sheep's cheese called *brach* there, too.

Yes ... but every time I have been in Tulle itself (which has a uniformly tragic history from the frequent battles of the hundred years' war to the slaughter of a hundred hostages by the Nazis, and which today has a grim-looking arsenal) there has been something wrong—heat, cold, sluttish hotels, the awkward contours plastered with raw new buildings, or a local fête (though *not* the celebrated moonlight procession on midsummer night) which closed the banks, stopped the buses, and deafened me with ceremonial detonations. Maybe, on some enforced return, I shall fall in love with Tulle. Until then, *anathema sit*—apart from the narrow-gauge.

*

There is no spot of great tourist importance on the line between Uzerche and Tulle itself. But near to the pretty little modern manor at Seilhac where the 140 road becomes the 120 (and near to a place called Tintignac which boasts some roman remains too) it throws a spur northward to Treignac—for the southern *-ac* ending, signifying of course water, is now becoming monotonous. And Treignac is a place in its own right. Equipped both with antiquities like a castle, old bridge and pretty square church (there *were* two, but the other has become a cinema) and with natural curiosities such as some Vézère gorges which seem to belong above its 1,600 ft, it is a steep and striking township even though rather grey, ill-arranged and over-rebuilt, a poor man's Uzerche. Finally, on its way to Treignac, the departmental railway has served a township of some gastronomic fame—le Lonzac.

Heaven knows it has no other claim to fame, though it runs up a long and quite attractive street, where typical little wells stand at every door, to a new and alpine-looking church. I have promised not to speak of individual hotels here, and just to show how right I am the Michelin recently transferred its almost meaningless rose from the pub I stayed in to the one next door. But I remember le Lonzac as holding one of the very, very few inns of France—not an *hôtel-brasserie*, not a *café-bar*, not a concrete caravanserai or bogus-English-stockbroker's-bogus-Tudor roadhouse, but an *inn* in the noble and Saxon sense of the term here in the often inhospitable and impersonal heart of France. I remember Madame knitting, and the smell of her hams in the cavernous copper-glowing kitchen, and a greenery-yallery sunset wandering vaguely across the hills east of her doors.

*

This is what lies north-west of Tulle, on this amazing metric system. But the tracks continue south-east too . . .

So the type stood until a few months before this book was finally revised. But we wrote too soon or published too late; for at last this noblest limb of the narrow-gauge in Corrèze has gone down. Rather than resort to denigrating footnotes, however, it seemed best to quote from the original as if from a yellowed antique document. And so . . .

'They continue south-east too, beyond where the Corrèze river is lost in hill-streams, as they climb over a route so fantastic that —though I had rather inaccurately written about it—I hardly believed it existed until I came across it in a clearing in the heart of a timber forest. This was somewhere between Clergoux and Marcillac-la-Croisille and la Roche-Canillac and St Martin-la-Méanne down towards the Dordogne.

'I knew the narrow-gauge line spanned a vast *étang* on an unexpected truss-bridge. But I did *not* know (for the fact is hard to read from the Michelin 76 map, on to which one has now trespassed) that it still dared a ravine-crossing on a tunnel-to-tunnel suspension bridge below Lapleau called the Roche-Taillard—an incredible *arc-en-ciel* 300 feet high, a bowstring of hope which makes the Swiss Landwasser (and most of the main-line viaducts of France too) look like stepping-stones. But it does do so, the autorails even being arranged so that you can get out and back in a day. And so I beg every tourist in this last, highest and most exalting corner of Corrèze to abandon his car for a few hours and take this route through the dizzy spaces.'

*

But it is all too late now. The viaduct is silent: the tracks are being lifted: and by car it will have to be.

Even in the last years of the branch, though, the tracks ended at Neuvic d'Ussel rather than at their logical, original terminus of Ussel unsuffixed. For with typical French illogicality their last few miles were axed only a few years after having been painfully relaid to

make way for the hydro-electric works of Triouzoun—an outlier of
the Dordogne scheme which makes all of this frontier area a maze
of artificial lakes.

But still, Neuvic is a pleasant if unexciting cantonment in itself:
it has, for instance, some ecclesiastical fragments, an odd tower with
ancient childish carvings, and a plethora of municipal belvederes,
follies, gazebos and ha-ha's for hoping to see the Puy-de-Dôme (now
only some sixty miles east-north-east) *from*. It is the market centre
too for all the southern slopes of the 3,000-ft Monedières, a satellite-
range of the Millevaches made of schist, gneiss and similar geology,
which is rather enigmatically described in a hand-out as 'a realm of
winds blowing over a thousand springs which ooze drowsy in their
heathy cradle, the realm of shaggy moors edged along by juniper
trees and the greener battalions of pines'—and also for such castles as
that from which Ussel's dukes came and another which saw the birth
of two popes.

And since Ussel itself, up to the north now beyond Liginiac and
Chirac-Bellevue has already been dismissed as a worried eagle; and
since there is not much except a technical college at the warm-roofed,
academic-looking township of Egletons away to the west on the 89
coming up from Tulle, it is time to close all these explorations of
frontier lands and to approach—if not, yet, to attain—the department
of Puy-de-Dôme itself.

The Pastoral Ocean

Whether the departments of France have much more significance than as an *aide-mémoire* is debatable. On the whole I think the topographer-encyclopaedists did a good job of dividing France into eighty-nine pieces of similar size; for though I set out to write this book with a contempt for all such artificialities, I have more often than not found the dotted border-lines corresponding to real changes of feeling. But inevitably the men of the revolution had to make their compromises between history and geography. And just such a compromise is Puy-de-Dôme, the northernmost department which is wholly of the Massif.

This is the nearest equivalent the modern map affords to the ancient Low Auvergne, though it extends farther south and takes in less of the outlying regions. But even so it is more homogeneous geologically than visually. Its name may have all the purple overtones of 'Basse Auvergne', of the deep volcanic centre of France (if not of the Massif) which statistically it is. But about a third of it—a wedge cut in its north flank—consists of the Allier-watered meadowlands called La Limagne.

The Limagne (for there are other similar but smaller alluvial valleys or plains given that name with a suffix) is the oldest cul-de-sac in France. A last land of fertility and prosperous markets before the valley tightens at Clermont like hands at a man's throat, it appears to today's southward traveller almost as it appeared to the pleasure-loving Bishop Ausonius—an acute, if rather gushing, travel-writer. That is to say, it is an *océan pastoral*, an opulent, billowing world of grass and grain, of root vegetables and orchards and such unexpected crops as tobacco, sugar-beet and angelica, of rich river-washed soil, of woodlands and leafy lanes, of farm-houses as proud as palaces and of

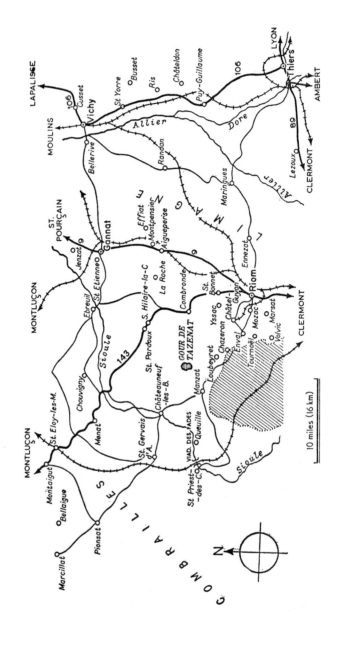

LAPALISSE

MOULINS

106
Cusset
Vichy
St Yorre
Busset
Ris
Châteldon
Puy-Guillaume
106
LYON
Thiers
AMBERT

Allier
Dore
89
CLERMONT
Lezoux
Allier

Bellerive
Randan
Maringues
Ennezat
Riom
CLERMONT

ST. POURCAIN
Gannat
Effiat
Montpensier
Aigueperse
LIMAGNE

Jenzat
St. Etienne
La Roche
Combronde
St.
Bonnet
Guyon
Mozac
Marsat

MONTLUÇON
Ebreuil
St. Hilaire-la-C
143
S. Pardoux
YssaC
Châtel-
Envol
Tournoël
Volvic
Marsat

Sioule
Chouvigny
Châteauneuf
-les-B.
Loubeyret
Chazeron

GOUR DE
TAZENAT
Manzat
Queuille

MONTLUÇON
St. Eloy-les-M.
Menat
St. Gervais
d'A.
VIAD. DES FADES
St Priest
-des-C.

Montaigut
Bellaigue
Pionsat
Marcillat

COMBRAILLES

Sioule

10 miles (16 km)

N

the last fine vineyards you will meet before you smell the Mediterranean 200 miles beyond. It is hard to realize the titanic forces out of which the Limagne was born, unthinkable centuries before men saw it, since today the only people it does not delight are tidy-minded topographers. For it is typically confusing that this entry-valley, so historically Auvergnat, should be structurally quite low and so flat that one can still envisage the days when it was a vast lake.

One's first sense of the Limagne as it now stands is that it is a simple funnel of eroded alluvial land, itself a thousand feet up, fifty miles long and enclosed between steep and narrowing hills. But the map shows it is more like a sack hanging from St Pourçain, with Clermont at the bottom left. Two ranges sprawl to its west and three to its east, whilst a different countryside brings up the rear. The Allier itself runs well over to this flank; but it was the west side which used to be considered the more fertile, since volcanic ash benefited *cultures* and marshes did not. Going into the plural the peasantry distinguished *bonnes* from *mauvaises Limagnes*—though, from either, a man with a hand-plough observing the feudal strip-cultivation which still obtains can gain a living.

This plain—a part of Puy-de-Dôme, a smaller part of the Auvergne and a scratch in the central plateau—is the historic gateway to them all. It is a cleft, narrowing from thirty to less than ten miles, between the lobes of the heart-shaped highlands. And only in relation to it do Clermont and the mountains behind make sense.

The Limagne may be found along any of the roads which lead south from Montluçon.

*

Neatly across the north-west frontier of Puy-de-Dôme (and there *is* a frontier here, if it is defined only by the sudden decline of the road surfaces and the slower decline of housekeeping and husbandry) run the Collines de Combrailles. These, dividing the basin of the Cher from that of the Allier, rise to nearly 2,500 feet; but they are a gentle range, covered with fertile clay and cultivated to their tree-clad crests with stook-dotted arable fields and watery pastures. With their new cultivation by tractor and co-operative they have a look of Swiss lushness, if not always of Swiss neatness.

Three roads from Montluçon towards Clermont cut through the Combrailles—one from Marcillat in Allier by way of Pionsat, St

Gervais d'Auvergne, Châteauneuf-les-Bains and Manzat, another past Ebreuil and Chouvigny, and the central 143 which runs by Montaigut, the coalfields round, Menat, and Combronde. There is nothing of real note in any but one of these places, though St Gervais with its landmark-suffix has a pretty church with a prospect, Manzat one with woodwork. Menat has the remains of an abbey and an old hump-backed bridge too, and Marcillat is close to the abbey remains of Bellaigue, vast even in the English sense. Combronde is the centre for the little bathing and fishing lake of the Gour de Tazenat (which is the northernmost of the Auvergne's volcanic craters) and boasts two village crosses as well, and Châteauneuf —which is a collection of villages with only a few hundred inhabitants between them rather than the residential spa it claims to be, despite its attractive old part up on the so-called peninsula of St Cyr —bottles a celebrated mineral water whose primary witchcraft is rheumatism.

But the outstanding town is Ebreuil on the Sioule, one of the old 'thirteen towns' of the Limagne, with its fine if chopped-up abbey church, its silver reliquary of St Léger, and its romanesque frescoes. However, all these places—and such smaller ones as St Pardoux and St Hilaire-la-Croix too—have their flavour of vine-hung barnyards, village greens, dusty side-roads, half-dead handicrafts like lute-making and marquetry, and (of course) views.

*

But the route south I would choose if it were possible would not be by road at all but up the Sioule itself—up a valley which winds for a hundred miles or so, back from its confluence with the Allier by St Pourçain, to its source west of Clermont. For the Sioule, though little renowned outside France except to fishermen, is one of the most beautiful of all in a land of beautiful rivers.

It flows along the eastern edge of the Combrailles and the western edge of the Limagne; and here and there it is flanked by a highway or trackway which glimpses its glory. But for most of its way it is on its own, broadening and narrowing or quickening and becoming placid as one climbs from the plains of the Limagne to those eroded, porphyry-streaked and granite-guarded upstream reaches which so worried Montaigne—an easily-worried essayist. And at last there

74

are only ruined towers, hydro-electric stations such as Queuille, and inaccessibly-perched villages to watch it.

But despite these natural splendours the greatest spectacle of the river is a man-made one. It is the Viaduc des Fades, near St-Priest-des-Champs. This is more than just another of those bridges which once brought new life to the plateau and now take only two or three trundling railcars daily. For, despite the fact that the Combrailles are gentle hills by Auvergnat standards, this is the highest viaduct in (depending on who you believe) France, Europe or the world.

The technical data are that it was begun late (by Vidard in 1901) and took eight years in the making; that its simple steel girder is over 400 feet above the river and 1,500 feet long; and that it contains more than a million rivets. But there is more fun than that to be got from the guide-book which they sell in the viaduct hotels—hotel*s*, for only France would have not just one inn but three at the bridge, dedicated to the pleasure of looking.

This little hand-printed publication has sketches by local school-children of the-labourers working like fellahin for 3d an hour on the great piles, and of the flower-decked inaugural train: it is full of reminiscences of the men who drank a bottle of rum—*à la suite d'un pari*, too—before falling to their death from the high girders, who cut their shot-holes a yard deep by hand in the middle of space, who broke their twelve-hour day with sheep's-head soup and con-certina-music in a wooden canteen where the bearded *patronne* threw men out with her own mighty arms. And even with all this period colour forgotten, there is more to the Viaduc des Fades than was seen by the child who wrote '*C'est très haut. En-dessous, il y a de l'eau et des poissons.*'

Yes, it would be pleasant to travel the Sioule in solitude. The next entry into the plateau is far from solitudinous, for it is the medial artery of the Limagne, of the Massif and of France, this route where the 9 and a loop of the Bourbonnais railway of the old PLM pass amid the last trees of Allier and enter Puy-de-Dôme just beyond Gannat.

*

Gannat is a place of about 5,000 inhabitants, if one includes the at-tractive *faubourg* of St Etienne with its half-ruined, tenth-century church. It is characteristic of not merely the Limagne but the whole

Auvergne in that it does not stand at the centre of a region but as an interchange-market between the plain and the hills. But it seems to me a frontier-station of the Massif in a wider sense, and perhaps the town where one comes across the most sudden change of feeling of all. That feeling may be a subjective one, based on some confluence of dusty evening light, cropped acacias, bead-curtains and the sound of cicadas and *boules*. Here, one says, the south begins: here the land deepens into lizards. But it is all as puzzling as the history of Jacques II de Chabannes de la Palisse, who was born—despite that mighty title which belongs fifty miles north-east—in Gannat in the late fifteenth century.

This marshal of France—gallant as a soldier, and not without fame as a philosopher—was taken prisoner at Pavia in a rather unimportant war. But whose prisoner he was became the subject of so violent a debate that an incensed Spaniard shot the marshal in cold blood rather than lose his disputed prize. At which Jacques' followers chanted:

> 'M. de la Palice est mort,
> Mort devant Pavie.
> Helas! S'il n'était pas mort,
> Il . . .'

Well, the last line originally went '*Il ferait encore envie.*' But some ass of an editor made it '*Il serait encore en vie.*' And if that was not the start of that curiously Anglo-Saxon kind of nonsense-joke which the French call a lapalissade (and I doubt if it was, very much), it is at least as good a story as anyone has concocted about the origin of the limerick.

For the rest, Gannat is a charming town whose church of Ste Croix is a fine patchwork of every century from the eleventh to the seventeenth and which houses a treasure of an evangelery belonging to the ninth. It has a bit of a Bourbon castle, too, and some gastronomic repute. But if one does not wish to linger there, nor to visit such pleasant outlying spots as Jenzat, it is an easy journey south—though one which should not be taken too swiftly, for there is much of interest along the way.

*

There is, for instance, Aigueperse—'Egg-purser', for you are not in Provence yet. This spreads along the main road and hangs out a few antique shops and cut-out chefs—and even a *salon de thé* advertising the local marzipan—to beguile the traffic. But it is a place of diverse attractions. *Item*, a mainly fifteenth-century church of Notre Dame which, though restored and making too much use of lava-stone, has its quality. *Item*, a Ste-Chapelle not easy to visit (perhaps because one ingenious tourist, posing as a photographer, stole the rose-window) but rich in renaissance woodwork. *Item*, the jaquemart-clanging tower of the Hôtel-de-Ville, as charmingly incongruous as a bit of Inigo Jones' nonsense leading to an Oxford quad. And, *item*, a flavour all its own.

That flavour is at first taste Burgundian; but Burgundy lies far to the east beyond the high woods, and in fact Aigueperse only concentrates a feeling which permeates much of the Limagne and coincidentally appears to belong further east. Still . . . The courtyards hung with vine or creeper, the cobbled alleys, the towers and turrets punctuating the long, distinguished high street, and above all the Hôtel-de-Ville itself, a former Clairine convent which rises above a stone-arcaded basement to a half-timbered and gabled attic, are all oddly reminiscent of (say) Beaune. It seems fitting that the only important vineyards between Touraine and the Languedoc, between Bordeaux and the Lyonnais, are found south of Aigueperse.

These are not as important as they were, for since the phylloxera two-thirds of the vineyards of the Limagne have been lost. I fear too that the prodigious thirsts of these parts may have diminished under the impact of *santé-sobriété*: the daily ration of half a pot a day for an idle man and a whole pot for a worker, which applied only a generation ago, may not sound excessive—but a Limagne *pot* held four gallons. But perhaps behind their doors the men of the *treize villes* still hold that a good lamp needs little wick but much oil.

*

Another influence on these parts has been the monastic one: lights burn before Virgins in street-corner niches as ubiquitously as in Italy, and there always seem bells sounding—even though they may only be advertising a cinema show. The southern Limagne even has its own saint, the recently-canonized and rather obscure Louise de

77

Marillac. But for all that the outstanding figure in its history was a secular one—Michel de l'Hospital, the great and tolerant sixteenth-century chancellor of France.

Three castles within sight of Aigueperse conserve his memory. The nearest, at Montpensier, stands ruined on its afforested hilltop, though it gave its name to the duchy whose capital was Aigueperse—and also to the absurd 'Grande Mademoiselle'. The second, at Effiat, is now essentially a renaissance manor, formal-courtyarded and tower-flanked, inhabited but visitable: its ruling house, whose most infamous member was the boy Cinque-Mars, included several of the grubbiest of those parasites, rakes and traitors who characterized the court of the detestable Richelieu. But it is the third castle, La Roche, which most preserves that intriguing blend of the military and the domestic which one finds at (for instance) Stokesay.

Built and rebuilt from the eleventh to the sixteenth centuries, this is associated with the Black Prince, Buridan (who 'fust geté en ung sac en Saine'), and the house of the treacherous Connétable de Bourbon, as well as with Michel himself. But always its military character was dominant, and today the formidable guardroom, and the terraces for pouring hot lead from, remain more impressive than the small dark parlours.

More impressive than either, however, is La Roche's impregnable situation. Stand in its courtyard and look out through the great gateway at the Puy de Dôme, miles away across lonely heathland but seeming little higher than you are. Even if one discounts the legend that the Limagne castles were once linked by tunnels (which, if it were true, would represent the greatest engineering feat of the middle ages), La Roche and its sisters are still haunting places.

*

Ten miles or so southward brings you to a bluff on the western flank of the narrowing Limagne, to the 12,000-strong *sous-préfecture* of Puy-de-Dôme, and to one of the golden cities of the world.

There are two ways of approaching Riom, as any *ville d'art*. The first is to treat it as a formal guide or guide-book must treat it—as a collection as carefully arranged as the exhibits in its museums. There is the Ste-Chapelle, for instance, a perfect provincial analogue of its Parisian namesake and a reminder of the days when Riom was the judicial centre of the whole Auvergne: it still retains some special legal functions in commemoration of that era. There is the late gothic church of Marthuret, with its infinitely-renowned fourteenth-century statue of Our Lady with the Bird (and, almost incidentally it seems, with Our Lord too), and St Amable as well. And there are all the domestic survivals of Riom's prosperity, which began in the thirteenth century with the great norman ruler Philip Augustus, continued through the fourteenth thanks to that mad patron of the arts Duke Jean de Berry, and flowered fully in the fifteenth.

This is certainly one way of seeing the place. But I think it would result in even greater disappointment than usual, for little in Riom is individually very satisfying. The church of Marthuret has a couple of old windows and other works of art but is in itself a low, shapeless and much-restored building: romanesque St Amable (named after a fifth-century evangelist and patron of those bitten by snakes who is venerated early in June by a folklore procession) is loaded with sixteenth-century mistakes and nineteenth-century woodwork. And even the S-curved Vierge à l'Oiseau—whose image possibly relates to the charming apocryphal legend of the Christ-child fashioning living birds from clay and being consoled by His Mother when one of them pecked His finger—does not seem to me quite to merit the panegyrics heaped upon Her.

No: Riom is a town, a whole town. It is its roads—the ringway which follows the ancient ramparts and the main streets which expose prospects so deliciously changing in all dimensions. It is the little squares and fountains, the towers, the market-town industries, and above all the medallioned renaissance *hôtels* and doorways and courtyards which make Riom a city with only one peer in Europe—and that peer far off in Westphalia.

*

All about, amid orchards of cherry and apricot standing a thousand feet above the sea, there is a ring of things of interest or beauty which are both satellites of Riom and part of the solar system of Clermont. For example, if Riom itself has no great ecclesiastical treasure the lack is filled by the contiguous village of Mozac.

From the road this is only a picturesque and rather squalid tangle of barnyards and masons' yards; but at its edge, down by the stream, stands a romanesque marvel. If one would not suspect this approaching the place unlettered, it is because the church of Mozac was in origin conventual: unlike the vast majority of revolution-surviving churches in all parts of France, it stands not hemmed-in by houses at the heart of its parish but like an English cathedral in secluded water-meadows without the walls.

It is a low building in a low valley, invisible until one has come upon it through dung-plastered streets which must have changed little since abbatical days. Even then the exterior is less than distinguished. This quiet church of St Peter appears at first a patch-work of stones, flint and mortar; it looks a mess of unfinished arcades and crumbled buttresses and tympani gutted of whatever survived a fifteenth-century remodelling on the cheap—and *then* the age of reason—to fill the cold museums of France.

But bow your head and enter. High above loom the norman capitals, many still in their original colours. On your own level—whether in the baptistry or the *musée lapidaire* outside—rest their fallen sisters, each almost as tall as a man. The initial, interior impression hammers home the fundamental marvel of quarter-tons of intricately-carved stone hung in space. Only after that does one begin tracing out the iconography. And only after *that* does one notice the fifteenth-century woodwork and glass, the monastic outworks, and the sacristy which holds the reliquaries of St Calmin (who is supposed to have founded *une abbaye bénédictine* here several centuries before St Benedict) and of St Austremoine. This latter was the Auvergne's first priest, and was borne hither on the shoulders of Pepin le Bref: both he and Calmin are venerated by annual processions, as is the skull of Pepin himself. At every stage, this church of Mozac remains one of those places where the heart stops for centuries.

*

So, taken in conjunction, Riom and Mozac provide almost all that a man has a right to ask. It could all, of course, have been spoiled by deciding to create a spa. But *that* was left to Châtel-Guyon, up in the hills amid the square *tonne* houses of the vignerons.

Châtel-Guyon lets you know it is one of the greater spas of the Auvergne the moment you arrive at its station. This is imposing enough to be a main-line terminus, boasts the kind of lavatory one

Chaudes-Aigues (*left*) would like to become a spa like Royat (*right*).

17

Romanesque glories of Puy de Dôme: the church of
St Nectaire (*above*) and a capital from Orcival (*below*).

18

expects at a spa, and has a special guichet labelled 'places de luxe'. It is as easy there as at Biarritz to envisage the parasoled *beau monde* descending from clerestoried through-cars hauled down from Paris by a high-stepping Edwardian engine.

After that opening Châtel-Guyon never lets up. Hôtel Grande, Hôtel Splendide. Hôtel Superbe—seventy-five of them—rise in concrete cliffs amid the cliffs of nature or stare from a hundred windows across the heathy country: Maison Primavera, Villa Neptune, Pension 'Home' fill the gaps. This pip of an old village (it is hard to realize that there was once a castle and a Guy to name the place), plumped-out by a lush peach-flesh of gleaming hypochondriac-houses and casinos, is one of the most single-minded of all such creations: it is not surprising that it was France's most favoured wartime funk-hole.

Its speciality is the grand miseries of the guts, which 10,000 fools a year come here to cure. But at a pinch simple *santé* or even *beauté* is good enough for Châtel-Guyon, whose aim is to be *nonchalant et féminin*. Nor are its claims confined to its thirty kinds of worthless water; for along the main street the oddest of regimes are offered, including *pyropharmacie* and a selection of herbal cures. There are, for example, heather for its diuretic, antiseptic and anti-putrid properties, *souverain dans les cystites*: burdock, the *plante à pénécilline*: and worse still.

After all this it is rather a relief to breathe the open air of the hills again, hills which are clad with terraced vineyards and riddled with cellars below the town, and above it pine-afforested.

*

North of Châtel-Guyon the village church of Yssac is worth a stroll: west of the spa, and approachable by a lovely birch-clad valley winding up to Loubeyrat, stands the castle of Chazeron. This is still inhabited, but has a sad air and a dishonourable history (Gamelin was imprisoned here in the Vichy days, for example, at the same time as de Lattre de Tassigny was escaping from Riom jail) and at the end of a long climb it comes as something of a disappointment. What with the ugly seventeenth-century brick orangeries about its old stone heart and the surrounding woodlands it is difficult to grasp in the round—and even more difficult to see over, despite the advertised *circuits touristiques*.

So perhaps it is best to leave Chazeron in its solitude, where many high round towers look over the Limagne—north to the little village of St Bonnet where there is magnificent woodwork in the church and a magnificent crucifix in the *curé's* backyard, east to Ennezat where again there are rich ecclesiastic treasures (in the days before the Limagne was drained, they called its great rambling church of SS Victor and Couronne, which may be the birthplace of all norman-Auvergnat art, a cathedral of the fens), or south to Marsat with its miraculous byzantine Virgin and strange annual offerings of helical candles to Her.

*

The paths west from Châtel-Guyon run out to a still more famous castle. For past a huge sanatorium, and gorges and waterfalls (such as those of Enval) which here hardly merit a star but which would be the stopping-place of a dozen charabancs elsewhere, they rise to Tournoël.

This elaborate and impregnable *tour abolie* has played its full part in history from Merovingian times, being rich in legends of a lady who became a very merry widow before she was of age and of a gentleman who filled it with his bastards: few places in the Auvergne, indeed, are so charged with tales of the middle-middle ages, of the courts of love and war. But today it is simply a romantic fragment atop the forests, dressed up in season with all the splendours of *son-et-lumière*—the twentieth century's own addition to the world of fairy-tale, and one which would certainly have delighted the castle's flamboyant Françoise de Talaru.

Just up the combe lies a small town with a celebrated name, Volvic. And here one exchanges the shrill of the cricket amid sweet-chestnut and birch for the whirr of wire on stone, the cockerel for the chisel, the shot-gun's blast for the thunder of dynamite, and a grass track underfoot for roads which are powdered with glittering dust in the rare fine weather but usually runnels of grey mud. For Volvic, below the renaissance calvary which witnesses a great May pilgrimage, is the place where the volcanic lava of the Puy country makes its north-easternmost thrust across the Combrailles to the Limagne, and comes most readily to hand.

*

It is not a beautiful stone, being essentially a rather superior kind of pumice: nor is it all that durable, affording a gleeful foothold for lichens. Like the chalk of Touraine, it has made for a profusion of renaissance carving in unexpected places; but one's first feeling is that it is better used as an industrial catalyst, or as a base for such enamel-work as forms the standard road-signs of France. Still, it *is* easy to work; and hence for eight hundred years it has provided not merely the disfigurement of as many churches as Purbeck marble but Volvic's sole industry. Off the streets of the town lie the masons' yards where grey slabs are worked up by hand into divers (but mainly funereal) shapes. In its squares stand numerous crucifixes, images, fountains, war memorials and columns to nothing in particular. Its graveyard is a sumptuous place, where the poorest families lie under tombs whose artifice must be the envy of those whose dear ones departed this earth from its less malleable outcrops. And a good deal of what was left over is plastered about the town promiscuously in the form of bas-reliefs, pilasters and pediments serving no purpose except as trade-cards to advertise the sculptor.

The church of St Priest was mercilessly knocked about in the last century, and today the grey lava-stone with its hard white pointing gives the effect of a Wesleyan chapel in Huddersfield. Even the arches look pinched and narrow, as if their builders or rebuilders did not trust their material to bear those titanic romanesque weights; and the tower rises only to an overhanging entablature as grotesque as the hat of an Orthodox bishop. But the choir escaped, and contains a fine series of capitals—one of which is conspicuously signed, showing that the local love of lapidary publicity is more than eight centuries old. Elsewhere in the church are some Carolingian remains, the shrine and instruments of martyrdom of St Priest himself (a much-venerated bishop of Clermont who was put to the sword in the seventh century) and a fourteenth-century Madonna. There is also something which you will find in church after church from here to the Mediterranean—a spritely, vernacular and bacchanalian image of St Verney, patron of vignerons, carved in wood in the seventeenth century and wearing the broad-brimmed hat which grape-gatherers wear today.

Further on down the series of basalt tongues which run out from the west flank of the Limagne are other places of note. But beyond

Volvic, as at some spot nearer to moon than earth, the tug of gravity is reversed. The pull is no longer towards Riom but towards Clermont itself, now little over five miles away where the Puy-de-Dôme blocks the sky like the burial mound of a god. And before that pull is succumbed to, the right flank of the Limagne waits to be explored.

*

There is not, in fact, so much to be said of the eastern edge of the great plain, for the water-meadows of the Allier held few attractions for abbot or seigneur. It was not until the seventeenth-century, indeed, that wealth flashed like lightning across the cornfields and a little town (all that is left of it now is a single tower) became Vichy *la royale*, queen of spas.

It is not for me to challenge that title. In size alone, this *sous-préfecture* of Allier has a resident population of over 30,000 (which is greater than that of all the other Auvergnat spas combined) and accordingly has a year-round life. It is the oldest of them, if one forgets about those romans—older even than Bath, though its prettiest buildings are of the early nineteenth century. It is the most gracious of them, with its charming parks and rotundas and pavilions and little go-carts for the kiddies; and the liveliest for *spectacles*, too, if you like that kind of thing. (Vichy, for instance, is easily the northernmost town in Europe to stage regular bull-fights.) It is the most thorough of them, for here are all the specialities for all the livers in the world: be they twisted, swollen or softened in the extreme, they will be cleaned, scraped, washed, treated by *bains, douches, bains avec douches soumarines, douches sur le lit, douches massages dites de Vichy, bains de vapeur et de lumière, aspiroclyse ...application de boues végétominérales, massages à sec* and others I could mention, and so returned to digest once again the richest of bad cooking and a full daily ration of raw alcohol. Finally, Vichy has two oddities.

The first is its church—or churches—of St Blaze. Of the ancient building little remains unchanged except the head of a black Virgin, now re-christened Notre-Dame-des-Malades; but a very modern basilica has been grafted on to it. The exterior of this is monstrous; but inside it is at least interesting, and the glass is unqualifiedly good. There is, incidentally, an aura of *real* faith-cures at Vichy, though it is mixed up with the bogus-medical witchcraft on heart and stomach and gout and diabetes: each August, for instance, there is a quasi-religious procession of *touristes et curistes*.

The other curiosity lies beyond the sandbanks of the Allier in one of Vichy's suburbs. (There are several of these, Cusset being the largest, most attractive and most historic.) The gimmick here in Bellerive—apart from the 'Omnisports' fun-fair—is an *intermittent* source: water which comes up from thousands of feet underground meets a sharp temperature gradient on the way and gets past it like a spurting kettle. The emissions come only about every three hours, and as nobody publishes a time-table you have to take your chance; but I was lucky and can report that, though the warm white gusher rises from its iron pipe only a foot or two instead of the twelve promised by the guide-book, it is an interesting and even rather exciting thing to watch.

On the whole I like Vichy with its Napoleon III *snobisme*, and for better reasons than that it is the only Auvergnat spa *on the level* or that one of its few mildly eminent sons, the poet Valéry-Larbaud, shared my fondness for trains. It is a haunting place out of season, especially during the lunch-time hush: then, wandering past its three hundred and more deserted hotels and three thousand lodging-houses, you can successively imagine yourself in Seville, Andermatt, Baghdad or wherever else their Sunset Boulevard architects had in mind. One could pleasantly spend a couple of days there, I think, with excursions up into the hills; but not longer. For here is what Mme de Sévigny had to say.

'*J'ai donc pris les eaux*,' this eminent seventeenth-century rheumatic wrote of her baptism. '*Ah! qu'elles sont mauvaises. On va à 6h. à la fontaine . . . on boit et l'on fait une forte vilaine mine, car imaginez-vous qu'elle est bouillante et d'un goût de salpêtre fort désagréable. On tourne, on va, on vient, on se promène. Enfin, on dîne . . . on va chez quelqu'un . . . on va se promener . . . on soupe . . . Et l'on se met ensuite dans un lit chaud, et voilà ce qui guérit.*'

The great lady was mistaken about the saltpetre, for Vichy water is simply bicarb. Furthermore, ten degrees above blood-heat is hardly *bouillante*. But dully gleaming through the words is the infinitely elegant boredom of all spas from the Grand Siècle to the present day.

*

After Vichy, What? a headline of the city's shameful years might have run. The present answer is that the highway labelled 106 (and with it a branch railway) runs down along the Allier into Puy-de-Dôme with the little towns of St-Yorre and Puy-Guillaume on it, and Ris and Châteldon just off it, for twenty miles to the Limagne-head. Of these places only St-Yorre, with a bottled-mineral-water renown and castled Busset nearby, comes in for much glory today. But old Châteldon is a pleasant enough spot even if you do not like home-made astronomical clocks. And Ris, now a crumpled village with a tiny crumbling church and suspension bridge, once produced a wine so great that it was used at a king's crowning.

Finally—away towards the centre of the plain on the diagonal Vichy-Clermont route—there are two places of more importance in Randan and Maringues. The former has the hotels and an enclave of prehistory nearby: the latter is a most charming township with old tanneries overhanging a stream which comes across from behind Riom and a norman-and-late-gothic church with good bosses and woodwork. The only other important feature of this side of the plain is that the Allier sheds (or accepts—for it is always difficult to think straight when working against the flow of a river) a tributary to the south as *it* itself swings over a little to the west.

This tributary is the Dore. It is important topographically, but perhaps the most interesting thing about it is its name, which is a witness of a heritage older than Rome. For *dore* (or *ore*) is Auvergnat for water, and stems from something Sanskrit or Indo-European or Turanian or Altonic or whatever, and so is cognate not only with *acqua* and *eau* but with all our Afons and Avons and Usks and Ouses and Exes and Wyes—with the Dourbies of Touraine, the Doves of Derbyshire and the mistranslated Golden Valley of Hereford, perhaps with Dover, and certainly with 'whisky'.

*

The whole Limagne is now defined, so far as one can define a tossing sea. For a stone's throw south, as straight as a dyke across an estuary-head, the 89 road and its associated railway form the highway which takes the big stuff from the Atlantic coast through to Lyons, and Grenoble, and Switzerland.

The road itself bears such a tight channelling of cross-country traffic that the short twenty miles east from Clermont seems an unbroken string of *étapes des gourmets, relais des routiers* and similar road-houses which one skims past, fearing the hills to come. One maybe notes from the guide-book that Lezoux of the belfry and norman chapel was in roman times the centre of an art-pottery industry which fed Britain and Prussia—an industry, based on the Limagne clay, which survives in the important but humdrum form of making those hollow ceramic building materials of the French. But before one has time to think much about it one is in Thiers.

*

Thiers precisely marks a corner of the Limagne sac. The roads south from Vichy and east from Clermont join under it, and snarl together up its main street at the start of a thousand-foot climb. Here, one is certain, one will find a city of note.

There are in fact three cities. The first is the ancient stronghold built about the shrine of St Genès, a mule-mounted local martyr. This is represented today by his own church (a broad, sloping and much-cut-about bit of romanesque, whose treasure is a fascinating merovingian mosaic), by the historied but somehow unconvincing church of Moutier in the even older quarter across the river, and by several ancient houses—including the one of the Seven Sins—of which the best is the so-called Château de Pirou. Rather remarkably, this and all the handsomer things in Thiers are not of carved stone but half-timbered; and this fact gives the steep corbelled streets of the city a northern-gothic look such as you will find nowhere in the Auvergne except in this neighbourhood. There is also, I think, an Italian note to the interiors of the old houses with their flat roofs. Thiers has several links with Piedmont: they even tried to grow rice here until the death-rate from malaria got out of hand.

The second Thiers is the town which makes knives and all kinds of knife-like things. Beginning—they say—with secrets brought back from the first crusade, the trade of stamping and sharpening blades spread up the valley until Thiers' little stream drove 130 mills. Today, in the age of electric power, stainless steel and plastic handles, there are 1,200. . . .

For—improbably enough—this town of *pittoresque chaotique* has not let its industry dwindle into a craft but has maintained its quanti-

87

Illustration 8

tative lead. It is rural Thiers, not Lille or Paris or Lyons, which is responsible for 70% of all the cutlery production of France—much of it exported. (Thiers confesses to having dies stamped 'Toledo' and 'Pittsburgh': it also, I think, has some marked 'Sheffield'.) Even more surprisingly, the industry has through co-operation retained the craft flavour it had when the grinders of Thiers lay on their bellies in the open beside the water-mills, their noses literally to the grindstone and their dogs on top of them for warmth. Even in Sheffield the majority of cutlery works still have a payroll of less than ten, but the *average* Thiers knife-works today employs just five men, and many of these are outworkers or part-timers.

The third Thiers is a synthesis of the others. It is the tourist town, with its hillside site (they like to pun that this is a town of tiers), its wide views over the local hills, its black-and-white houses and glittering cutlers' windows, its well-stocked museum and its half-sophisticated neighbours up the valley. Thiers is not merely the most beautifully-situated manufacturing city in Europe but also, I think, among the most intrinsically beautiful. Forget about the grimy secrecy of our own northern industry. Thiers, which never knew a dark Satanic mill nor any coal except the *houille blanche* of the Auvergne, treats its trade as a tourist attraction.

This *sous-préfecture* of Puy-de-Dôme—population 17,000—is a unique place. It is also a show-piece for those who believe that self-employing craftsmanship is fully compatible with modern manufacture. I cannot quite *like* Thiers, I cannot find it a place to linger in. But it is most certainly a place to be seen.

*

So closes the Limagne. Stand on the terrace of Thiers and look for the last time over the great plain to the north-west. There is nothing as flat for a hundred miles in any other direction.

Three Ranges and a Valley

To the east of the Limagne, in echelon, are the Madeleine, the Bois Noirs, and the Forez... It is very easy to write something like that. But it is harder to define these three ranges which have much more to unite than to separate them—and which were once, indeed, combined as the province of Forez.

All are granite ridges. All are thickly afforested, except for the pasture-lands of their lower slopes and the heaths of their extreme crests; and if one accepts the British army's splendid simplification of arboriculture—that there are only pine-trees, bushy-topped trees, and hedges—then pine-type trees win. (The bushy ones are mostly beech or the sacred hazel.) Their crest points *do* climb steadily as one moves southward—3,800 feet for the Madeleine, 4,300 for the Bois Noirs, and 5,400 for the Forez—but it is not a spectacular difference. And, finally, they are divided from each other by cols (one of them important, one not) rather than by wide distinctive valleys.

Thus these hills—the first truly Auvergnat ones of this book, though politically their north was once Bourbon territory—present themselves as a single system. Their upper edge is defined by the 7 road from north of Vichy to Roanne, and their lower by a departmental frontier, so that they measure well over fifty miles from tip to toe. Laterally they are contained by the Dore and the Loire, which here flow almost parallel (and almost due north) some thirty miles apart.

*

Climbing east from Vichy and its own backyard hills, by the minor roads which run beside a pretty stream and an abandoned tramway bed marking part of the huge system of secondary railways which once laced these parts, one may come after about fifteen miles to four

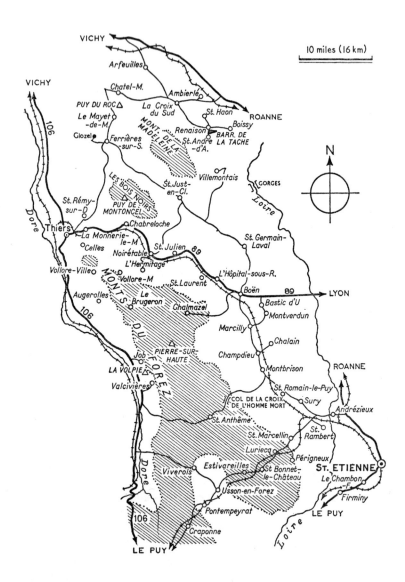

VICHY

10 miles (16 km)

Arfeuilles

VICHY

Chatel-M.
Ambierlé
PUY DU ROC △
La Croix
du Sud
St. Haon
ROANNE
Le Mayet
-de-M.
Renaison
Boissy
Glozel
Ferrières
-sur-S.
St.André
-d'A.
BARR. DE
LA TACHE

Villemontais
GORGES

St.Just-
en-Cl.
Loire
LES BOIS NOIRS
St. Rémy-
sur-D
PUY DE
MONTONCEL
Chabreloche
St. Germain-
Laval
Thiers
La Monnerie-
le-M
Celles
St. Julien
89
Noirétable
L'Hermitage
L'Hôpital-sous-R.
Vollore-Ville
Vollore-M.
St. Laurent
Boën
89
LYON
Augerolles
Le
Brugeron
Chalmazel
Bastie d'U
Montverdun
Marcilly
Chalain
Job
PIERRE-SUR-
HAUTE
Champdieu
LA VOLPIE
Montbrison
ROANNE
Valcivières
Col de la Croix
de l'Homme Mort
St. Romain-le-Puy
Sury
Andrézieux
St. Anthème
St. Marcellin
St.
Rambert
Lurieca
Périgneux
Viverols
Estivareilles
St. Bonnet-
le-Château
ST. ETIENNE
Le Chambon
-F.
Usson-en-Forez
Firminy
Pontempeyrat
LE PUY
106
Craponne
LE PUY
Loire

N

little towns to the west of the crestline of the Madeleine and so still in the department of Allier. These are—reading down the map—Arfeuilles, Châtel-Montagne, le Mayet-de-Montagne, and Ferrières-sur-Sichon. All are about 1,700 feet up, have a thousand or two inhabitants and one or two hotels, and are separated from their neighbours by only five miles: their fishing is supposed to be good. Ferrières has two small claims to attention in the shape of a fairy grotto (most of its stalactites have been stolen, but they are busily looking for more), and nearby at Glozel a museum of prehistoric oddities now considered bogus, and perhaps the more interesting for that. Châtel-Montagne has a major claim, in the massive, clear-cut and only discreetly restored shape of a church whose lonely site epitomizes all the awe and remoteness of the high romanesque. This is not merely the most important building which all these forests can show. It is great by the standards of the Auvergne, which is to say of all Europe which knew the normans: it is the peer of the more famed basilicas south of Clermont, and its west front eclipses theirs.

The energetic, having feasted on this cluniac masterpiece, can either climb the Puy du Roc close by for a general panorama of the area from almost the 2,000-ft contour (*puy*, in these parts, means just a peak and not necessarily a volcanic one), or set out on a tour of numerous minor norman churches. The rest can drive on, over the spine and the frontier, into the department which is—at first surprisingly—named Loire, and so past a node of the region called La Croix du Sud down to Renaison.

Renaison is on the extreme eastern shelf of the Madeleine. Almost washed by the artificial lake of la Tâche which very elegantly collects Roanne's water, and overlooking the plains of the Loire, it is a tourist centre. It is also a centre of viticulture, producing an elegant *rosé* which will stand up against anything made beyond the river. But more interesting are its neighbours.

There is Ambierle, for instance, so far away on the northern shoulder that you can see it from the St Germain-Roanne railway. Its wine does not quite rival Renaison's, whatever they may say; but it has a fine eighteenth-century house which enshrines an unusual museum as well as a striking, clean-lined and individual *flamboyant* church of cluniac foundation with a tower attached. This church —as purely architected as any church I know—enshrines a thousand

91

Illustration 12

square feet of superb if confused late-medieval glass, mainly in the five great *chevet* lancets which stretch from floor to ceiling in a blaze of colour which almost kills Ambierle's other treasures—a Flemish triptych of the same period and some painted bosses. In this isolated village on the extreme north of the plateau (where there was recently a *cause célèbre* between the fifth republic and the schoolmistress) is the finest glass which it can show anywhere.

St Haon, nearer to Renaison and with the 'o' silent, has no monument of this status; but is a remote, fortified, half-ruined and highly-explorable town with all the piquancy which comes from a prosperity which was already vanishing in the seventeenth century. Then, just east of Renaison, there is the gracious manor of Boisy—the house of Jacques Coeur, they call it, for the name of this merchant prince who financed the half-imbecile Charles VII (and hence, indirectly, Joan of Arc) is as celebrated here as in Bourges itself. Finally, to the south on the way down to Villemontais, St André-d'Apchon has a renaissance castle and some most precious renaissance glass in its church.

Good wine: quite good food creeping up from the Roannais: glowing glass: turreted manors and crumbling walls: and up on the heights hellebore and gentian, wild carnations and geraniums, stonecrop, gillyflower and wolfbane: there is a richness here surrounding Renaison.

•

One does not find it as one moves back to the south-west, across the little valley which divides the Madeleine from the Bois Noirs. These latter, at their crest of the Puy de Montoncel, support the triple point of Allier, Loire and Puy-de-Dôme. But so small and unpopulous are they that there are perhaps only two things to be said of them—that of all the Black Forests and Black Mountains which I have seen between Wales and Bohemia these really *look* black except when the sunset turns them translucent, and that they have a presentable tourist centre, 2,000 feet high and with an old quarter surrounding the still higher castle, in St Just-en-Chevalet, at the combe-head and well into Loire.

So one comes down to the latitude of Thiers and the main lateral valley of these hills—the valley which takes the 89 road and the branch railway through from Clermont on the direct but tough way to Lyons. Both the cutlery (there is a rattle of forges everywhere here) and the tourist industries of Thiers straggle steeply and densely up into the hills, with St Rémy-sur-Durolle, la Monnerie-le-Montel and Celles as the main centres; but they, and with them Puy-de-Dôme, end at Chabreloche. This is again more than 2,000 feet up and marks the end of the steep climb: the route has only 300 feet more to go before it reaches the crest (which even the French do not call a pass) at Noirétable, in Loire again.

Apart from a few megaliths such as stud all these hills, and a surprisingly lush hotel, Noirétable on the open plateau has not much of interest: men even seem to have forgotten the outlying castles which once gave it a tourist fame. But its site is a watershed and something more: it divides not only the Allier basin from that of the Loire but the two northern ranges from the Forez. And so one must leave Noirétable, and the 89's descent to the plains through a series of pleasant villages (like St Julien and l'Hôpital-sous-Rochefort and St Laurent) to discover what these still higher hills—pronounce them how you like—can offer.

*

This, I am afraid, is little more than a series of holiday-villages, places with one simple hotel and a few Swiss chalets. The Forez is notably higher than the Bois Noirs—as you discover when, with your heart pounding from the climb, you try to light a cigarette in its thin air: it climbs through the tree-line to contours almost a mile high, has the first serious snow-sheds of the region, and is visibly more alpine than its northern neighbours. The chalets—which, I suppose, have brought a kind of prosperity to otherwise failing hamlets—are thoroughly bogus and clash with the traditional buildings of low, whitewashed stone; but the peasant's way of life has the flavour of even higher ranges. There is, for instance, a kind of *Alpaufzug* (which does *not* mean, as a learned professor once translated it, a train for going up mountains in) between the inhabited belt about 3,000 feet high and the summer pastures which begin above the trees at 4,000 or so. The High Stubbles, they call these latter; and so high and broken by spines of rock are they that there is no presentable

motor-road running east and west for thirty-odd miles south from
Noirétable. The holiday-hamlets hence tend to be dead-ends, in at
least the literal sense.

Most of them hang from the west, or Puy-de-Dôme, side of the
hill (which is here, reversing the situation in the Madeleine, the
steeper one). Vollore, *Ville et Montagne*; le Brugeron; Job; Valcivières; there they are, between 1,750 and 2,750 feet in altitude but
offering little except that *flaîcheur* so loved of the French, their possibility of winter sports, their situation (particularly happy for the
last-named) and their excursions to nearby rocks and waterfalls like
those of la Volpie. The Vollores boast a few antiquities of their own,
and there are others at l'Hermitage and Augerolles. But mostly it is
just heights.

One height, however, should not be forgotten. This is the one called
simply the Pierre-sur-Haute. One cannot climb every peak, and I
have never climbed this. But I wish that I had, for just now and
then one needs to desert these main-road panoramas which are
sucked in as effortlessly as a moving train sucks in water, and to
get *up there* the hard way—partly to survey the land and see where
one has been and where one is going, partly because men need
(though not too often) to delude themselves that they are birds or
aeroplanes or gods, however their aching limbs tell them that they
are not.

The Stone On High was a holy place to the Gauls; and still, I
believe, there is a service of blessing there on Assumption Day and a
Stonehenge-like gathering on midsummer morn. Furthermore, if
the guide-books speak truth, you can from this crest of all the Forez
see the Dômes and the Dores to the west, the Cantals to the south-
west, the Velay and Vivarais southwards, and all round the eastern
horizon the Alps—and even the Jura—rising behind the hills of
Roanne and Lyons with perhaps the dawn exploding behind them
through the mist. The contour map suggests they *may* be speaking
truth.

*

On the Loire side of these much-watered uplands there seems only
one town which anybody has noticed: it is called Chalmazel. But
before moving a few miles south, a few hundred feet down the

gradient, one should perhaps ask if something is not slipping away from these high woods and crystalline rocks where men once said that land was worth a penny an acre and life was nine months of winter and three of hell.

They are no place for the luxury-lover; and lovers of rustic solitude may either deplore their little attempts at sophistication or come to love unsophisticated rusticity rather less. But there is a genuine feel to the area. Feather-beds; neat farming on forty-five-degree slopes; stone cow-pens called *burons*, fine strapping girls and old men deformed by goitres; ox-carts, sacred fountains, and perhaps the glimpse of an eagle's wing; timber-yards with clumsy water-towers; one bus a day if you are lucky and one a week if you are not, curtain upon curtain of hills before you (I have counted eight here, though the last *might* have been cloud); sweet tawny wine and great dreamy skies and the sun and storm fighting from slope to opposing slope; this is the Forez. Perhaps these impressions hold for any upland country, but they are combined in different ways. Perhaps there is not much more to say of the range, for there is never much to say of solitude. But I should hate to be thought blind to its pine-scented charm, even if I feel it a land to be passed through by many winding lanes and crests and cols rather than to be lingered in.

Those who fancy passing through it by an easier route have a respectable way a little further south, where the cross-country road is well-surfaced and serves the real town of St Anthême. This is admittedly a very *small* real town. But it is the easternmost cantonment in all Puy-de-Dôme, as well as being the support of several ski-hotels and in general a well-sited place. And so, I suppose, it is entitled to some respect.

The road, of course, is not all that easy. One side of St Anthême is the pass of Dead Man's Cross. The other side there is a lake called, simply, Hell.

*

One must change Michelin sheets, and pass over the cantonment of Viverols (which maintains an ancient look though it no longer attracts a procession of penitents) before one finds the last of these mountains, where they slope down to another traversal road and the branch railway which twists beside it without much topographical excuse. These mark the cleft where the granite Forez merges into the higher and more famous limestone mountains to the south; but they also run into unexplored country to the west, and so it seems best to follow them—for a change—from right to left of the map.

St Bonnet-le-Château is the first town met on coming this way from the eastern versant, where there are scattered, semi-mountain resorts like St Marcellin, Périgneux and Luriecq. And suddenly, just as one has decided that the only places with a real look of past glory in all these ranges are to be found on the northern edge of the Madeleine, one discovers a gem on the southern edge of the Forez— and nearly 3,000 feet up, too.

St Bonnet no longer has a château, and holds only the dimmest memories of the eponymous saint who passed this way—albeit dead —in the eighth century. But it does have a granite church which dominates the landscape for miles and is no disappointment when one reaches it. Outside this may appear a little lopsided, pinched by its site and cluttered by stairways; but within it is simple and spacious. It houses some excellent frescoes, divers *objets d'art,* and (they say) mummies.

Leave it and you find a terrace with a view. It is a good view, and perhaps a great one: you can clearly see Mont Blanc and the slopes of Italy from this lovely northern-gothic building. One wishes that English hill-towns would more commonly provide this simple but civilized amenity, and counts those which do: Bridgnorth, Lancaster, Rye . . . it is hard to fill one hand.

Behind, the town of St Bonnet has its own charms. There is a good chapel, a gateway and wall, and certainly the most attractive streets in the whole Forez—and the liveliest too. Despite the fact that its traditional craft is that of the gunmaking which has now moved down to a greater city, some *fleuri* spirit out of Touraine or the Lyonnais or even Perigord seems to have blown into these primitive parts: symbolically, the stationmaster's garden is planted with dark cypresses on one side and high papery hollyhocks on the other. I can think of no reason for this enclave of grace other than that the presiding spirit of St Bonnet—as so often in the heights—was a woman. She was the lovely Anne of Dauphiné, Countess of Forez at the close of the fourteenth century.

They have taken my happy St Bonnet out of one tourist guide in favour of some dreary lake or other. But for the diligent there are some dubious druidic remains to be found nearby.

*

'Nearby', moving south-west down this charming and curiously neglected vein of communication, takes you through walled Esti-vareilles to Usson-en-Forez. By comparison with St Bonnet this is a humble spot, though it has the castle-remains, the roman road *and* the tourist hotel; but the sense of a hushed and holy corner of France persists. I was perhaps brought to these parts only by a sense of duty, but I shall return for pleasure. The cooking is simple but satisfying: the wine unadvertised but surprisingly good.

Over Pontempeyrat—the next halt down the line—I draw a curtain. It is near the triple point of Loire, Puy-de-Dôme and Haute-Loire—a point which lies, unusually enough, in a hollow. It is historically a frontier-town, where the calvinists gathered to assault Le Puy; and it also seems to have the best hostelry in the region. But I came down into its 1,000-foot combe on foot with the August sweat streaming out of me—and went on up again because I had not observed that The Train ran only on Saturdays.

'Craponne regardless,' I remember muttering then. It was the kind of stupid phrase which runs round in a mind near to sunstroke, for Craponne is the last town down this road. It seemed then mostly saw-mills, and I did not even visit its presentable-looking church. But it was cosmopolitan enough to have a bus, a bus with pink and blue windows which technicoloured everything, a bus which whisked me for the last time out of these beautiful—but, perhaps, rather *dull*—hills and on to the cardinal, central, turntable plateau which divides four or five regions of the Auvergne.

*

And that should be the end of a brief chapter. The Auvergne, they say in their arbitrary way, ends at the crest-line of the Madeleine-Bois Noirs-Forez complex, and everything east of it is something else. But they do not say *what* it is (for it is certainly not yet the Beaujolais): there is no change in way of life at the watershed and little at the foothill-line: and historically the plain was always linked to the hills. I have already hinted that the country of this book continues down to the undercliff of the Loire: now I go on to suggest that it does not end until the river itself.

For you cannot define a range without its flanking valleys any more than a football field without its touchdowns. You must always ask what is on the other side of the hills; and in any case this basin of the Loire—left and right flank alike—is a most interesting one in its own right. It would be an exaggeration to claim that the alluvial plain which runs the whole length of the three ranges forms an independent land like Andorra or a hidden fertility like Shangri-La; but it *does* have a private quality to it. And there is a good topographical reason for this.

Almost every great river of central France (like most of those of the world) follows a standard pattern. It rises in sweet cow-tinkling uplands. It accepts tributary after tributary, gathers strength, becomes a torrent and slices through a gorge which is essentially a structural crevice worn deeper by the stream itself. And then it finds the plains and becomes just another river flowing away to the Mediterranean or the Atlantic. The gorges usually occur fairly high upstream, which is why very few of the starred clefts of the plateau are found in the department which bears the name of their river. The Dordogne gorges are in Corrèze, for instance, and those of the Tarn mostly in Lozère.

But the Loire *had* to be different. Born in the very heart of the highlands, it has a more complex relation to them. Moving south, west, and then north, it knows its 'innocent water-meadows, Where the trees lean low, complaining', and one if not two sets of true gorges too, before it breaks out of the hills—after having lost half a mile of height in the country of its birth. But instead of then heading easily for the Rhone, it continues north for a long, long way before deciding (it seems) that its end awaits in the sunset as an Atlantic river. And for half that northing it becomes a *boundary* of the plateau.

This cannot be plain sailing all the way, and at one point the Loire has to find another passage—to cut through a gap in its adolescence as well as its childhood. The point comes just southeast of Roanne, where the Madeleine and the Beaujolais are fused together 1,500 feet above sea level.

The narrows are not very terrible. The basin behind is on a latitude with the Limagne and at the same altitude of about a thousand feet: the resulting gorges are hence hardly gorges at all by Auvergnat standards. They are flanked only by hillsides, *panachées* with poplars, which curve down to a quite broad and already northern river: you are through them in ten minutes by the train from Roanne to St Etienne. But the road which follows them is little more than a mule track, and one has a sense of entering an enclosed land as one moves upstream into this lower-upper, or upper-middle, basin of the Loire.

*

With no particular reason (for the whole thing is as symmetrical as the intersecting arcs a schoolboy draws with his geometry set) all the riverside *towns* south from Roanne lie east of the chord of the river. Even that bank was once politically attached to the Forez, which indeed had its capital at Feurs; but one must take a line, and they do not belong here. On the left shore there are only villages, and the towns are drawn back against the undercliff.

There are no more than three of them. The northernmost is St Germain-Laval: there is nothing to be said of that, for its few antiquities are in a sorry state. The second is Boën, a tiered little place which rolls some mild-steel slabs: there is not much to be said of that. And the third is Montbrison, second capital of the Forez and second *préfecture* of Loire, of which there are several things to be said even if one discounts its gastronomic claims. It shows, for example, a most charming and terraced face to the little stream which waters it and which it spans with Venetian bridges. It has a thirteenth-to-fifteenth-century church, Notre-Dame d'Espérance, which is the best bit of gothic for many miles and has that warm, worshipped-in, *receptive* feeling which no guide-book mentions and which one is almost afraid to mention oneself lest it be an illusion. And it has its *Diane*.

La Diane (and the name has nothing to do with the goddess, but derives from *doyenne*) is of rather uncertain origin but is basically a fourteenth-century guildhall. The interior is rich and heraldic, but I almost prefer the atmosphere which crept in when it became the headquarters of the local cultural organization, artisans' institute or steam-improvement society. Viollet-le-Duc's façades, incorporating some ancient corbels, indeed strike one as the most perfect example in France (with the possible exception of that pagoda near Amboise) of an English, Strawberry-Hill-Gothick type of folly.

*

Such are the towns. But this half-moon sector of the Loire-side plains, thirty miles long by eight (at the most) broad does not depend for what distinction it has on towns alone.

There are, of course, the mountains—the Auvergnat ones which curve round the western horizon, the blue-bloomed winehills beyond the river. And even down in the plains themselves things are not quite as flat and *étang*-studded as they look from the map. The whole land has indeed an odd (and quite superficial) resemblance to both the middle Rhine valley and Lombardy—if one can conceive of Roanne standing for Strasbourg or Milan. And here, as there, there are numerous nippled hills supporting their half-ruined castle or church. Many of these are only a bow-shot from the river itself.

Montverdun: Marcilly: Champdieu: renaissance Chalain: and above all Bastic d'Urfé which bears the name of the great house of these parts and enshrines their most famous manor: these are only a handful of the villages which stud these plains or hang against the sun-rise edge of the Forez. If you want your own favourite, it will not be hard to find in this curious basin of scattered, loosely-built factories and mud walls which is crossed by Roman highways. And you will not eat and drink at all badly during the finding.

*

Beyond the villages of St Romain-le-Puy and Sury (which are both worth pausing at) the basin ends at St Etienne—*the* St Etienne.

It ends there because the Massif suddenly bulges out as voluptuously as a film starlet's bosom. South of St Etienne—which is itself about 1,700 feet up—whole ranges thrust violently to the east and the Rhone, so that the present-day *préfecture* of Loire, though well away on the river's right bank, is a true guardian-town of the plateau.

But what can one say of St Etienne itself? It has nearly 200,000 inhabitants, which is half as many again as Clermont; and it certainly does not act like it, for a naturally great city can never be challenged by one with a single richness. Since St Etienne is built only on coal and ironstone and sweat and muck and knowhow, one can do no more than compare it to its compeers. Trade-wise, the likeness would be to Sheffield for the alloy steels or to Birmingham for the guns and (for a man called Rudge introduced the French sacred animal here) the bicycle frames. But authority-wise it can only be to Manchester. St Étienne even has a shambles quarter round its church.

Of course no free man in his senses would pause here longer than it takes to put in a gallon of petrol or change trains, not with that sulphurous grit in his mouth, those slag-tips ringing the sky, that straight, straight street going on for ever—or, literally, for four miles. Yet in some ways St Étienne is not unpicturesque, with its jumbled Victorian tenements (ghastly—but how much better than Hulme) and its new buildings rounding over the hills (ghastly—but how much better than High Town). It has pleasant squares, the usual art galleries which salve the conscience of such cities, and Loire-side suburbs such as St Rambert which have a vine-hung grace such as you would not find at Glossop. One of the prettiest of these is Andrézieux, which was the old port of St Etienne and the site of the first railway in France, opened in 1828.

The objective awfulness of St Etienne as measured against the other black countries of Europe is perhaps impossible to assess: so much depends on the weather. Bibendum, even in this spot, goes looking for rocks and gorges; but for anyone who cares about the souls of cities the most impressive thing about St Etienne (as of so many mansions of the damned) is its passionate local pride. One is not a *Stéphanois* or 'black fool'—and certainly one does not play in its first-division football team—for nothing.

*

And that is the end. South-east of St Etienne a mountain mounts the sky behind the smokestacks and blast furnaces. Southwest the trolley-bus lines straggle back to the Loire through unspeakable suburbs (and here even Stockport wins) like le Chambon-Feugerolles and Firminy. But Firminy is at the start of a country into which only the hardy would push a canoe, a country where the Loire enters its real gorges, a country of hay-scented heights at St Etienne's back door. And one is again south, far south of Clermont and the central mountains.

Churches, Castles and Cure-Houses

he happiest approach (and how long one has had to delay it)
to the city of Clermont-Ferrand—the *préfecture* of Puy-de-
Dôme, the old official capital of the Low Auvergne and unofficial one of the whole Massif—is on a summer's night and by rail
from the west. Then the floodlit châteaux under the tremendous outline of the mountains, and the lamps along the boulevards hundreds
of feet below, draw one into a city of fairy-tale.

Clermont is no such place, of course, not by a long piece of lava.
But it is a distinguished enough city, with the air of being one of the
great crossroads of Europe. Here traffic from the north to the Mediterranean has immemorially met that from the Alps to the Atlantic;
and here each has paused for breath or trade, said its prayers, checked
its load and left its alms. By its mountain-foot situation alone Clermont was bound to grow great as Munich and Milan grew great.

It is worth remembering from the start that it is Clermont-*Ferrand*,
and so called not merely to distinguish it from a dozen other lesser
Clermonts but in deference to an ancient rivalry as bitter as that with
Riom. For when Clermont was first a bishopric the secular centre
was gathered about a volcanic *puy* a mile away. In time episcopal
wealth, politics and the lie of the land reduced Montferrand to its
present status of a rather grubby-looking suburb in the gasworks
quarter the wrong side of the tracks, being to Clermont what St
Denis is to Paris, or in urban terms repeating the story of Auch
and Bordeaux, Bourbon and Moulins. But Ferrand is still very well
worth exploring even if you miss its February fun-fair; for many
echoes of the days when it mattered still sound about its spacious,
wood-rich flamboyant church and the numerous old *hôtels*—to me far
more attractive than the contents of dead museums—which surprisingly line a gridiron of streets which looks unattractive enough on

the map but in fact dates from the sixteenth century—from the age of the beginning of Montferrand's decline, or preservation.

Ferrand stands to the north-east of Clermont. A balancing wart on its smooth face—though hundreds of feet higher—is the spa of Royat to the south-west. This is so close to its mother-city that most people overlook Chamalières, whose locked church (which includes carolingian, as well as almost every other period's work) and buried history lie between them.

Royat climbs up a long, steep gorge which is watered by a stream destined to feed the industrial quarter of Clermont but which here clatters as pleasantly as its name. Water, indeed, seems everywhere: it flows together, divides, splashes over cascades, runs through natural and artificial tunnels, drips from cliffs, foams with dissolved gases, rises into grottoes and thermal basins. Its sulphur content (the boon of a laundering industry as well as of sufferers from cardiac diseases) is discernible in the air, and together with the scent from the precious Sévigny chocolate factory gives to Royat a most characteristic aroma. It is strange to remember that only two centuries ago this ultra-sophisticated spot was regarded with horror as the entry into the terrible mountains.

But the late-Victorian spa quarter, with all its oddities of petrifying springs and caves where a dog dies of CO_2 suffocation and a man splutters from SO_2 (the place was once regarded as a literal gateway of hell, but the stifling of curs to amuse tourists belonged to a more enlightened age) lies only at the lower end of Royat. Above the white hotels a steep old town climbs up both sides of the ravine in a picturesqueness of houses and bridges which—with the woods and *puys* behind them—made it the delight of many a Victorian water-colourist. (The ancient furniture of these houses is now mostly to be found in the folk-museum on a bluff above.) And over it all, putting to shame the quaint and the queer, the gimmick and the gimcrack, crouches the great basilica of St Léger.

This is a fortified romanesque church, quite different from its neighbours: the side which you see, for instance, (for the north abuts on abbatical ruins) is as completely machicolated as any in France. But this does not mean that there is anything graceless about this marvellous building. The thick curtains of rubble-and-mortar hang as lightly between their arched ashlar buttresses as the glass walls of

Illustration 14

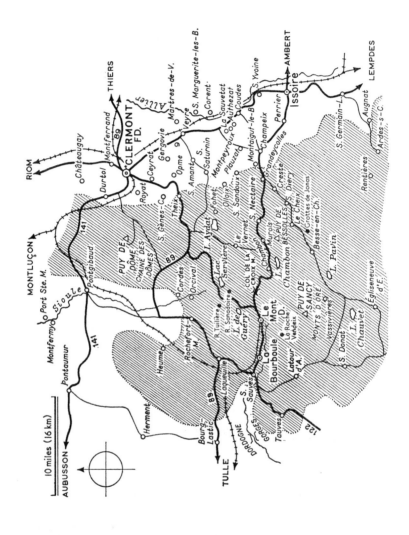

Gloucester; and though this is norman architecture—almost military architecture—the exquisite sandstone lantern lifts above it all as load-lessly as a saint's aureole. I am quite aware that this last was added in the nineteenth century: it *had* to be added.

The perfect balance and symmetry, the feeling that St Léger is built more of space than stone, is echoed within. Turn splendour inside-out, and for once it is still splendour. It is allowed to stand alone, too, for there is no heavy furniture to distract the attention and no clutter of chapels. Even the capitals are subdued, the best being small and at eye-height in the calm little crypt. The same good taste which has restricted exterior maintenance to a dressing of quoins without glaring repointing has left the interior to make its own triumphal resolution of substance and space. Architecture abso-lute, a monolith as surely cut as the opals, agates and amethysts which they gather in the hills behind, is this greatest (for me) of all the great churches of south-central France.

*

So Royat and Montferrand stand like black pawns guarding their bishop. And below the former's Avenue Thermale stands the bishop itself—the city to which the capitalate of the Auvergne slid down, Clermont-Ferrand.

It is no mean city, this of St Martin (who got out of Augustus' Clermont fast, scandalized by its luxury) and Sidonius Apollinaris, of Gregory of Tours and Blaise Pascal. And all its long history re-mains curiously alive today.

Clermont is essentially a *provincial* city: it remembers proudly the Grands Jours of 1665 when Louis XIV helped it to throw off its pirate barons, and despite a fivefold expansion in the last century it remains of a reasonable size with about 125,000 inhabitants. Its tempo is neither frenetic nor somnolent and its history is in the main one of wisdom and tolerance. It has been only mildly Hausmannized, too, and the tangle of streets behind the Place de Jaude preserves the right late-medieval air: they may smell a little of *ordures déposées*, but that is no worse than the rubbery emanation from the great tyre factory which saturates industrial Clermont with scents less appetiz-ing than those usually associated with the portly Bibendum. The market town, the university city, the bishopric, the regional capital, the many-hotelled centre for tourists and transients, the crossroads of transport and the industrial conurbation—all are in balance here. And all are interesting, even the industry; for was not Clermont's wealth in rubber technology founded on a Franco-Scottish romance? In the bankrupt age of the Bourbon restoration a girl made rubber balls for her children as she had seen her uncle make them, and founded a little trade. Her uncle's name was Mackintosh: her grandson's name was to be Michelin. With the exception of Grenoble, there is no major French city in which I more happily find myself than Clermont-Ferrand.

Clermont's major *monuments public* are simple to catalogue, for they consist only of the cathedral and Notre-Dame-du-Port. The former is a large and perfect specimen of *haute gothique*. It was built in the second half of the thirteenth century, on the original and five-times-sacked Clair-Mont where there was earlier a greater norman church than Notre-Dame-du-Port itself. It is the only cathedral made of Volvic lava, even though the stone's compressive strength proved well suited to gothic engineering. Its stained glass—particularly that in the two rose-windows—is first-rate. And that is almost all that anybody has ever thought worth recording; for the cathedral of Clermont is as lifeless as it is beautiful and devoid of detailed interest, local accent or the maturations of time. This was not le Duc's fault either (for his towers are the best part of the job) but rather an inevitable result of transplanting the style of the Ile de France whither it had no roots. Any gothic purists who believe that the great age ended with the Black Death might be chastened by comparing this building with—say—the splendid cathedral of Nantes, which was not begun until the late fifteenth century but which is as alive as Clermont's is dead.

The church of Notre-Dame-du-Port—the centre, for pilgrimage-hunters, of a May manifestation—is another matter. For it is a classic example of that style which is the Auvergne's own and sole great contribution to the arts of Christendom—a variant, owing less than the art-historians would make out to Burgundy or the Saintonge, on that architecture of the eleventh and twelfth centuries which we call 'norman' or 'romanesque' and the French '*roman*', '*Roman*' or even, in their most confusing moments, '*Romain*'.

*

This book is no treatise on architecture. But there are things which should be recorded here so that they do not demand to be recorded several times over at the peers of Notre-Dame-du-Port.

At the opening of the eleventh century, then, a number of factors coalesced in the Auvergne. The land had reached a stage of richness and urbanity not known before and its princes had money to spare: its monks were in a springtime mood to build: legends of local miracles were tempting pilgrims to take the hard way to Compostella: and the normans were marching. Out of all this there arose, at the close of the century, a school of architecture whose influence has already been discovered in this book at Mozac, Volvic, Châtel-Montagne and Royat, which could also be found as far afield as Toulouse and the purely Auvergnat church of Paray-le-Monial in Burgundy, but whose classic expression is in four buildings in the diocese of Clermont which are physically of only middling size but architecturally immense.

The exterior hall-marks of this school are the spired octagonal lantern which surmounts a hipped transept tower, and the eastern chevet which far more than compensates for the starkness of the weather-assaulted west front and of the lateral porches. Elsewhere outside there is only a dog-tooth cornice and perhaps a Judgement tympanum: but eastward, like basalt prisms, the inter-related apses and ambulatories and semi-circular chapels soar to their shell-like roofs of tile. Nowhere is the architecture of the twelfth century more calculatedly adventurous than about the altars of the Auvergne, and one's feeling is that 'norman' is almost as much of a misnomer as the idiotic *roman*. There is something byzantine here: Clermont is as near to Ravenna as to Durham.

The interior characteristics include simple hoops of polychromatic stone which punctuate rather than sustain the immense weight of a plain barrel vault which is in fact buttressed-up by the aisles— usually with some sacrifice of light. Only at the east, where the ringed chapels lend support, are tall lancets possible, their light falling on the superb capitals which are the sole structural decoration.

Such is the basic *style roman auvergnat*; and it may well be that in the beggar-haunted Notre-Dame-du-Port at Clermont it finds, despite the still-older work incorporated, its purest expression. But the church suffers from its site. For it lies buried away in a rather grimy quarter of the city, the old volcanic *ville noire*, and so little light penetrates that the whole church is almost as dim as the crypt where a reproduction Black Virgin is anually venerated.

Still, one is likely to have time enough to explore it, and the minor attractions of the city—several museums, a lively renaissance fountain, some old squares and houses, some modern statues including a weighty Vercingetorix surrounded with the only trees to thrive on Clermont's chemical water, the catalpas; petrifying springs whose mildly gassy produce is sold at 2s a glass as lemonade and which, if you wait ten days, will turn a coin dirty; and a few minor churches as well. For to anybody travelling the Auvergne its capital is an inevitable centre; and unless you are the purest bird of passage (in which case you will probably gather a rather unfavourable impression from the ring-roads) you will spend many nights in hotels outside which the lorries hum with the romance of the modern *routiers* and the trains (so many of them that one suspects the SNCF is using an effects-record) swap their loads in the night.

*

The term *région clermontoise* is a vague one, but the highlands and lowlands which form Clermont-Ferrand's home-park have an allegiance of their own. And before journeying south towards the numerous things curious or beautiful, natural or artificial, which stand within a score of miles, it is worth exploring that shaggy, low, volcanic ridge which crosses the Limagne-head between Clermont and Riom and marks the old level of the uneroded plain.

It is especially worth it if one loves wine. For if one discounts Corent, produced in very small quantities to the south of Clermont, it is from the slopes of these most recent of volcanoes that derive the only two *crus* of the Massif to qualify for the connoisseurs' guides.

These are Chanturgue and Châteaugay, and both come red, white and in-between. Their character—not surprisingly—is intermediate between that of the wines of St Pourçain and of the Beaujolais, and though they rarely carry detailed credentials they provide at about 6s a bottle (restaurant price) a most smooth and satisfying alternative to the *ordinaire* of these parts—itself a pleasant enough *rosé*.

Chanturgue produces the rather more distinguished and expensive bottle. But it is only a name, whereas Châteaugay would still be a place of remark on account of its fourteenth-century castle. This—the only one in the whole Auvergne whose keep Richelieu spared—is rich in memories of love and war, of mediaeval murders and of the far more terrible bloodshed of the revolution which the grisly Lafayette here plotted.

It is odd that the château of Châteaugay is marked as ruined on the map, for in fact it is as inhabited as any castle could be. Within its *enceintes* are half-a-dozen farmhouses; and up and down the twisting vices, in and out of the vaulted rooms, chase children, chickens, tourists and flying ants alike. This castle of Châteaugay (which has some sort of Rhenish or Blarney-stone legend about wishes and fairies and hearts and wine and eternal happiness) is indeed freer of inspection and easier to reconstruct in the mind than any guide-rattling manor. You could even use its ancient privies, which are one degree superior to some contemporary French sanitation in being holes *with seats on.*

View, history, everything else apart, this half-living castle of Châteaugay is wonderfully Auvergnat in its sense that nobody cares any more except the state authorities who are knocking it about in order to floodlight it. And having recorded this, and the fact that Châteaugay must have undergone as many renamings as any place in France, there is not much more to be done save admire its charmingly vernacular renaissance chapel and then drink its health in that excellent *rouge.*

*

So at last one leaves the sunlit plains and foothills, leaves behind the mildly interesting Clermont outliers like Durtol, and faces the passes and night mists and drenching rain beyond.

It was never an easy change for travellers; and it is no easier a one for the travel-writer. For many roads tangle amid the crucifix-crowned hills between Clermont and the departmental border. The only way to treat their features, I am afraid, is as everybody else treats them—as a round trip, a sharrer bunfight, a *circuit touristique.*

You begin southward then, up the Allier valley where the arteries of the 9 road and the Nimes railway begin to close together. And hardly are you away before you pass, on the right, a shoulder of land. Despite the uncharacteristic vagueness of the *De Bello Gallico* and the doubts of some scholars (which doubts are, of course, hushed-up hereabouts), it is most probable that it was near here that, in the spring of 52 BC Caesar camped with 30,000 men to attack the ramparts of the basalt bluff itself. He almost won it, but was counterattacked and routed by the twenty-year-old Vercingetorix, chief of warriors, with his ragged Arvene force. It is certainly the shoulder which men today call Gergovie.

It rises only 400 feet from the plateau—which is here itself 2,000 feet above the sea—but it has the same dominance and look of being bent below piled centuries of watchfulness as has White Horse Down. These battles long ago leave deeper marks on a land than fosses and entrenchments, and the site—which, by an inversion of relief typical of the Auvergne, was in origin a river-bed—remains in the eye long after your car has rumbled on south. I think that Gergovie *is* Gergovia.

Mourn Vercingetorix here, then, even if you do not visit the local museum; for the noble Caesar later captured him, dragged him in chains, and tortured him for six years before strangling him. And then pass on to a cluster of habitations just west of the Allier—les Martres-de-Vevre with its picturesque little streams, Veyre itself, and Ste Marguerite-les-Bains with its curious claim to spa-dom.

The valley closes in a little: the *puys* and ruined castles climb above the high-road past la Sauvetat and Authezat and Montpeyroux and red-roofed Coudes under its round tower and sandstone cliffs and then St Yvoine: and at last comes Issoire. This is today (amongst other things) a centre for the hand lace-making which still quietly survives. But it was once as bitter a centre as the whole of Auvergne remembers of the wars of religion.

'The little Geneva' men called at St Austremoine's shrine around 1540, when the church itself became a battlefield and the heroes were the protestant martyrs. But after St Bartholomew's Eve the new faith took not one eye for an eye but two; and with the detestable Captain Merle—less cruel than some of his subordinates, but still a man compared to whom Thomas Cromwell was almost clean—reigning in Issoire, simple death was the best a priest could hope for. It is a Graham Greene subject; for five years later came the last reversal, led by the half-pseudonymous Monsieur who was in fact the Duke of Orleans—brother of Louis XIII, son of Henry IV, husband of

Madame and father of the grotesque 'Grande Mademoiselle'. The catholics returned by a trick (for who would trust a royalist calling himself 'Mister'?), burned the city, and scrawled above its sacked and smoking ruins '*Yci fuſt Issoire*'.

But—as always and everywhere—the vandals were wrong. The Issoiriens built again; and even when *bâtissant de boue comme l'hirondelle* aimed to provide a setting for the wines and the girls once famous alike for their sparkle. So today this tidy *sous-préfecture* of about 8,500 people looks ancient and mellow, picturesque and at peace, and not much different from the days when it gave François Premier his chancellor. And the romanesque church which Merle put to the axe and Monsieur to the flames still stands, not conspicuously restored apart from some hideous paint-sloshing and with its individual, zodiacal medallions and great choir capitals unblemished, as one of the masterpieces of the Clermont ring.

It is not the least of Issoire's tragic ironies that this is now dedicated to St Paul....

*

The church is visible from the railway; and that is significant, for though Issoire stands in a basin or *limagne* of its own it feels like a distant gateway of Clermont. Beyond it, past old le Broc up on the heights and on to the former local capital of St Germain-Lembron— a town set in gentle country with a de-luxe restaurant but not much else of note—the land may not steepen suddenly. But it does change character as the Allier valley climbs steadily into another world.

So the tourist-circles of Puy-de-Dôme snap westward from Issoire on a cross-country road which runs through the village of Perrier (where there are basalt columns, a sky-hung ruined tower, mastodons' bones, troglodytic caves, a belief that St Austremoine was assassinated on the spot, a good white wine and all else that an Auvergne village should have) to picturesque Champeix—where there is another castle, a mildly interesting church, and two silent letters. And there, at the longitude of Clermont and as a more direct road from it comes in through Plauzat amid the apple-orchards, but some fifteen miles south from the big city, they start to wind up in earnest through the tangled passes which separate the Allier/Loire basin from the western valleys. This cross-country road offers a succession of interesting hamlets such as Montaigut-le-Blanc and

Grandeycolles as well as dolmens and rocks galore. And near its crest it comes to St Nectaire.

St Nectaire (which makes surprisingly little fuss about its famous cheese) is the epitome of Puy de Dôme. It is small, consisting of only two villages related like those of the riviera—the low and new, the high and old. These share some secular junketings on the *quatorze juillet* and the Assumption, but otherwise have nothing in common. For the former is something of a spa, and the latter has a good deal of a church.

St Nectaire-le-Bas, then, is all hydros and hotels, dank grottoes and waters *excitantes, régulatrices de la nutrition,* and *rénovatrices des tissus* for those with anaemia, albuminuria, nephritic kidneys, growing pains or (a nice touch, this) addiction to alcohol: it is the second smallest of the important spas of the Auvergne but not the least self-conscious. -le-Haut, a mile up the sunless valley, has a truer fame. The lady Madeleine of its colourful ruling house—a typical figure of Auvergnat legend since young, beautiful, virtuous despite her bodyguard of sixty lovers, a protestant and a widow—would alone have lent it some lustre: she almost won Riom and Clermont from the calvinists, after all, and Henry IV lifted his helmet to her after she had killed his lieutenant in equal combat. But a greater glory derives from the romanesque church of one of the Auvergne's great evangelists, which lifts its ragged front high on the promontory with a small old village behind. For this is another of the outstanding four of the bishopric—over-ornate inside, perhaps, despite its superb deep capitals, but certainly the most nobly-sited of them all and with a treasury well worth the visiting too.

*

A mile or two more (and you are now 2,750 feet up, and ringed by volcanic crests advertising their views, megaliths, waterfalls and divers caverns) brings you to Murols—or Murol, for even the Michelin cannot decide on the spelling. A castle as deep-red as old blood and locked in a square enceinte crowns a volcanic hill here: it is a wildly romantic pile—perhaps the finest in all the Auvergne—which was commenced in the thirteenth century, expanded by an unusually literate baron called William of Sam, later decorated by a charming renaissance pavilion and towers, sacked (of course) by Richelieu, and

Illustration 17

19

Sights of the hinterland of the high Auvergne are Murols (*above*) and
St Saturnin (*left*). The castle of Val (*right*) has a softer site.

20

21

Alleuze in Cantal (*left*) and Crussol in Ardèche (*right*)—two lonely castles of the southern Massif.

left—after it had harboured outlaws as late as the revolution period—
to become one of the sights of the region, with the Puy de Bessolles
towering behind it. Murols is indeed one of the most favoured resorts
of the area: with only a few hundred inhabitants it boasts four or five
hotels and likes its region to be called the garden of the Auvergne. Just
beyond it, too, lies Lac Chambon—one of the largest and best-
furnished of the lakes which litter these parts, but a shallow and rather
unmysterious one since it was formed by a lava-dam across the valley
rather than in a true crater.

The village church of Chambon and its parvis are interesting, and
there is also a pretty legend associated with a 300-foot cliff to its
north called the Saut de la Pucelle. The maiden, fleeing from some
panting cad, leaped over its edge to save her honour at the expense
of her life but was miraculously preserved. When nobody believed
her story the shepherdess went through it all again. This time the
consequences were fatal. The moral is that you should never trust
to a good gimmick twice.

✳

Beyond the lake of Chambon the road grinds on and up round the
edge of the Dent du Marais by impossible hairpin bends. And then,
when it seems the engine can take no more, you are at a brief tunnel
nearer 5,000 than 4,000 feet above the sea. This is the crest—the Col
de la Croix Morand, Diane, or Dyanne.

As usual in the Auvergne it is a pass in little more than name,
being only a few hundred feet below the nearby peaks. Everything
may well be veiled in mist, and it is never easy to pick out one
mountain from another in this landscape of heaving heights. Even
the volcano which begat it all may be only a southward haze from
here—the 6,250-foot Puy de Sancy at the crest of central France which
is a giant but a conquered one, since a motor road and a cable railway lead up to its great viewpoint. Even so, however, this pass of
Morand's Cross—which, they say, used to claim a man every year—
may be a fit place to wait while the engine cools and to wander amid
the uplands of harebell and phlox and marguerite. This is not, frankly,
my Auvergne: it is far too cold and touristy for that. But it is *the*
Auvergne, like it or not.

✳

Illustration 19

For the ancient rock-flanks and sedimentary plains are left behind now, and one is solidly based on basalt. Northwards from the pass, past Clermont and almost to Riom, it extends for a matter of twenty miles. But further again to the south there heaves, like a dinosaur's back, the gnarled massif of lava which has hitherto been met only as outcrops.

The wandering, narrow line away to the north is the Chaîne des Dômes, the Puys des Dômes or the Chaîne des Puys; the chunky main range at hand and far to the south are the Monts (or Mont) Dore (or d'ore, or d'or: remember again that all this has nothing to do with gold). The two ranges are geologically quite distinct; for the Dômes—all rounded, though differing in cultivation and topsoil —are so much more recent that they erupted less than 100,000 years ago and are by comparison with the ancient sierras of the Dore tree-clad and fertile. But topographically there is no sharp break, and the panorama has well been compared to that of a herd of cattle (perhaps of the local red and white-spotted *vaches ferrandaises*) half-drowned in mist and with only horned brows, rounded shoulders and sunken haunches showing. Either way, there are seventy dead volcanoes on either hand.

The whole form, from Clermont to Cantal, can be grasped only from the air, from the great isolated crests, or from a few viewpoints along the roads. It is a form composed of clustered volcanoes of classic shape, domed volcanoes with their craters filled by magma, double and triple volcanoes, *égueulés* volcanoes which exploded at the side like the one which was replanted in the nineteenth century by an historic proto-Commissioner called Montlosier, volcanoes which filled a dip in land now eaten away called 'necks' and 'dykes', and —especially to the south—the eroded fragments of old volcanoes, soft and tree-clad or jagged and bare. Even the valleys are lined with the two forms into which lava crystallizes—the basalt prisms produced by pressure and the shaley 'phonolith' or clinkstone which results when it solidifies freely. Here at the pass, it is difficult to realize that nobody suspected the volcanic origin of the Low Auvergne until 1750, and that for a century after that there were sceptics.

And then all this is eclipsed as one enters the western valley. It is stern enough itself, yet it encloses a stream whose name takes one to a different land. For it is the valley of the upper Dordogne.

Just as it begins, another road *s'amorce* (and that is an explosive word) back to the north-east. It passes near to three solitudinous lakes—Guéry, cratered Servière, and the lava-carved Aydat which is the largest natural pool in the region and is distinguished not only by its underground streams but by memories of Sidonius Apollinaris carrying the lamp of Rome down a dark century in his island hermitage amid the heather and juniper-trees. It also passes by the rocks of Tuilière and Sanadoire, dramatic enough as glimpsed from the road but again only grasped in their relation to the land from a high-level view. And eventually it joins the 89 cross-country highway before running through a brief tunnel.

But apart from the village of Theix in the parkland of St Genès-Champanelle there is nothing of habitation along it, except ruined fortifications and mist-ringed farmsteads whose slate roofs are green with damp lichen, until one passes the western flank of the Gergovian plateau under the village of Opme (an attractive one, this, with its church and castle and fountain) and re-enters the outskirts of Clermont itself—suddenly exchanging basalt for granite—at Ceyrat and Beaumont beyond the gorges.

Immediately west of this road junction, however, two most curious and celebrated townships almost touch each other. They are the ones called le Mont-Dore, and la Bourboule.

*

'Spas of Europe' I exclaimed, in another book and a puzzled moment, 'so astonishingly alike . . . from Matlock to Montecatini. Peeling Italianate stucco: deserted bandstands: icy pumphouses: brooks running through dankly mossy grottoes in public gardens: seasidey shops: steep streets (for all spas are steep, especially those devoted to diseases of the heart): mist driving upwards over limestone outcrops and into pines (for all spas are damp, especially those devoted to rheumatic diseases): these images recur and recur between the Pennines and the Appenines. . . .' And if the sleazy sophistication of spas is oppressive enough in an isolated town, it is far more so when a whole countryside is involved as it is here in the Massif.

The geology of *les eaux thermo-minérales* of the Auvergne (and elsewhere) is simple and mildly romantic: water, whether from infiltrated rain or condensed vapours formed within the world, seeps

115

Illustration 13

below the surface, becomes lukewarm, and escapes at a spring which is normally (though *not* at the Dore spas) associated with a geological fault. The chemistry is simple and extremely dull: during its passage the water picks up the much-advertised *deux gaz* (carbon and sulphur dioxides, the two characteristics of a stuffy room) and a few innocuous minerals like bicarb, rust and sand, Epsom, Glauber's and common salts. The pathology is, perhaps, more in dispute: but certainly the only thing in any of these costly fluids which could not be put together from a child's chemistry set is arsenic. There *is* a certain glamour to the ancient water-worship of the Auvergne, that land of earth and air and fire as well. 'The body has its blood, the plant its sap, the rock its water,' they used to say, and every disease or disaster had an accredited spring. But today the things are more outmoded than herbals, and it all simply will not do.

It is true that, several decades ago, the more enterprising medico-publicists of the Auvergne picked on the magic word 'radioactivity' to add a few scintillations to the wares for which they had sold their professional souls. But it is doubtful if irradiation at this low level has the slightest effect on the human frame, and certain that if it had it would be a detrimental one. In our age of Aldermaston and strontium fall-out, when some are even worried about the stunted babies of Cheltenham, one may expect to hear less and less of this particular claim.

What then remains? A faith-cure of course; and I concede that this is a fine kind of cure, better than any highly-paid plungings of the carver's knife. Of course some poor, idle old Englishwomen feel better after a bellyfull of cochineal and sugar on the NHS: of course some poor, pious old Irish nuns feel better after a dose of Fatima: and of course some rich, overfed old French *mesdames* feel better after the herbal tea and *régimes* of the Auvergne. It is the pseudo-scientific gloss which the spas put on their pagan water-worship which distresses me so much. A reasonable man can believe that a special grace of Our Lady resides in the springs of Lourdes: a reasonable man can *not* believe that a few milligrammes of magnesium chloride is 'sovereign against paludism, amibiasis, pre-cirrhotic states, enterohepatic syndromes' or any of those other diseases which could only be invented, christened and cared about by a nation whose eat-ing and drinking habits are less than eupeptic—a nation which recognizes the profession of *curiste*....

*

Even if the waters had any virtues they could be enjoyed as well in Vauxhall as in Vichy; and in fact the Auvergnat spas export their bottles at the rate of 130 million a year. But this is only a fraction of the 2,000 million which gurgle up from springs which are classed with the absurd self-consciousness of Bordeaux wines and priced like railway classes *circa* 1910, springs which are housed in pagodas of curious device, or in dripping grottoes, or in domes which look like launderettes from outer space.

If one is sceptical of the medicinal values of the waters of Puy-de-Dôme, these spas have little enough else to offer. There is only the pump-room with its mob-capped attendants where you drink or gargle or sniff or splash from 5 a.m. till 11 a.m., the so-called casino with its palm-court orchestra, the funicular, the elephantine archi-tecture of the great infirmaries, and an infinite shivering boredom accentuated rather than relieved by *le bridge* and *le ping-pong*. Had these shrines of hypochondria the grace of Bath or the *brio* of Baden-Baden, I could understand the fact that thousands of healthy people choose to stay in them. But, as it is, there is only scenery to draw one—that and the fact that their whole atmosphere makes a pretty sick person like myself feel pretty fit by comparison.

In many ways there is little enough to choose between these two most famous of all the Auvergnat resorts. Both claim to have been founded by the Romans (who hadn't, after all, the benefit of Boots for their ills), and both draw intriguing pictures of carolingians lapping up health amid broken pillars and cracked pavements. The little Dordogne flows through the streets of both. And, finally, both are today nineteenth-century accretions of hotels and boarding-houses—well over 500 of these to a joint resident population of some 5,000.

However, a sharp eye *can* detect differences. Le Mont-Dore, for instance, is a round place up a combe which goes in for winter sports, waterfalls, ravines and dancing in the streets: la Bourboule is a straggly place along a valley and nearly 700 feet below. L.M-D. is the terminus of a branch-line where the grand *Thermal Express* ends in a very rural way: L.B. is one station further towards sanity. L.M-D. is fairly single-minded about asthma and breathing: L.B. claims the nose, the blood, diabetes, the skin (including lichen and pruritus, from which I would hate to suffer), allergies and—in general—the children and the sick young folk who give it its peculiarly sad gaiety. L.M-D. is older: L.B. is generally better organized (except for winter sports), as it has to be since even the Michelin cannot take very seriously its wars of the wells, its tales of indecent exposure and its claim that the most poisonous water in Europe tastes of beef soup. L.M-D is wetter.

But both enterprises are dedicated to the cult of sickness, to (and I quote) 'thoracic affusions, nasal douches, the sniffing of thermal gas through pipettes and other operations of an agreeable and re-laxing nature'—including *insufflation tubotympanique, nébulisation d'aërosols, douches filiformes, crénothérapie éthétique* and other horrors they do not translate. There is, if you are in the mood, a lot of rather macabre fun to be got out of these places. But my memories of the two of them are of snotty-nosed children, harsh municipal flowerbeds, wine served in polythene carafes, and—an odd, prevail-ing image this—of a little homosexual sipping soup at ten in the morn-ing in a bar filled with the glossy theatrical photographs of eminent French queers.

This country of pinewoods and small and casual waterfalls *is* beauti-ful. Why, then, does it have to pretend to be healthy too? Why does it prey so on the irreligious and unscientific superstitions of the silly rich and the even sillier *bourgeoisie*?

*

If you want to escape from these questions, there is a different land waiting behind the Puy de Sancy—a land where there stand oak-trees planted by Catherine de Medici and Marguerite de Valois and where the viewpoints cover the cardinal departments of both Auvergnes. This deeply glacial land is sometimes called the Artense plateau, and its flavour is given by the Roche Vendeix, just off the Mont-Dore-La-Bourboule road but so isolated that it became the headquarters of the most successful of all the land-pirates and *routiers*. To penetrate it by any road not marked *parcours difficile ou dangereux*, however, one has to take a turning to the south far sooner, between Champeix and St Nectaire. And even then one must pin back one's ears.

For along this secondary road, past Creste and St Diéry and le Cheix and those curious caves called the Grottes de Jonas about which the archaeologists have still not made up their shadowy minds, the bus-drivers search the hillsides for stones to use as chocks whenever they stop. There are the usual gorges and castle-towers, ever-climbing bends like the snakes on a snakes-and-ladders board, and views which take the ground from below one's feet. And then at last comes the rather extraordinary market town of Besse—Besse-en-Chandesse.

Whatever the Chandesse is (for no other villages bear the suffix) Besse is its capital. It is a good one, too. A place of surprising importance in the middle-ages—though now as depopulated as any in Puy-de-Dôme—it retains quite a few memorable *monuments historiques* to complement its lovely situation and its minor importance as an ecological station. Notable are a twelfth-plus-sixteenth century church dedicated to St Andrew whose romanesque stone and renaissance wood stand comparison with better-renowned things, several good lava-stone houses, a fine belfry, and two palaces whose look is quite peculiar—handsome sixteenth-century manors in the centre of the town, with castellated defences which might have been some use three centuries earlier slung from them as decoratively and uselessly as a ceremonial sword.

Besse also boasts the usual water-works, an echo, and a pair of religious festivals which—though only recently revived—are typical of the Auvergne and as fervent as any in France. In early summer, at the *montée*, a figure of the Virgin is borne up to Vassivières, which is westward along the road and higher too. And with autumn, at the *dévalade*. She returns with Her cows to the valley-habitation—itself 3,500 feet up, and one of the highest real towns in France outside the Alps.

With so many minor attractions, this remote mountain-town should have remained a collector's piece. But it has turned itself into a *station d'altitude*. It is not a spa (though it has had the bright idea of advertising itself as a place in which to recover from spa treatment); but in the desperation of French tourism it has become a resort whose numerous hotels try hard, with their gothic lettering and their varnished wood and their trailing plants, to be Swiss. Besse keeps fairly busy, anyway; for in summer there are the walks, in winter the sports of winter, and even out of season there are the mountaineers champing in and out at reduced terms and tottering to bed at half past eight.

*

They could hardly choose better country. All about swell the Monts Dore; and though from the main road one sees mainly the fractured face of their gorges and valleys, by-ways and mountain tracks lead to the crests of this scoured land only recently won over to cultivation. Best, of course, when a sunlit day is passing into an evening of stormy sunset and then a pure night, these hills are tremendous even in the prevailing rain. Horizontally this sweeps in curtains like theatre scrims, dividing the country into zones of depth: vertically it drifts about the valleys and leaves only the great domes breaking through like bubbles on an infernal sea. But either way, though it may detract from the tourists' comfort, the weather lowers its own majesty on this land which always knows majesty.

For this is the very heart of the historic Auvergne. West of Besse, for instance, the road swings round past the spectacular but far too frequented Lac Pavin (fifty fathoms of deep-green, this one— but its name does *not* mean 'terrible') and the rather less famed Lac Chauvet, which are themselves only outliers to a number of other lakes up in the hills. And then, beyond the turning for St Donat, it drops a few hundred feet to Latour d'Auvergne itself.

The name of this place—especially with La Tour split as two words—is charged with romance and wind and the clash of arms: fittingly, one feels, one finds it all over France. But unfortunately (as with Thiers) the streets and restaurants and hotels are named after a person rather than the town—or at least after a family, the ducal one which bore Catherine de Medici. And Latour itself, despite its lovely setting, is less than exciting. It does not even have an ancient church (though that lack is fulfilled by a series of high-towered gothic edifices close by), and the castle which was the core of its power has literally gone underground, being now only a hole in the municipal park. So I remember this high and open town mainly for its views and its mountain air, for its roofs of random slate and its great basalt columns, for the kindness of a *madame* who sheltered us in winter when the reputed hotels were closed as we came in soaked from mountain mist, and above all for a name which rings in the imagination like Ethandune or Roncesvalles.

*

Beyond Latour the road comes back again, like a man returning from an opium-misted dream, to a spot west of La Bourboule called St Sauves: though on the Clermont road, this is notable only for the remains of its church being worked up into a folly. A little further down is Laqueuille, a road and rail junction where two routes to the south-west divide: the statue in its square is of the inventor of the Auvergne blue cheese, of which Laqueuille remains a centre. And further again along the rejoined 89 comes Rochefort-Montagne. This is itself a lively and rather attractive market-town with three or four minor romanesque churches nearby—most notably at Heume. But few tourists linger there. They take the by-road to Orcival, which holds the last of the four mighty churches of the Clermont ring.

One's first impression is of how much the similarity of them all is modified by situation. For whilst Notre-Dame-du-Port stands in a slum, St Paul d'Issoire in a trim township and St Nectaire like the wind-breaking prow of a ship, Orcival rests on its hillside at the edge of the village as quietly as a Somerset wool-church. Turn your back on the little cluster of shops and hotels and you have only woods, upland meadows, and this great basilica amid them, barely touched by time and hatred and earthquakes but for the truncation of its tower.

The silent spaces are within, too; for this is a many-windowed, large-choired, uncluttered building where light blows like a breeze across white storied capitals, chains left for votive offerings by freed crusaders, and the dark byzantine Madonna enthroned which is the object of the usual pilgrimage—here on Ascension Day. It is the airiest, the slenderest, the most gracious and feminine, of all this corona of churches.

There is nothing else in Orcival itself. But a kilometre beyond there is something almost as unforgettable—Cordès, a norman-cum-renaissance *gentilhommerie* which is not only perfectly preserved in itself but set in the most formal of Le Nôtre landscaping. It is a sweet place, and an intriguing outpost of the disciplines of the north

Illustration 18

too. Trespassing in its grounds by the headwaters of the Sioule, it is hard to realize how many stormy decades of miles these have to run before they find, beyond the purple heights, the silvers of Touraine.

*

The most direct return from here to Clermont is by a road which winds desertedly up and down about the 3,000-foot contour until, just before the outskirts of Clermont, it throws off the turning for the Puy de Dôme itself.

This is a legend. The oldest, the most famous, the easiest of access, and by 1,500 feet the highest of the volcanoes of the chain, it names them all—and the department too, though they were going to call it 'Mont-Dore' before a deputy pointed out that that might lead revenooers and similar sharks to think that there were piles of *écus* in much-taxed Basse-Auvegne. (It was easier, he said, referring to Pascal's experiments, to weigh air than gold about Clermont.) More even than Mont Blanc above Geneva—which, they say, is visible from here through a gap in the Forez—the Puy de Dôme seems at the end of every street in Clermont and part of the city's soul. It is stained on the renaissance windows of the cathedral; it was there— and somehow very appropriately too—that the Friars Minor per- formed those elementary-text-book demonstrations of barometric pressure; and still the locals tell the weather by seeing whether the Puy *porte son bonnet* of cloud or not. In this context, I like Henri Pourrat's eulogy: 'Le Puy de Dôme, qui attire les nuées, les absorbe ou les accumule, fait ou défait les orages, n'est plus un dieu, mais demeure un prestige.' *Prestige* is a marvellously equivocal word: I think I would translate it by saying that the Puy de Dôme is a signal beacon. It is less than 5,000-feet tall, and hence only shoulder-high to such uncrowned peaks as the crest of the Forez, let alone the Puy de Sancy; but like the South Downs it appears to dominate a far vaster landscape than physical dimensions can explain. Its details, I swear, are visible from a train running into La Souterraine—and that is a long hundred miles away.

You can, of course, go up the mountain—not now by the charming spiral railway which once offered a regular service, but by coaches in the season or by car on a toll-road. And at the crest, above the tangle of berry-bushes, you will find the kind of thing which marks such eminences—an observatory, a scatter of wooden-hutted cafés and souvenir shops, a radio mast (a disputed amenity, this; but in the mist it will pass for a norman turret), and a tremendous sunset view down on the whole lunar landscape. This view covers a radius of almost 200 miles, a dozen departments, an eighth of France, and half the territory of this book.

Yes . . . But one could get much of the view from the towers of Clermont itself. Perhaps, after all, the mountain should be left as a distant prospect. There is a sense of desecration here, as on the Jungfrau, Snowdon, the Brocken and all the over-conquered crests of Christendom—a desecration the sadder for the fact that, from long before the Romans built that temple to the Auvergne's god Mercury which was so romantically rediscovered, until almost yesterday, this was a sacred mount.

*

There are still some left-overs of Puy-de-Dôme in this sector to the west of the capital. First come two bridge-towns between fifteen and twenty-five miles from it along the 141—a road surprisingly serpentine for such comparative lowlands but otherwise noteworthy only for some springs where, they say, there is ice in high summer. These towns are Pontgibaud and Pontaumur.

The former, at the tip of an outlying *coulée* of lava, has a decent church and a brown manor-house; this succeeds, and partly incorporates, a castle associated with the Countess Brayère who (they claim) lived off salted children until the lowing of a calfless cow turned her stomach against infanticide. There is a charming church and water-mill (*se méfier des vipères*, you are warned) at Montfermy, a few miles downstream where the waters of the Sioule make a remarkable ox-bow and chime as pleasantly as the Belloc poem which—apart from the Thursday gathering of chicken-farmers en route for Clermont market—gives Pontgibaud its only other claim to fame: it is also the centre for the little lost ruins of the Chartreuse of Porte-Ste-Marie. Pontaumur is rather dull.

Only slightly further west, beyond Herment on its basalt bluff, one comes to the Montluçon-Eygurande branch-line where, amid dozens of watershed tributaries of the Cher, the Sioule and the Dordogne, the land slopes back into Creuse or Corrèze. This line I have already taken as the edge of the border-country. And not far from its southern end, in the most confused and glacier-scoured part of all the plateau, there is another pair of twin cities—Bourg-Lastic, of the fluorspar mines and an OK name for Auvergne, and Tauves. Each is over 2,500 feet up on the 122 road and has a minor church, but they are separated by some tree-clad Dordogne gorges.

However, though Puy-de-Dôme has already filled most of three chapters it is not yet exhausted. There are, indeed, three more whole zones of it. First come the mountains which stagger on and up, south of Besse and Latour and west of St Germain-Lembron, through a whiteness on the map broken only by symbols which mean that Egliseneuve d'Entraigues—on the departmental border and at an altitude of 3,150 feet—has a small hotel, that Augnat and similar spots have little norman churches (and maybe other curiosities), or that Ardes-sur-Couze (an ancient and once-fortified ducal stronghold) has lashed Rentières valley. But this land of high enclosed farmyards lies along the end of the map, where also begin the Cantals.

Then, in the heart of the country and bounded by the tourist circuits, there soar some 300 square miles west of the two-castled hilltop town of St Amant where the shotgun goes *pan* on misty September morns. High behind dripping cliffs, up where the Michelin does not trouble much to blue the views or star the gorges, over where the runnelled roads climb about lonely *puys*, there is something which only dedicated men like Paul Bourget (born in Amiens, but the star novelist of these parts) will ever fully explore. Few go there; and those who do do not speak much of it, though wildly-picturesque St Saturnin has not only an outstanding romanesque church (less ornate than its big sisters, but also less restored) and a castle of the barons of Latour d'Auvergne, but a little bohemian colony too.

I have also heard the hamlets of Fohet, le Vernet-Ste-Marguerite, St Sandoux and Olloix well spoken of. If ever a man wanted to lie low from the cops, civilization or the promptings of his conscience, he might choose worse places than these.

All these places are part of Puy-de-Dôme. But still this single department, no larger than any other in France, refuses to be exhausted. For its south-eastern corner, *a forestière* land in two senses, is a region of its own.

124

Illustration 20

7

The Forgotten Corner

Most of the many mountains which comprise the Massif, blend and blur as they may, have at their heart some unique personality. After a little practice one could tell, dropped blindfold from a helicopter, whether one were in the Combrailles or the Madeleine, the Dômes or the Dore. But if there is one range which seems to me to lack this individuality, it is the Monts du Livradois.

A dog barking from versant to versant: men threshing corn with hand-flails all a hot summer's day: myself sitting on a mountain-top and watching the equinoctial thunder-heads fire down on Clermont in the plain: the barber coming round on a Saturday night to ply his pudding-basin trade in the village bar: an ox at twilight under a white harvest moon standing whiter than an ox-ghost: these images I recall from the Livradois. But they are not *typical* of the Livradois, and I know of almost nothing which is. Sometimes the churches (usually handsome, middle-sized, symmetrical and norman-to-transitional) look like acquiring a trademark. Sometimes the hills seem nippled with the ruins of black lava castles of unusual disposition. Sometimes the pines, now exploited only for telegraph poles and pit-props, retain the majesty of the age when their 100-foot high queens were reserved as masts for the King of France's navy. Sometimes the villages (and there is nothing larger than a big village in the whole range) appear to be throwing up a particular school of Volvic carving or their market-crosses developing a characteristic look. But it all seems to vanish by the next valley.

I cannot blame anybody—except the gliding enthusiasts for whom, apparently, it is all a veritable paradise—for never having heard of the dim Livradois. After this introduction, I cannot blame anybody

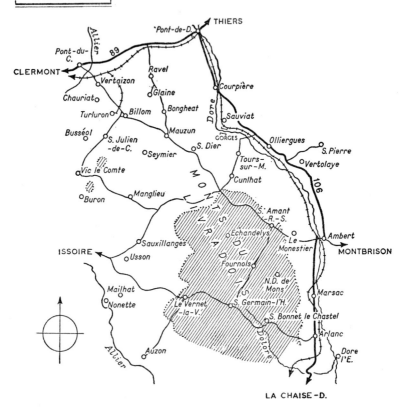

10 miles (16 km)

THIERS
Pont-de-D.
Allier
89
Pont-du-
C.
CLERMONT
Ravel
Vertaizon
Glaine
Courpière
Chauriat
Bongheat
Dore
Turluron Billom
Sauviat
Busséol
Mauzun
S. Julien
-de-C. Seymier S. Dier
GORGES
Olliergues
S. Pierre
Tours-
sur-M.
Vertolaye
Vic le Comte
Cunlhat
106
Buron Manglieu
MONTS
S. Amant
-R.-S.
LIVRADOIS
Echandelys Le
Monestier
Ambert
ISSOIRE
Sauxillanges
Fournols
MONTBRISON
Usson
N.D. de
Mons
Marsac
Mailhat
Nonette
Le Vernet
-la-V. S. Germain-l'H.
S. Bonnet le Chastel
Allier
Dolore
Arlanc
Auzon
Dore
l'E.

LA CHAISE-D.

for not *wanting* to hear of the damn Livradois. But there are a few things of real note, a number of things of interest, and above all a sense of utter remoteness a few miles off the tourist routes, in this range. A kindly couple, giving me a lift only ten miles from Clermont, stared at a peasant crippled over his Millais field and summed it all up: '*C'est un coin perdu.*'

*

The forgotten corner is structurally easy to define. It is the land, mostly in Puy-de-Dôme, between the Allier and the Dore. The obvious follow-up to this is 'Between the Allier, the Dore, and what else?'; for as things are usually arranged a river and its tributary move ever farther apart as one heads upstream. But this pair have the peculiarity that—separated by some thirty miles at their farthest —they close together again like the Severn and the Wye until the source of the Dore is only half that distance east of the Allier.

So the Livradois (which was in the tertiary period a lake-floor) takes the shape of a rough, squat ellipse. It lies between the same latitudes as the present Forez and is similar in size, but it is to the west of it and is substantially lower. It is truncated to the south by a dip in the land and then a marked rise, and in the north too there is a chord. Purists might extend the land right up to the union of the rivers not far south of Vichy; but all that part has been washed down as flat as an omelette if not as a pancake, and so belongs to the Limagne. The northern edge of the hilly Livradois hence lies along the 89 Clermont-Thiers road and the cross-country railway, in a belt where they recently searched for oil but struck (of course) water. And its apices, only a dozen miles apart, are Pont-du-Château over the Allier and Pont-de-Dore over . . . well, over the Dore.

*

From Pont-du-Château itself one can sense the *otherness* of the Livradois. Stop the car at one of those main-road pull-ups, walk a hundred yards south into the town, and there is a fine transitional church on a hilltop, a late-gothic chapel, ring upon ring of tumbled round-towered houses above the Allier which have not been rich since the town lost the distinction of holding the only bridge for fifty miles, and memories of a typical local figure too. (He was one of the

127

wickedest of the wicked barons hanged by proxy at the Grands Jours de Clermont, and sounds a good pacemaker for the Marquis de Sade.) A hundred yards more takes you on to the seventeenth-century manor of the town's name, now the *hôtel de ville*; from its terrace there opens out a view of much of this asphalt land trapped between higher and more famous ranges. It is a curiously satisfying balance of hillscape, as you stand here with your back to all that is more renowned. And it makes, perhaps, the starred views from Clermont and Thiers on either hand look a little cheap.

One would like to feel that one had Pont-du-Château all to one-self, and with it those northern foothills of the Livradois which seem almost a continuation of the Limagne—a brackish estuarine reach of that sea trapped behind a cob, a liripipe of its cowl flung over Clermont's shoulder. But tourism is creeping in. A few years ago, for instance, nobody except students of red-brown, decorated roman ceramics had heard of Ravel which stands a few miles east of Pont-du-Château. But now its castle is on the *son-et-lumière* circuit.

I am not sure that this elevation is quite justified, for from the out-side it is a dull-looking building with the hollow tooth of its medieval glory filled with routine eighteenth-century constructions. But in-side there are some amusing *bibelots à la chinoise, style Louis XVI*, for those who like that sort of nonsense. And it has an odd history.

Its main oddness, I suppose, is that it is full of names which mean little outside the context of this particular countryside. But it was one of the few Auvergnat castles to be definitely captured by (rather than burned-out by, starved-out by, bored-out by, or simply given up as a bad loss to) the British. In 1377, that was; and almost exactly four centuries later Ravel had its revenge. It was then a seat of the great d'Estaings whose hobby was revivifying castles—they also owned, at this period, Effiat—and the admiral Charles Henri Hector of that house was on sea almost what his fellow-Auvergnat, Lafayette, was on land. He sailed to Savannah; and what happened thenceafter is one of those things which French tourist offices have to word carefully so as to attract the Yanks without alienating the Limeys. Perhaps we had the last word after all, though; for on his way to the Terror's scaffold the admiral said 'Send my head to Eng-land—they'll pay you good money for it there.'

For me, the most interesting reflection on the whole business is

24

Grim, grey, ancient and rain-washed are the round-towered lava towns of Cantal, such as Salers (*above*) and Vic-sur-Cère (*below*).

25

26

St Flour: the high-set
black cathedral (*above*) and
one of its lava
sculptures (*below*).

27

that, in France as elsewhere, the great sailors come from high, dry spots hundreds of miles inland.

*

Ravel also has a presentable gothic church, as do several nearby villages such as Bongheat. It is indeed a particularity of the whole Livradois that there is a high population of good churches, if few which Aldous Huxley's young prigess would call quite first-rate. For in the neighbourhood ecclesiologists can also find romanesque Chauriat, rich in polychrome and capitals and furniture and with a neighbour which is now a wine-cellar—and also Glaine under its minor castle. Glaine is amongst the most ancient of all the Auvergne's churches, since twelfth-century work counts as a restoration there: it marks, indeed, a unique transition from carolingian to true norman and puts one in the right mood of ancientry for the pre-Christian cemetery close by.

So far as these mild hills have a capital it is Billom, though not for the last four hundred years could Billom have claimed to be the capital of *anything*. Gentle and *triste*, it is a city of memories—memories of the days when it was a university centre of learning and disputation with nearly 3,000 scholars, memories of the rise and fall of the first Jesuit college in France, memories of busy markets now silent and of many treasures lost.

But it conserves some ancient towers, a renaissance mansion or two which just get a mention in the guides, the minor church of St Loup and the major, if rambling, one of St Cernauf. This, perhaps, has little strictly architectural merit left; but it is a treasury of vernacular work in wood and iron and stone and marble and lava, dating from the eleventh to the nineteenth centuries: the pearl is a sweetly naive nativity, norman but carved by some mason who for once forgot the terrible discipline of the Mozac capitals. In general, Billom retains a most haunting atmosphere of the middle ages, with many of their delights and with such of their squalors as only the French can still endure. And it retains a railway too.

I mention this because it is so *right* that what is almost the last standard-gauge, steam-worked, private railway in France should lead to Billom. One or two times a day (not at particular times—just times), an ancient engine and single passenger coach trundles down the five miles from Vertaizon on the Clermont-Thiers line (itself worth a visit) and stops—not because Billom is a terminus, but because after that the tracks go still deeper under the grass until they end at a roadside below some romantic ruins called Turluron. (*Where* were they heading for, one wonders?) It is the most appropriate approach possible to this queer, lovable, absent-minded township which may still make a few bricks but which has quite forgotten what time it is.

*

South-west of Billom there is a castle—one of the dozen or so hereabout—which epitomizes the region. It is called Busséol. Once it boasted '*Je suis Busséol—je vois du pays largement*': now the guidebooks warn you not to penetrate for fear of its falling down. Of this, too, it might have been written:

> 'Your time's a time of memory, like that hour,
> Just after sunset, wonderful and grey'

But on reaching even Billom one has dipped into the deeps of the Livradois, and like an inexperienced swimmer is suddenly out of one's depth. For from what seemed to be only the shallow end of the basin one has been swept away into these profound waters which are also the high land. It is time, then, to haul over the easy distance to the western side of the learners' pool, and to gasp for breath alongside a familiar rope.

As usual, though, the swimmer has made more ground than he quite anticipated. He is past the ambiguous reaches of the Allier by now, south of the Clermont suburbs and into that Veyre country where there is such a fascinating contrast between the burnt but wine-planted hills west of the river and the unused eastern slopes.

The cardinal entry to the Livradois here is at Vic-le-Comte.

*

Vic lies in a small basin, cut off from the main valley and surrounded by its own green hills mounting to 2,500 feet yet bearing little trace of their volcanic origin. It was the capital of the Comté, which has kept the accent which the town has lost; but this county was a tiny one, only a few miles square, and now men have mostly forgotten even what it was. Vic itself is essentially a dull place, and on the whole less interesting than some of its less-famed neighbours: its church, for instance, is a merciless mess. But it holds one treasure—the late-gothic choir which is all that is left of a castle which Catherine de Medici used as one of her *petits trianons*. From the dizziness of near-renaissance carving and rich glass within this Ste Chapelle there stands out, *parmi les lys de la France, le glorieux chardon écossais*. For its builder's name was John Stuart, count of the Marche.

Students of the roman religion might care to note that in the nineteenth century an under-clothed Adam and Eve were pulled down in Vic (and God the Father with them) to make way for a plaster Virgin. Students of military architecture may well be deflected to Seymier or Buron (this name, of course, means a cow-pen of stone) where there are ruined towers. Diligent ecclesiologists will find something to interest them at St Julien-de-Coppel. And for the rest, a few miles to the south-east over one of the granite ridges which divide this belt of the Livradois into dozens of independent cantonments, comes Manglieu—only a village off a minor road now, but once the seat of a benedictine abbey. The church (unusually) has been scraped and restored outside more vigorously than within; but it is still an impressive building, and one with an odd coherence considering that the choir is tenth century, the portals romanesque and the nave as late as the sixteenth century. Inside there are some very ancient tombstones and similar relics.

*

The roads wind up and down amid a host of minor villages, but there is no centre eastward until one arrives at Cunlhat. This is a place of some size (if a rather small one) and has a certain bourgeois solidity: it also boasts the only tourist hotel for some distance around, which shuts at 9 p.m. But Cunlhat is hard put to it to advertise itself as a holiday centre. '*Distractions—Cueillette de champignons*' says its hand-out hopefully. But even with the local fungi called *myrtilles* and *morilles* thrown in for the lovers to search for, I feel that more than that is needed to ensure happy times.

Cunlhat does, however, have some typical old streets and a good norman church, and there are even better ones (early gothic this time) at Tours-sur-Meymont and St Amant-Roche-Savine—which latter village takes its name from some rocks up on the 3,000-foot heights. Finally, away on the road which leads back to Billom, there are two other curiosities—the painted and fortified norman church at St Dier and the dark castle of Mauzun which once boasted nineteen towers, one for each village which depended on it, but which now (having served as first an episcopal palace and then an episcopal prison) crumbles into weedy romance. Both these are good of their kind in a part of the land where the general standard is not striking.

*

But at St Amant one is not only well over to the Dore side of the Livradois (where there are still more churches to be found) but on a new latitude south, that of Issoire.

Issoire's most important neighbour to the east is Sauxillanges, which has a church, a procession of penitents, and a hotel. I have been to Sauxillanges. I was even involved in a passionate, colourful but quite unfatal car-smash there. But if ever I made any notes about it, other than that it has a certain ancientry, they have been washed white in the tempestuous waters of its streams.

The only other place of note hereabouts is Usson, not so very far north of its namesake in the Forez though thirty miles or more to the west. This village has a church of many treasures and a famous pilgrimage statue, even though the great castle of Queen Margot (the learned, pious and amorous Dumas heroine who led Henry of Navarre such a dance) which once crowned the triple tiara of towns was almost totally razed. There are one or two spots of interest around the holiday hamlet of Echandelys further east, but in general this strip of the Livradois which runs along the parallel of Ussel, Latour d'Auvergne, and Vienne on the Rhone is so dim that one might as well forget all about it, go back to Issoire, and begin again on a slightly more southern road. This generally runs through 2,000–2,500-foot, rather than 1,500–2,000-foot, country and takes in two small resort-towns favoured by those who believe in sheer altitude— le Vernet-la-Varenne, which was once famous for its pipemakers and amethysts and so had a life of its own before tourism came to it, and—rather more important and over 3,000 feet up—St Germain-l'Herm.

At the Allier end this road passes through château-country, but

for the most part it is high enough to afford views of the neighbouring hills—views which are rare in this continuously undulating
belt. Woodlands and heathlands, arable lands and park lands, climb
up together to a forest of *pins* and *sapins* (I am never sure of the
difference between these trees, even in English). One passes below the
crest-point of the Livradois, which is Notre-Dame-de-Mons and supports a pilgrimage chapel nearly 4,000 feet up. And then, by way of
St Bonnet-le-Chastel, one descends again.

*

Up and down: it seems a fairly monotonous job however one crosses
the Livradois. But here, where one exchanges Michelin sheets for
the deeper 76, is no place to abandon the venture. For south of the
roof-tree of the range, south of the border from Puy-de-Dôme (for
this was *still* Puy-de-Dôme) into Haute-Loire, back in the Allier
basin but only an easy day's stroll due west of the sources of the Dore,
there stands the curious town called Auzon.

It is curious if only because its old and up and its new and down
parts are as sharply separated as anywhere I know. The low town
is dense with the localized coal-mining which seeps from across the
Allier: the high one is so remote that even a taxi-driver who must
have been to the village every day of his working life had to ask
the way to its collegiate church of St Laurence. Anybody, one would
have thought, would have known that the answer was 'up'.

This is a fine church *as* a church: it is like a little le Puy with its
rocky and naturally-fortified site insisting that the capitals come at
the wrong height and the porches spread in the wrong directions. It
also houses one acknowledged treasure in a Virgin classed among
the classics of France. For anyone who feels, as I do, that the late
fifteenth century is a curiously unattractive period for sculpture,
there is a superb wooden crucifixion of the twelfth century, fourteenth-century frescoes like medallion glass, a pulpit with a runic or
lombardic inscription which is so old as to have baffled the de-
cipherers, and even some fragments of its fifth-century foundation.

I find such things more exciting than any sophisticated eve-of-
renaissance Madonnas. But, whoever is right, this church of Auzon
guards the south-western extremity of the Livradois.

*

133

There is little left to say about the ridge itself. But there *is* something still to be said about its flanking valleys—and notably about that of the Dore.

For the Allier is easily described. Between Usson and Auzon (if one neglects Mailhat's ancient church) there is indeed only one place of interest amid the rolling green hills east of the river. This is Nonette, which beetles—if ever a town beetled—700 feet above its valley of abandoned marble-quarries. It has a church with romanesque carving and a fine fourteenth-century head of the Saviour, if at this stage you are still in a mood for churches. But its main interest is in a castle almost more inaccessible than the church of Auzon.

Perhaps it is not the château itself which is interesting (for it was *very* thoroughly ruined) so much as its memories; for it was on this easily-defended granite promontory that the nastiest of all the Auvergnat barons held out. Astog the Red Bull sounds foul enough, but Amblard was worse. They called him 'The Winterless' because he would not hibernate from evil, and legend says that it was from his rape of a nun (presumably a *small* nun) that the village takes its name.

There is not, however, anything nasty about the Allier valley as it mounts lazily out of Puy de Dôme as if conscious that it has still *un long voyage à faire*. It is a steep valley but not—as a Jane Austen heroine would say—not yet really *horrid*. The procedure of the Dore up from its bridge on the Clermont-Thiers road is rather more complex.

*

For the Dore has no great journey to make, and moves like a man doomed to premature death with all its alternations of tumbling raffish gorges and tranquil reaches. There is first a quiet bit, beside the 106 road and a branch of the north-south railway, as far as Courpière. This is not the most celebrated town of Puy-de-Dôme, though it claims a certain spa-dom; but it is a picturesque one with a fine, lived-in-looking and thoroughly Auvergnat norman church hemmed in by old houses. The gothic tower has an asymmetrical wrought-iron bell-lantern, at first reminiscent of Provence but in fact characteristic of the Dore valley.

Then the gorges come, swinging round the hilltop church of

Sauviat to Olliergues—a not unpicturesque place, sprawled and tiered along the valley, which is proud of sending its railway-workers all over France. And then, just as you are expecting something spectacular, the river opens out again by Vertolaye into a reed-waving solitude of dragonflies and water-snakes which continues for at least the next fifteen miles to Ambert and quite destroys thoughts of the winter-sports villages like St Pierre-la-Bourlhonne which stand more than 3,000 feet up in the hills to the east.

Ambert, like all these towns on the right bank of the Dore, is not strictly of the Livradois: that ends at the old hamlet of le Monestier to the west. But it has set up a megalith of mountain granite in its square, and it has several claims to fame. Historically it has its forti-fied-looking church of St Jean (a fine, if patchwork, piece of over-ripe late-gothic), its town hall (which is an odd rotunda which looks as if it would be more at home in Harrogate), some other mellow old houses, and memories of the wars of religion almost as tragic as those of Issoire twenty miles due west. Merle once held the place by tear-ing the images from the church, dressing them up in uniform, ranging them along the parapets, and so frightening the catholics into believing that an impregnable army faced them.

Ambert's past citizens include Michel Rolle, an early algebraist, and the composer Chabrier. It also had recently—and for all I know may still have—a remarkable number of local traditions: the memory of Fr Gaschon, for instance, or the custom of blessing but not conse-crating a special wine at the feast of SS Come and Damien which is particularly fascinating to amateurs of liturgy. But even more varied still is the town's industrial history.

In the sixteenth century Ambert was a great centre of paper-making, with more than three hundred mills. Dore shares with Thiers' stream the doubtful honour of being the first thoroughly exploited French river; but Ambert did not adjust itself to the industrial revolution as Thiers did and its skilled sons, including the Montgolfier brothers, scattered across France. Today only two hand-mills remain open in souvenir of an art older than printing, one which—they claim, as at Thiers—came west with the Crusades. The factory which you can-not visit has a genuine and unbroken tradition lasting in its dark, damp rooms: the one you can (which is marvellously situated at the bottom of a tributary valley) is rather a reconstituted showpiece,

135

Illustration 7

though there is something satisfying in the idea of a watermark dated 1326. But both are exclusively concerned with a craftsman's product rare in the world today.

When its paper-trade faded, Ambert (which is a *sous-préfecture* of 7,000 inhabitants) had to take to other activities. It had the great cheese which remains its own contribution to that *table d'Auvergne* of which it claims to be the capital, a cheese speckled blue within and red without which comes from byres cleansed in the Augean way; and it made a tidy corner in wigs and sabots too. But the industry which won was religious trinkets.

Every year now Ambert exports a quarter of a million pounds' worth of *objets de piéte*, mainly to the USA. It sounds ghastly: but in fact the quiet, lime-shaded little city has great good taste and there is hardly a rosary to be seen. Ambert, in fact, is a happy town, and with its pleasant inn it is one of my favourites in all Puy-de-Dôme.

*

For a moment more—a mere ten miles—the Dore runs softly beside the road south, in a basin so broad and fertile that they speak of the limagne of Ambert. It wanders past Marsac with its two sinking and southern-looking churches. And so it comes to its last town.

Arlanc is a *long* place—over a mile long, long enough to be two entities. The lower, unexpectedly, is the older. This is the *bourg* of the lace-makers, and is enchanting in a thoroughly Auvergnat way: it is not surprising to find another version of the virgin-shepherdess-escape story relating to nearby shrines here. But the norman lava fountains on dung-strewn village greens, the decrepit houses and (especially) the romanesque church of St Pierre are yearly subsiding into weeds. If I were you, I would visit old Arlanc while it is still there.

The upper *ville* (and it is a killing climb, though the *route nationale* goes right up the high street) is a long string of restaurants and garages, broken only by a couple of renaissance buildings. They seem to say that it is time to re-fuel while you can, for there are steeps ahead. And they are right.

For just south of Arlanc, above Dore-l'Eglise (which, for once, *has* an *église*) the river—and with it its beautifully-christened affluent the Dolore—bend back like a cedilla into the hills and there fall into their death agonies. With them ends all that can be called the Livradois. Behind Arlanc now there rises an immense cliff which implies for travellers on the 106 a succession of hairpins beyond counting and for railfarers a long but lovely detour.

The escarpment also corresponds here to the frontier out of Puy-de-Dôme. Beyond it lie great things, but different things. Everything is becoming dramatic, the land is assuming a form. And that, for the *coin perdu*, will never do.

*

For only a morning's walk south from Arlanc, high on that tree-lined cliff, stands the abbey of la Chaise-Dieu, the house of God.

'If ever too great a title might be excused it is this,' wrote Belloc in an essay on this 'church of granite, enormous, forsaken and alone'. I think that this is a true saying. I know that I shall have more to write of the Chaise-Dieu, up there on what I have already called one of the cardinal, turntable plateaux of the Auvergne where many ranges meet and several lines of transport unite. But this is not the place to write it.

For if the northern transept of this fortress-shrine looks down upon the Livradois, the southern stares across Velay. And that is another land; another chapter.

137

8

The Sunlight on the Farms

Vienne, Vézère, Corrèze, Dordogne, Lot, Aveyron, Tarn. . . .
I began the chapter which dealt with the north-western
marches of the Massif with that marvellous litany of Atlantic
rivers, and I do not apologize for repeating it here to introduce the
south-western corridor. For the seven words are a magic charm, not
merely beautiful in themselves but a potent help when one is perplexed about the shape of the land.

Like most spells, however, they must be used with discretion; for
the valleys do not, for the most part, run due east and west. The
great southward race of the Vézère for example, formed a western
boundary of that earlier chapter; and the Dordogne itself has so far
been only briefly glimpsed as its sunless headwaters flow past the quays
of the spas of Puy-de-Dôme. What has gone before, in fact, has
ended with a latitude rather than a valley—the latitude of Tulle on
the Corrèze.

I am sorry that it did so, for Tulle was never one of my cities. I
would have liked, even then, to have followed the Corrèze, the
89 road and the cross-country railway less than twenty miles further
west—past towered Cornil, past the church and cromlech and gorges
of Aubazine (a magnificently picturesque village, this), out of the dark
cliffs of granite or jurassic limestone and down to that sandstone
basin of market-gardening and fertility where it and the Vézère
meet. But I could not then justify a knight's move of two squares
west if it implied (as it *did*) one square south to within a day's march
of the province, miscalled Dordogne, which is black and prehistoric
Perigord.

However, what was lost on old roundabouts can be won on new
swings. And so this chapter, which follows behind Chapter 3 like a

holiday relief train which, perhaps, carries more interesting passengers than its predecessor, can at least begin with the queen-city which stands two-thirds of the way down the great Paris-Toulouse artery, where the 20 comes in from Donzenac and the railway from high Allassac. This is Brive, Brive-la-Gaillarde.

*

I approve of Brive, with its fine Italianate symmetry; and I hope that Brive approves of me. *Le riant portail du Midi* it pronounces itself in flowers and stone, at the station where the big trains stop; and though it is anybody's guess where the south begins, Brive-la-Gaillarde, (for she deserves her full style and title) is both a mighty crossroads and a smiling city. I have drunk coffee at dawn on her quays after an agonizing night in an undergraduate vintage car: I have washed up here from numerous rattling buses: and I have broken my rail journey south many times at this city whose name means simply 'bridge'. She has never disappointed me.

Anciently of lace-making fame, Brive is today essentially an agricultural city; and even its thriving manufactures (such as that of building materials) depend in some way on the land, though I wish I knew just how '*le noyer alimente les fabriques de galoches*'. As a tourist centre, perhaps, it has not over-much to offer, though the food tends to be good and Brive is reputed to be the centre for two really off-beat liqueurs, *bleu* and *léonie*, which I have not seen advertised and certainly have not tasted. The high narrow transitional church of St Martin (who may have been martyred here) is restored and less than distinguished: the norman chapel which is the town's only other church is somehow suburban: and the sandstone grottoes where St Anthony of Padua prayed are tucked away on the wrong side of the tracks. There are some charming renaissance courtyards, and the suburb of Malemort out on the Tulle road is worth a visit. But the one unique thing in Brive is its ancient seminary of Labenche, now used by some kind of learned institute for museumizing sea-shells. Here the discipline of the late middle ages, of the *trivium* and *quadrivium*, comes to life as vividly as anywhere in Europe.

Yet Brive—the laughing gateway, the strong and merry, *la tant graciousa*, the shapely, comfortable, ringed town of 35,000 inhabitants—is, I think, the pleasantest place of its size in all France. And

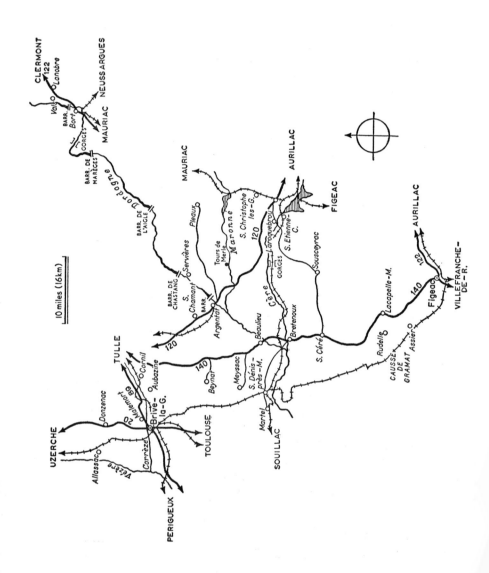

behind that smile there is strength and pride; for Brive was the first
city in all France to liberate itself from the Nazi occupation by its
own force of arms. I share its anger that through the ages not it but
Tulle—dim, dull and much smaller—has been the official capital of
my beloved Corrèze.

*

Immediately beyond Brive the great Toulouse road drops out of this
book once more; and fascinating as is the countryside of Collonges
and Turenne which follows, it does not belong here. So one must
turn east again, past a church or two and several strongholds and
then across the 140 road, for twenty-five-odd miles to Argentat.

'*C'est pas mal*' was the best they could say in Brive—and with a
patronizing shrug at that—when I told them I was going to this
place. But in addition to its amusing castle, the legends which surround its menhirs, and its warm and likeable personality, Argentat
has four claims to individuality.

One of these is that nearby, up the Maronne tributary, there rises
a many-splendoured spot linked to the great house of Uzès called
the Tours de Merle; near it the rebuilt castle at Servières is also
worth a glance. Another distinction—for me at least—is that Argentat is the terminus of the last of those narrow-gauge railways of
Corrèze of which I have written so much elsewhere—the one which
comes straggling south from St Chamant beside the 120 road from
Tulle. The third lies in the charm of the mellow, half-timbered
houses which mount grassy levees beside the river. And the last
(*c'est pas mal, Argentat*) is the river itself.

For this is the Dordogne.

*

Argentat, indeed, is the very fulcrum of the Dordogne river, and I
would love to give it a Janus-figure to mount upon its bridge. Glan-
cing at the map, the eye travels downstream—a mere fifteen miles
south-westward as the river runs, and little more than half that
en vol d'oiseau—to the bridge of the 140 road where the golden
names begin. The temptation to follow it down these magnificent
reaches is already present, and soon will have to be faced again. But
for the moment the movement must be reversed—north-eastward,

below the Corrèzian villages which fringed an earlier chapter, against the stream and back to the mountains from whence it came.

The Dordogne means many things to many men, and we are not all archaeologists or rich *touristes-gastronomes* specializing in truffles and good living. For the engineer, for instance, the river is a puissant source of power; and Argentat is the frontier-station of that change of viewpoint. For just above it one finds the first of the great barrages; and from there for seventy-five miles it is just one dam thing after another.

*

Argentat: Chastang: the Eagle: Marèges: Bort: these are the treads on the stairway. A twenty-five-year-long programme, involving barrages across tributary rivers and long tunnels as well, has now virtually reached completion and its seventeen power stations produce 2,500 million units a year. A tenth of all the hydro-electric energy of France, indeed, derives from this one stretch of the Dordogne and its affluents which forms the boundary between Corrèze and Cantal (and almost reaches Puy-de-Dôme) in its climb from 500 to almost 2,000 feet above sea-level—a greater difference of level than all the way down the Rhone from Geneva to the Mediterranean.

They have, of course, altered the aspect of the walnut-clad and essentially domestic valley, these great walls of concrete a mile across which themselves weigh up to three million tons and retain perhaps 300 million tons of water in a lake fifteen miles long. But I do not think they have impaired its beauty, except perhaps at low water when a French river is a sad sight anyway. For the power derives from *current* rather than *potential*, and there are none of those hideous pipes which scar the Alpine and Pyrenean valleys.

During construction these works were certainly a confounded nuisance with their meccano-like workshops, aerial ropeways, industrial chug-chug and roar of blasting. But it has all settled down now, and the Scotophile French like to think that they have made lochs in one corner of their land—though in fact they have made Windermeres. A few dull villages were drowned and a few minor ways of communication inundated. But above the winding Dordogne (which in any case has often changed its course from natural causes) the rocks and bridges and castles and waterfalls and viewpoints are still there: the Michelin, for instance, gives fifteen references to the sights of the valley. And the castle of Val is more there than ever.

Val is a few miles above the town of Bort, near the pretty norman church of Lanobre where the 122 road comes down from Clermont over a legendary and glacial plateau. A few years ago it was just a medieval castle on a bluff above the river, charming enough with its six pepper-pot towers and its galleries but not a great *but de voyage*. Then the waters of the uppermost of all these artificial lakes rose (and one can almost hear the argy-bargy between the Ministry of Fine Arts and the Cie. Hydro-Electrique de l'Auvergne going on all the time) until they lapped its courtyard. But they rose no higher; for at that level there awaited the ski-jump of the barrage.

The result is that Val has been transformed into a castle of fairy-tale. It is water-ringed except for the causeway which gives it access; and the waters which ring it seem those which surround Elsinore and Camelot, even if they only got there to supply their 150,000 kilovolt-amps. All I regret is that Val's lovely chapel is now used as a boathouse, a transformation which would have worried its builders on more than one count.

*

But Val *is* above Bort; and 6,000-strong Bort (on the right bank of the Dordogne, and hence just in Corrèze) is not a place to be over-looked. It has its 250-feet high cliff of lava-prisms above—crystallized, they say, like organ-pipes and so giving to the town its traditional suffix of 'les-Orgues'. It has the usual gorges about, and a devil's kitchen, and waterfalls too—though these have been bled by subterranean tunnels for hydro-electric ends. It has a leather industry, a thing like an English butter-cross, a passable church, a speciality in *croquants* and a wine called Clairgay which is *rosé*, smooth, but not (as the pundits say) very vinous. And above all—literally above all, the only thing besides the *orgues* which *can* overlook Bort—it has that dam, the most accessible of all the series.

This has made of Bort a boom-town (though not really an industrial one), and has pulled up its hotels—though they still want to go to bed at ten—to the standards of Essen or Scunthorpe. It also gives a Thurberish sensation to a night spent in one of them. Of course, one thinks in the dark hours, that is only a tap dripping: the dam

143

Illustration 21

can't break. But still . . . one thousand million cubic feet of water are pointed, like a shotgun with the hammers back, at the grey roofs of Bort and . . . *I tell you it's only rain, the dam can't break.*

There is one other curiosity to be noted of the town. It *had* a through train from Paris, running down twenty-odd picturesque miles of a tributary valley from Eygurande-Merlines in the north, until the hydro-electrics drowned its track so deep that even the keenest lover of abandoned railways will not find it without an aqualung. The Germans would have cut a new roadbed at a higher level: the British would have trusted to buses: but though France no longer builds railways, to take off a link with Paris is almost a breach of the Code Napoléon. And so Bort still has its through-cars, though they must be trailed round, by way of the Toulouse line, over a detour of more than a hundred miles.

*

Such is the upstream terminal of this power-packed reach of the Dordogne; and all the sinuous way back to Argentat there are an infinity of viewpoints. But there are no towns which belong to this chapter; and to move in any other direction from Bort leads one into sterner lands; and so one is again faced with the temptation to drift downstream from Argentat.

It *is* a mere fifteen miles more south-west, after all, to the bridge-town which stands where the 140 road has come down the twenty winding miles south from Tulle without a village on it—though with the small holiday centres of Beynat and Meyssac in the hills to its west. This bridge-town is Beaulieu, a place as happy as its name suggests and one with a magnificent and far-famed norman church. Then, only an hour's walk south, comes Bretenoux, equally enchanting at the crossing of the Cère; this spot may once have been defended by Thomas à Becket. And as far on again is St Céré, which switches the accents round to show that it is *not* on the Cère but a third river. It is in this place, perhaps the most *sympathique* of all these picturesque triplets which dominate a corner of land fantastically rich in castles and manors, that Lurçat holds his school—and Poujade his political rallies.

These towns are not of the Massif, despite the fact that they lie (rather than stand) twenty miles inland of the 20 road and the

latitude of Brive: the contours of the plateau have made their furthest
thrust at the sunset, and they are retreating now. But all three are,
I think true guardians to it, as is symbolized by the fact that the
frontier of the department of Lot—of the ancient Quercy—winds
amid them through a richness of market-gardening which resembles
Brive's. However, their situation is only fully appreciated by travelling (and here at last is the excuse) a little further yet down the
Dordogne.

*

From a height above history-stained, sun-baked, seven-towered Martel
on the Atlantic limestone shelf (which most people have heard of,
if at all, only because the branch-railway crossroads of St Denis is
près it): from the propitious rocks or even from byzantine Souillac
twenty miles south of Brive on that inevitable road-rail artery, look
back in anger or in love.

Look eastward—and, if you have the stomach, look at dawn. A
black line, mosaiced with purple and gold, rules the sky; and in
it there is cleft one gap as cleanly or terribly as with an axe. The
line, of course, is the edge of the central plateau. The break in it is
the Bretenoux basin where the Dordogne, the Cère and their many
affluents emerge and converge, the place where—they say—great
Roland slaked his thirst and the last Arvenes surrendered. I know
no starker entry to the Massif: with reason the French call this gap—
which is also the great amphitheatre of the hundred years' war—the
trouée héroïque.

And why, one asks, should one return to pass through that herculean gate? Here in Quercy is the land of—

> The days of halcyon weather,
> The oriole fluting in the cherries,
> The sunlight sleeping on the farms.

From here to Bergerac, and onwards half-way to Bordeaux, the
orchards toss their blossom about brownstone mills and the poplars
at the valley-floor are pale plumes in spring, eagles' feathers in
autumn, and in winter white incense-offerings. Here are the tourist-
grottoes, whether signed by prehistoric man, or natural, or simply
fake: here are the chiming names of the homeland of the troubadours,

and of Charlemagne. No countryside has had more lovers—and in particular English lovers, who have here found a deeper Wessex of greater hills and an ampler sun.

'Funny how you get a kind of craving to go back to a place like *that*,' I once heard a man say in a Dorset pub: *he* was speaking of Stockton-on-Tees. From the heroic basin of Bretenoux it seems as absurd to turn eyes eastward again to those forbidding steeps—to return up the Cère as one has already descended the Dordogne. *I* must do so, because the land of this book lies there. But nobody need follow me who does not want to know what dignity and symmetry lies over the hills and far away, under the high horizons, the white skies of dawn and the marbled clouds of sunset.

*

The Cère has quite a long journey to make, up from this clay basin through limestone gorges and then a pool of sandstone country, before it reaches the volcanic heights; and only its first reach belongs in this chapter. All along that it is followed by one of the unimportant branch-lines which keep going in these parts, but by no road at all—though the 120 closes in on its right bank some little way after it has turned east from Argentat. One or two villages amid the hydro-electric works which punctuate the Cère's sunless valley have a glow of warmth of Perigord or Quercy; and they say that there are some still-unfamed chasms here too. But for all the rest it is just solitude, and the uneventful border between Corrèze and Lot and then Cantal, until it reaches the old church-and-castle town of Laroquebrou. This remembers a legend which introduces one to the true Auvergne again; for once, when its *seigneur* died, there were so many poor pressing to share in the traditional alms-giving that seventeen were suffocated in the crush. Today it is a sound tourist centre with a local fête, centring on its huge statue of the Virgin, in early August.

Nearby is the small resort of St Etienne-Cantalès; and both these places stand on the shores of a strange lake. It is again an artificial, hydro-electric one. It is vast (containing 3,500 million cubic feet), comparatively shallow, more oddly-shaped than a natural lake could ever be and, with all its islands and promontories, very beautiful indeed. It has not succeeded in drowning the four-way rail junction

146

Illustration 4

of these parts, one spur from which—running north towards Bort past the village of St Christophe-les-Gorges whose church is now dedicated to St Omer—crosses another *retenue* on the Maronne near the attractive resort of Pleaux in Cantal: the whole journey is so spectacular that one wonders why the SNCF does not advertise these branches as the *route des barrages*. And finally its water-level is just above that crucial contour of 1,500 feet.

East of this nameless lake, in fact, the real steepnesses of Cantal begin. So, on its surface, an omen floats like a water-lily. This is to return in a beeline, making across the border of Lot again past the ideal, buried frontier-town of Sousceyrac, to the 140 road at La-capelle-Marival—which is itself a pleasant spot and gives access to the church of Assier and a neglected, fortified place called Rudelle.

The next town down the 140 road is Figeac.

*

Vienne, Vézère, Corrèze, Dordogne, Lot, Aveyron, Tarn—what has become of that great corridor? Figeac is barely even on the Lot, and there are two more rivers to cross. (The railway to Toulouse, indeed, traverses the Aveyron eighteen times.) But the contours of the plateau are pulling back sharply now, running nearer to the horizontal than the vertical as they approach their south-western point. And here the border-lands lose their identity, and what began as a countryside becomes a thin line or ends at a single point.

Look at the map again. Behind Figeac there is a dense woodland slashed with small streams, indubitably of the true Auvergne though technically still in Lot. Before Figeac there is a brief valley and then a very different land, that of the Causse de Gramat. The name and barren look both suggest that this too belongs to the Auvergne. But geology is doubtful, since the Gramat is of chalk interlarded with china-clay and flints rather than of limestone. And history gives a firm 'No'.

The Causse de Gramat, though visually similar to the true causses which are on the same latitude but fifty miles or more to the east, is a region of its own—a juniper-studded scrubland whose *fossez et citernes* have given cover to Muslim tribesmen, Christian martyrs, the enemies of Pepin le Bref, *routiers* and *maquisards* and outlaws of all kinds for twenty centuries, a holy land whose shrine is Rocamadour, today a tourist land because of the grottoes and mysterious waters, but not Auvergnat land.

And so Figeac, though a mere 750 feet above the sea, is locked away from the world: symbolically, it is lost in the corner of a Michelin map sheet. But, after so much beating amid the bushes, what kind of place is it? It looks a decent enough township (how often one uses *that* phrase) and is a sous-préfecture of 7,000 inhabitants (how often one supplies *that* information). It has a typical western-Auvergnat shape with its slope from station to river and up again, old houses, a picturesque waterfront, and two churches (St Sauveur and N-D du Puy) worth more attention than they usually receive. Finally, it is marked on the gastrophile's map as the eastern point of the truffle country, and on my own humbler level I have found it no bad place to eat and sleep.

But nobody without a penchant for falling for the ordinary would call Figeac *exciting*. And so it seems a pity that this tone-poem in two movements of the marches of the Auvergne should end on such a muted, if harmonious, downbeat.

9

The White Cantals

The Monts du Cantal are a continuation southward of the Auvergnat ranges. They could even be included with the Dômes and the Dores as themselves an Auvergnat range; for like the rest they are volcanic. But the Cantals are not a conglomeration of volcanoes. They are what is left of a single volcano.

A million or more years ago there was only one Cantal mountain —a single cone more than a hundred miles in circumference and two miles high, a massif, smoking like a farmyard dung-hill through a dozen chimneys, which was as large as an English county and as tall as Mont Blanc. It lost its form, not from some catastrophic and Krakatoan explosion standing like the fall of man at the start of time, but after it was extinct and through the patient erosion of glaciers and rivers and the pressure of upstart mountains knocking at its doors. But the form is still discernible, if more clearly on a relief map than on the land itself.

There is the fanged central tooth of the Puy Mary and the more rounded Plomb du Cantal, still rising 6,000 feet above the sea and at their peaks only 100 feet below the Puy de Sancy: I am not sure if these crests are really distinguished ones, since I have seen them resemble both a Japanese print and a slag tip. There are a number of needles nearby only a little lower, for the Cantals are far more jagged than the northern ranges. There is the great tent of fairly fertile volcanic soil which shelves away from these columns and crests —quite gently to the west, more sharply to the east, and to the north (whose utterly lonely heights, where a cow's horns can scale the 5,000-foot contour, bear their own name of the Cézallier) confused by the counterflow of lava which came down from the Dores. And about all there is a starfish of tributaries scouring down and radiating like the ribs of an umbrella on their way to greater rivers—the Rhue,

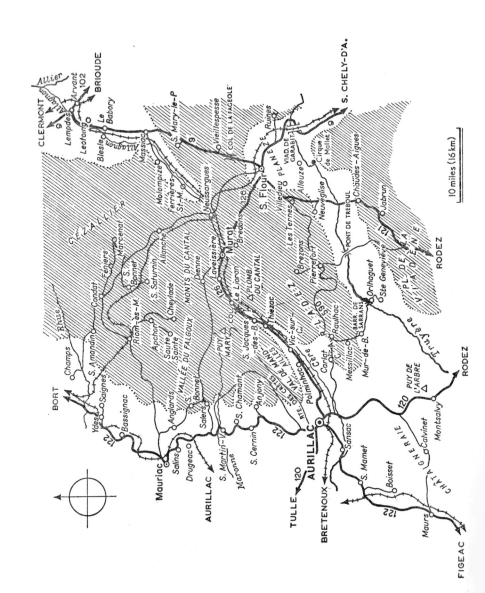

Maronne and young Cère towards the Dordogne in the west, the Allagnon toward the Allier in the east, and southward a number of less important affluents heading for the Truyère and the Lot.

Despite its geological unity, the area of this chapter is as hard to define as any; for contour-lines and boundary-lines fight all about its edges and recognizable rivers, roads and railways form the smaller part of its confines. But they have their own look, these true Cantal hills which fill out the department—already touched on its western and northern edges—*called* Cantal, which is itself the nearest a modern map offers to the land of the old Haute-Auvergne.

It is a look of immense emptiness, especially since today all the highlands are deforested. To open the Michelin sheet 76 at the top left, indeed, is like contemplating a Cantal cheese: the blue veins of valleys, the little patches of green which mark all that is left of the primeval forest, only emphasize the white spaces between. But the flesh of the cheese which is wrung from the cows which roam these open, thin but not infertile pastures patched by bracken and broken by granite is a distinguished one. And the mountains of Cantal are not the least noble in France.

I say this knowing that many love them passionately but without myself wholly liking the department. Its weather has always been unkind to me, and no landscape looks drearier than the most magnificent of mountains under lowering lifeless skies. Its public transport is miserably inadequate. And in fact I associate all Cantal with rain-lashed waits in transport cafés and with unwanted taxi-rides through 1/10th visibility. But if you follow the Michelin route, apparently, you can knock off Cantal in an afternoon. . . .

*

In this stark land beasts count for more than men. Pourrat, for instance, tells the story of the peasant with whom he commiserated for having lost his cow and his wife within a few months, only to be told that it was best that way since the *dot* from his new spouse would buy a new animal: the killing and roasting of a pig is indeed still a ritual matter. One does not, then, expect great architecture; and though Cantal has a few towns marked on the tourist map, they are not such as to attract travellers into the most Auvergnat part of France. There *is* an architectural trademark, I think, which derives from the outcrops of basalt *orgues* which here and there arise in their giant's-causeway hexagons and guard the department behind Bort: quarried, these prisms give a beehive look to walls all over the High Auvergne. But little of even passing note has been built from them; and it is quite misleading that only just out of Bort, where the pre-Roman highway from the Auvergne to the Limousin crossed this western frontier, there is a rich little corner of culture, castles and churches. The most famed places are only a mile or so apart; and though both get into the guide-books on the strength of their roman-esque churches, each *mérite un détour* in its own right.

Ydes is a village. But it *is* a village, and not a cluster of farms or a main-road straggle: its white cottages round the green, and the stream running through which has mercifully not been exploited for its mineral properties, have an English (or, for those who do not think the highest tribute to French landscape is to compare it to our own, a Norman) look. The church is fascinating outside, with some splendid though unintegrated panels of zodiacal carving. The interior, apart from the modern glass, is disappointing.

Saignes, on the other hand, is a real town. It has a *place* rather than a village green, and a very fine one too; for in addition to the church there is a perfect fifteenth-century *hôtel* which I covet almost more than any other small renaissance mansion in France. Failing that, one will be comfortable enough in the hotel which looks across the square as confidently as a Trust House in some spot like Olney.

I am sorry to harp on these homely comparisons. But—once again —the belt of land which runs south from Bort along the 122 is the purest of frontier-country and was once an English frontier. After this pocket of peace, however, you are reminded that this is *not* the lower part of Somerset (or even of Lot) by the many sharp hairpins which lead you, through castled Bassignac and a handsome countryside broken by isolated coalfields, over the twenty miles to Mauriac.

*

Of all the *-ac* towns which run down this slope of the Massif, Mauriac is the dimmest. The church is advertised as *le principal monument de l'art roman de la Haute-Auvergne*, the main effect of

which is to make an ecclesiologist despair of the High Auvergne,
to which in any case Mauriac only marginally belongs. Inside it is
a dreary building; but the exterior is not unimpressive with its
strong, fortified-looking tower brooding over a low, grey but quite
distinguished square. There is also a lava lantern of the dead
which once looked on the cemetery, a really exciting west portal,
and a moving legend concerning two captured crusaders who
prayed to the Vierge des Miracles of Mauriac so fervently that they
were transported in their sleep—chains and all—back to their little
home town. The chains are still there, though shown only during
the basilica's May fête and processions: the black Virgin more
regularly on display is several centuries younger than the legend.

For the rest, Mauriac is dark and unremarkable, save for two or
three presentable *hôtels*. One's impression is that this market-town
sous-préfecture somehow has ideas above its station, though physically it lies *below* its station, sloping down to the river in typical
Auvergnat shape. It has some pleasant inns, however, which are
useful enough resting-points before the next leg south.

*

Down from Mauriac, then, the 122 contorts itself; and so savage are
the changes in the contours around the 3,000-foot mark, so many
river-valleys and waterfalls like Salins' come searing down from the
bleached *planèze* highlands, that this is as spectacular, splendid and
terrifying a road as France affords. To its east, indeed, lies what is
recognized as the most alpine country of all the Auvergne. Habitation is not lost, for there are castles and churches above, barns and
mills below; but for the most one sees only quarried cliffs of basalt
or underlying granite, rounded slopes cropped by small russet cows,
snowploughs stacked against the winter, and the entries to valleys
such as the marvellously lonely one of the Falgoux just above
Mauriac and—far further south—the so-called Route des Crêtes and
the many-caved Mandailles valley which is so savage and lonely
that it is not surprising to learn that it has the highest emigration
rate of the whole Auvergne.

These are for road travellers only. But the road is at first duplicated
by a gossamer railway—a continuation of that long line which started
above Evaux, was lost in the upper Dordogne, and here continues

south before it bows away to the lake junctions of the Cère. In many ways this has a still more spectacular traject than the road. Already, before Mauriac, it has made a huge Z-bend to gain height, so that unwary travellers look up to see the sun setting behind the lilac hills of Perigord when it should be striking the purple steeps of the Dores. But either way of transport will take you past the gothic church of Drugeac to the upper valley of the Maronne, to St Martin-Valmeroux, and to a jumping-off point for Salers.

St Martin itself (formerly the bailiwick for the whole Haute-Auvergne) has had a little fame thrust upon it because its square—decent, but no better than many in these parts—lies on the main road: the church is presentable and for some reason all the guide-books mention the trees too. Salers, to my mind, has been grossly over-valued. It has a fine site and an attractive *place* with some attractive houses: it was in turn a military, judicial and pilgrimage centre, and in the fifteenth century gave the parliament of France its first president. Its fountains once literally flowed with wine; but when, in the eighteenth century, they put a stop to that, *le nombre des pèlerins diminuait sensiblement.*

Today again everybody goes to Salers, not so much because it still sports a procession on Trinity Sunday but because it has become a Burford-in-the-Cotswolds, a centre of the quaint and the olde-worlde. It is true there is nothing new and nasty in this faithful and never-sacked town (which is why it is as familiar to kinematomanes as Denham) and that even the hotels are ancient; but, unfortunately, the old is not very good. The church is a failure as a building, though it has some scattered treasures within: the village of St Bonnet has a better building, and little Anglards further to the north one quite as good.

I feel Salers to be a bit of a wash-out and nothing like as fascinating a place as (for example) Stirling; but maybe it was only washed out for *me*—literally by driving rain, spiritually by an excess of publicity. Others might find that very average square meriting one (though certainly not two) stars. The town lends its name to a brand of Auvergnat *gentiane*, and also—thanks to the comparative richness of its pasture—to the standard breed of cattle of the High Auvergne which, being paler than those of the north, give rise to the legend that these shy beasts are really Ferrandaises scrubbed with pumice.

154

Illustration 24

Parapluierie

Since it is an inescapable name, it is worth remembering that the final 's' is silent.

*

Unless you make a very small detour across this boulder-strewn and glacier-scoured land to see the woodwork of St Chamant (a village, like so many in these parts, fallen on hard times) the next town down the road is St Cer- (or Ser-) nin, where the church has some excellent woodwork probably removed from the aforesaid St Chamant. Hard by is the splendid castle called Anjony. Then, twenty minutes' drive further south past a few more villages with churches, comes the last of the major -*ac* towns, Aurillac. And though it is admittedly difficult to keep the mind clear between one and the other in a land where the names sound so similar as the -*villes* of Normandy or the -thorpes of Suffolk, this is the most substantial of them all.

The prefecture of Cantal and the largest town for fifty miles or so, Aurillac gave to Christendom one of the giants of the Dark Ages—Gerbert, the local shepherd-lad who became monk, horologist, astronomer, doctor, tutor, musician, mathematician, introducer of Arabic ciphering, begetter of the crusades, and at last the first Frenchman to wear the high tiara—great Sylvester II, *pape de l'an mille*. Among his innovations was gold-plating, which became Aurillac's first staple industry. This was so wastefully conducted, however, that many a shepherd made a little pocket-money by leaving a fleece in the stream to collect its burden; and it was eventually succeeded by the manufacture of lace and then of kettles. Even today the city's main job-of-work remains an individualistic one, highly appropriate to this drizzly edge of the Auvergne. Aurillac is the centre of the French umbrella trade. . . .

Savagely ravaged during the wars of religion, when the huguenots buried its monks alive, Aurillac today has no historic buildings of *grande classe*. There is a lopsided late-gothic parish church (oddly dedicated to Notre-Dame-des-Neiges) with a black Virgin, an interesting modern chapel-of-ease, a few much-restored renaissance buildings, a couple of museums and a huddle of old houses by the river. But they are all overwhelmed by the modern city of over 20,000 inhabitants.

This, however, has preserved most of the old planning and a pleasant un-Hausmannized look, and still shapes itself along the stream. A great agricultural mart and centre for tourists and transients, Aurillac has a flavour of its own. Ox-carts and lush cars with foreign registrations jostle in its streets, market-men play *boule* opposite neon-glistening cafés with *terrasses chauffées,* peasants in clogs hobble through the revolving doors of shiny banks and administrative offices. There is no larger, busier, smarter, shinier town between Clermont and Toulouse.

*

The 122 turns southwest out of Aurillac, past the pretty churches of Sansac and St Mamet and near to the resort of Boisset, to border one of those sudden enclaves which crop up here and there in the highlands. This one (and its centre is another little resort, Calvinet) is called the Châtaigneraie, and is a strangely mixed land. Geologically it is akin to the Forez and the Limousin, and so has its hamlet-habitations and its patches of pasture. But in essence it is an undulating mass of granite west of where the lava reached, infertile and thinly-populated even by the standards of the high Cantals. Only hair-thin valleys support those chestnut-trees which give the land its name; and after much deforestation to make gallic acid it is not at all the great green forest it looks on the map.

On the 122, the branch-line to Figeac and also the extreme western edge of the Châtaigneraie is the rather odd town of Maurs, which makes prefabricated building materials. This is a picturesque, symmetrical little place with plenty of distinguished history, some old streets and a charming fourteenth-century church whose most striking features are (outside) the tower and porch and (inside) a diverse, dusty and dateless ring of wooden statues surrounding the choir, as mysterious and inscrutable as the stone caesars of Oxford. But Maurs seems to have had an advertising agent more effective than accurate. He invented the suffix 'la-Jolie', in the place of the former 'de-Cantal' and christened the local countryside the 'Riviera Cantalienne': he drew a picture of vines and sunlight and flowers and silkworm farms: and he got all this accepted, with next to no historical or topographical justification, by supposedly objective guides.

Attractive Maurs undeniably is; and after a journey through the sunless gorges which surround it, its region seems warm enough. But it has only two very humble hotels, and the attempt to paint it as the centre of a *terra ridente* is, I think . . . well, misleading.

*

The eastern edge of the Châtaigneraie is defined by the 120 road below Aurillac; and the town there corresponding to Maurs is Montsalvy under the historic triangulation point of the Puy de l'Arbre. This has no high-falutin' ideas, but with its old gates, its amiable patchwork church and its augustinian conventual remains is quite as good a town. And from either place the third side is close at hand, for only a stone's-throw south is the departmental edge, the end of the Châtaigneraie, and that greatest of lateral clefts in the western Massif, the valley of the Lot.

The hinterland, then, awaits—the white highlands, all above 2,000 feet, which rise east of this shoulder strip of Cantal above deep chasms where the snow never melts. The most typical countryside is neatly contained by two branch-railways, virtually the only lines ever built in the whole department. One runs south-east from Bort, and the other north-east from Aurillac, and they meet at a place called Neussargues at the apex of this triangle which is a day's march along each side.

As a junction, Neussargues gets its name on quite big trains; and even the bit near the station, where the cicadas cry in the dusk and are answered by the slow deep SNCF gongs, has souvenir shops which suggest that the town itself a mile or so away would like to be a resort. Apart from its square it is not a distinguished one, though it boasts the usual small norman church and castle; but in its open combe, 2,750 feet up, it is certainly delightfully situated. I know of few pleasanter places in France to kill those three long hours between trains.

*

To reach Neussargues by either railway line from the west implies a long and savage journey, but the feeling of the two routes could not be more different. Out of Bort in the north most of the climbing is done in the first few miles; once you are clear of the many tributaries of the Rhue tangling south of the town of Champs with its strangely-shaped church there is no particular river valley and no

road of importance. The line doubles and snakes, tunnels and viaducts, all on its own.

Here, where the Cantals and the Dores press together to form the
Cézallier in a jumble of crests as tight packed as heads in a subway
train, is a wilderness-enow. But it is—when you can see it—one of the
most magnificent of all the highlands of Europe, and for such a bitter
and barren land the journey is amazingly unmonotonous. Amid the
enormous fields, drystone walls and picket fences, the squares of
gentian and the granite striking through the lava skin, one finds
sudden blazons of rhododendrons or flowering cherry recalling the
fuchsia-vales of Cornwall. Why, in this thin land—which (they say)
God touched only twice, to make and to abandon—are the low, whitewashed, slated and thoroughly wuthering farmhouses of some crumbling *domaine* surrounded by such pretty little gardens? One cannot,
so far up, look for an English or a Gascon influence: one hesitates to
use the psychologist's slick proof-by-contraries: maybe it is only that,
with nothing edible within gunshot, the peasant has to do *something*
with his spare time.

After a string of small villages with small norman churches you
come to the first, the lowest, the most important (and with its
cheese market, cattle trade, liqueur distillery and diatomite mining,
the most prosperous) town of these mountains. It bears the ancient,
ringing name of Riom-ès-Montagnes and is no bad place; but when
you have seen its romanesque church of St Georges you have seen
most of it. From it onward the railway makes a wild detour north
and almost reaches St Amandin. But it unfortunately fails to attain
Condat.

This is a small town; but it was once prosperous with weavers,
and is still the centre for a good deal of textile merchanting and
hence a surprisingly rich place. It has really sound hotel facilities and
looks like what it is, the capital of the Cézallier and the Rhue
country. Here the streams come down from Puy-de-Dôme through
waterfalls, green gorges and a reservoir in a very charming way. The
place is sometimes suffixed 'en-Féniers' in confused memory of the
great cistercian abbey of which, after a tempestuous history, something is still to be seen a few miles away towards the ancient-looking
resort and cheese-market of Marcenat.

For these corners of ancient sanctity crop up in the Auvergne as unexpectedly as in Switzerland, and remain holy ground. Only a few miles south of Riom itself, for instance, one finds the deserted village of Apchon. This gets into the tourist books mainly on the strength of a castle which was once the seat of the premier barony in the Haute Auvergne, and still affords as good a viewpoint as any over the Cézallier. But it also boasts a little-recorded local rite in the form of a quite modern annual procession of herdsmen out to the nine-teenth-century chapel of the Saute Sainte above Cheylade—itself a small mountain station whose much-restored church is famed for several treasures but particularly its curious Noah's-Ark decorations.

*

On a latitude with Cheylade, but ten miles to the east, the railway from Bort comes down over the Dordogne-Allier watershed past an-other St Bonnet and St Saturnin—down from the mushroom-round hills where clumps of mushroom-round trees stand as on some vaster Chilterns into the slate-roofed resort of Allanche which is still more than 3,000 feet up. After you have looked at its church, though, there is only a slip down through greener woods and closer villages and lower contours into Neussargues itself.

Reaching the junction by the other route from the west—the line which runs beside the 126 up the upper valley of the Cère—is a very different experience. It is to my mind a duller one scenically than the open spaces of the Cézallier afford. But even the hamlets have presentable churches, and the castles are splendid.

The first town out of Aurillac is Vic-sur-Cère, set over 2,000 feet up in a wide gentle valley of the greener part of Cantal. Vic is very far from unknown, for it has all that is needed to make a tourist town, even without its therapeutic claims about chlorosis and anaemia. There is history, associated firstly with Pierre—the 'mad monk' who preferred drinking-songs to the chant of the Mass, and made his tour of the courts of love, and swung his sword in the crusades and generally lived to the full in the springtime of the twelfth century when the Carladez (or lower Cantal) was an orchard and Vic's church new-built. Other great names are those of the princes of Monaco, whose palace survives and who reigned here in the early renaissance years when this Vic, like its namesake in Puy-de-Dôme, ruled a county; of Merle, who showed his usual sense of

Illustration 25

humour nearby; and of Marie-Angélique de Fontanges who was lovely as an angel and stupid as a basket and who bore Louis XIII so many bastards that she died—in action, as they said—at the age of twenty.

Vic also has some natural curiosities within hailing distance—a small, rocky waterfall, a chapel-crowned hill, and a pass with a view. But it is a green and tucked-away sort of place; and since it never made quite the grade as a spa it might be a good one to linger in.

Just below Vic there are three fine and fortified manors, the most notable being Polminhac under its basalt cliffs. And just above it is Thiezac—itself only one more picturesquely-sited village-turned-resort, but with a good statue in its gothic church and in the vicinity that gracious little painted chapel which had a reputation (which Anne of Austria accepted, with the result which Louise Quatorze proved) for curing sterility.

Then, beyond St Jacques-des-Blats (a *station de repos*, they say— but not with those motor-horns) come the stark rocks and the watershed between the Cère and the Allagnon. This frontier is called the Lioran, and it is one of the more notable end-on passes of Europe. Here, on a small scale, is the structure of Andermatt and the feel of the Arlberg. Road and rail must burrow, in parallel but one above the other, under this shoulder between the Puy Mary and the Plomb du Cantal. The road tunnel, a mile long and not far short of 4,000 feet up below the roman pass, was once the greatest in all France.

One's first feeling on emerging from it is of a dramatic change. The horseshoe of the eastern portal opens on to a world from which the last Dordognat thatch has vanished, and at the little skier's resort of le Loiran itself the scenery is as Christmas-card conifer as anything in Switzerland. It is only a momentary change; for as one slips down beside the glacial-grey Allagnon to pass through another *station de repos* (Laveissière) and south of a third (Dienne, where there is a good church) normality returns. But there remains the sense, characteristic of the Allagnon valley, of being in an enclave rather than an entry.

*

The largest town in this area (and, with 2,500 souls, one of the largest of all Cantal) is the next stop down the line. Murat is an open, tumbled, terraced and Alpine place of sunlight and mist over 3,000 feet up—one of the grey roofs of the mountains and the red roofs of the valley, of markets and of tourists. It was the home town of the Count of Anterroches, who in the hundred years' war coined (they say) a number of quixotic aphorisms including the one about not firing first; and its hacked-about church of Our Lady of the Olives houses a black Virgin attributed to St Louis' days.

I do not much like Murat, despite its few old houses, its long list of gastronomic specialities which are copies of other people's, and its heroic record in the resistance. But maybe I have been prejudiced by the weather, at whose mercy one stands more in Cantal than in any other highlands.

What no mists can wipe out is the fascination of the nearby village of Bredons on its basalt knoll. There is a fortified romanesque church here of striking charm, but the hamlet's great curiosity lies in the old subterranean houses now used as cow-byres. Even without these, Bredons would be worth the climb, for its mud-roads caked with dung, its somnolence shocked only by the quarryman's shot, its sheer peasant dilapitude, are astonishing to find in such an accessible place.

Murat is not very proud of Bredons. Murat prefers to advertise its tatty casino.

*

A cigarette further on the autorail runs into Neussargues again, and one has defined a quarter—the most populous western triangle—of Cantal. But this *is* a four-way junction, and the ways which lead east (which were P L M-Mediterranée ways) rather nearly saltire the rest of this depopulated department.

The northern track slavishly follows the Allagnon valley, to the north-west of which there is little of habitation. Even the first fifteen miles of the railway and the narrow highroad are not eventful: there is Ferrières-St-Mary ('Mary' in Auvergnat does not always mean Mary, but here it does), prettily sited but of no real note, and then Molompize, and then a greener valley, and then Massiac with its few old stones—a minor tourist centre for no more reason than that it stands where the 9 highway comes in, an Auvergnat gastronomic centre for no reason at all.

But here the river, road and railway *do* turn north, up towards their nearby junctions with the Allier valley and the Clermont axis. Massiac, indeed, is at the beginning of a change of countryside. But it is only at the beginning, and for another fifteen miles or so one is in a strange *zone franche*, the end of Cantal and the return to Puy-de-Dôme at the place where the Haute-Loire too bulges in.

The capital of this enclosed and castle-guarded region, just off the 9 and the railway too, is one of the most remarkable towns of the whole Auvergne.

*

'Il faut voir Blesle' they say, with a passion which makes one feel that they would add 'et mourir' had not Naples thought of it first. Initially, one wonders why. This is a satisfying enough town, with a curiously-shaped church of small and irregular windows which has good carving in stone without and in wood within, some striking military and religious towers, and a gentle richness of secular architecture—norman, gothic and renaissance too. But why does it bring that particular sparkle to the eyes, as to those of a commercial traveller speaking of Nottingham? Not, surely, for its antimony.

In the first place, Blesle was for nearly a thousand years ruled by an order of benedictine noblewomen who lived in superb grace and state if not always in a state of grace; and any town where the women have worn the trousers—even when concealed by a habit—conserves a characteristic sheen. In the second, Blesle is most elegant in its situation. The gorges about are not savage defiles but orchard-floored like the Wye country, and the uplands billow with grain.

Out of these favours, Blesle has culled an extraordinary flavour: one would never guess that it was so dismantled that at the Terror it boasted a church without a tower and a tower without a church. That flavour is not at all Auvergnat: it is more Swiss than the Swiss. Get off the train at Blesle's basalt-crowned station at le Babory, and there is a small bus waiting, driven by an extremely pretty girl who is light-hearted about fares. In the medieval streets children are playing ping-pong. In the cafés everybody is very young and helpful, the girls flaxen and the boys learning the hotel-trade. One rubs the mists of the Cézallier from one's eyes: this is Canton Uri.

In one's bitchier moods, of course, it is all too nice, too terribly gay, to be true. This holiday-village, this colony, is—one tells oneself

—an imitation of imitations. This town has no substance but only a Cause—a cheery and rather beastly Cause like Buchmanism or Mental Health or Students of the World Unite for Peace. And yet ... the birds fly higher here, the peasants in bluer smocks hobble home at evening more picturesquely, the cowbells chime sweeter and the light is more golden than a mere mile away. Some feather from an angel—or an exalted abbess—has fallen on the High Auvergne near to the triple point of three savage departments.

*

Up the road—up under the eagle's-nest of fourteenth-century castle Léotoing—one finds a tangle of hairpin bends and railway viaducts. The topography north of Blesle indeed resembles that south of Arlanc some twenty miles due east. Whichever way one comes upon it, this is the shelf at the rim of Puy-de-Dôme.

And so the road flows back to meet the country of Chapter 6 at Lempdes. On the departmental edge, and in a land where villages and features have kept their gallo-roman (an extraordinary equivalent of 'anglo-saxon') names, the railway's end is at Arvant. This is just a hamlet; but like Lempdes on the road it is a cardinal junction, for it is on the Clermont-Nimes line. Indeed, the journey up from Neussargues is here seen as part of the sister route to Beziers.

So a railfarer must return, back to Neussargues and out again to the south-east. The 9 takes a more direct but lonelier route, missing even St Mary-le-Plain and Vieillespesse, over the tunnelled 3,700-foot Fageole pass. But both meet again at St Flour.

*

After so much of unknown spaces, so many dusty townships, it is something to come to a place whose name is known to more people than have actually visited it. This fame is—as so often in the High Auvergne, of which St Flour was once the capital and bishopric—due to a combination of site and history. And the site and history are fundamentally linked.

High on a basalt bluff, 350 feet above a comparatively fertile, sun-tanned and wind-ringing plain (it is called the Planèze—which word, like Limagne, is only specific with a capital), and not far short of 3,000 feet above the sea, this land-locked Mont St Michel is still the

Illustration 26

sous-préfecture of Cantal, though its population is under 6,000 (or 3,000 less than in medieval times). It was an obvious stronghold, and an invincible one. 'A masthead of the world, a lone look-out', this was the frontier of France when the British held Guienne: it resisted twenty sieges against *routiers* and *rodrigars,* bandits and barons, Armagnats and huguenots: it made mock even of Merle. '*Nul ne te prit jamais de force que le vent,*' they said, before the revolution humbled a place then hiding as Fort Cantal.

The shrine and stronghold are both there as one approaches St Flour from the east and finds it buttressed above the new town on its cliff of black rock; but the shrine dominates, and the heavy twin towers of the cathedral *are* St Flour from a distance. Proximity lends disenchantment: the front is an ugly restoration and in general the church mirrors Clermont's in its alien and mechanical fifteenth-century bareness as well as in its black stone. For all the treasures of its spacious interior and the life which its July fête brings, it is a stark building, restricted less by its site than by lovelessness. St Flour has been unlucky with its ecclesiastical buildings: the parish church is now disaffected as a market-hall.

The irregular, arcaded square outside the cathedral is for me the best thing in the city. Only one *hôtel*—housing the museum—has any architectural merit, and the best things about *that* are the statues in the courtyard and the view from the ramparts behind it. But the rest of the grim, high, black buildings do not destroy the sense that nothing much has changed here since the sixteenth century. The *ensemble* is curiously impressive, even without the great bronze Christ whose lacerated side once wailed in the winds.

For the rest, some vestiges of an ancient commercial importance, religious veneration and military power remain in and below the streets of St Flour. But far more important seem its prowhead site and its sense of continuity with a tempestuous past—with the days when a new bishopric was carved out of the 150-mile-wide see of Clermont and fell to St Flour rather than Aurillac: the slightly later days when, as the key to the whole kingdom of France, it was granted the lily-flower blazon which it still bears: and even the far earlier days when the roman ways leading from the Arvenes in the north to the Ruthenes of the west and the Gabales of Languedoc divided here and a bishop called Flores (who was *not* martyred

Illustration 27

and, so far as one knows, worked no miracles) was unaware he was to christen a most notable Auvergnat city.

*

The satellites of St Flour are rich in castles, churches and pilgrimage centres, to which the guide-books will direct you. But all are mere villages, of which one or two have tourist hotels which make the best of a bad job by advertising a *cure de repos*. A few miles down the 9, where the railway soars above it and the Truyère, there is a great thing in the Garabit viaduct whose lovely *arc-en-ciel*, built by Eiffel in 1892 when iron bridges were still suspect, is 1,800 feet long and 400 above the river (soon to be a lake). But the nearest thing to a town which the whole region affords bears the rather sad name of Ruines. . . .

*

A line ruled west from Ruines would take one, after about thirty miles, back to Aurillac. It would also, *en route*, sweep a little south of the Plomb du Cantal through a land where the mountains shelve down into the tumbled, fertile, untravelled and beautiful hills of the Carladez or Carlados, which Aragon once owned.

These, south of Vic, take their name from Carlat, where a basalt rock supports what Henry IV spared of the cardinal western fortress of the High Auvergne—one associated with half the great names of French military history from Louis the Debonair on. They form the southernmost range of the volcanic Cantals, the most populous, perhaps the most gracious, and certainly not the least historic. Brezons and Raulhac by the splendid renaissance château of Messillac are sophisticated villages with a sense of the past about their battered walls and lava tiles, and there are two real towns in Pierrefort and Mur-de-Barrez. Pierrefort has the usual church and castle, but Mur formerly disputed with Vic the viscounty of Carlat (on which the Barrez depended) and today still has something to show for it. Those who love the not-quite-famous might appreciate a pilgrimage to the nearby birthplace of Cardinal Verdier, who tried to convert Paris to Christianity around 1895. But in its own right Mur is well worth the journey.

And it is also most picturesquely set, It would, in fact, be one of the best small towns in Cantal were it not that a kick-back of the frontier throws it technically into Aveyron. . . .

For you are here approaching one of the most confusing zones of France, as well as one of the most fascinating. One way on from Mur would be to move a few miles south across the valley and climb again, beyond Orlhaguet's strange fortified church and Ste Geneviève, into the wilderness of the Viadène plateau. But between lies the Truyère—a great river, a beautiful river, a curious and sinuous river which once flowed to the Allier rather than the Lot, and for all the hydro-electric works like Sarrans (one of the oldest and most complex in France) and its increasing number of successors including a subterranean station, still a most lonely river. Hardly a road skirts its granite shores for a hundred miles or so, and the border does so for only a brief while. But the Truyère still forms one of the defining creases of the Auvergne, and a return up it to the Garabit closes a landscape which I would like to know far better.

On the river itself there is little but a solitude, spanned by the spidery suspension bridge of Tréboul which replaces a fourteenth-century bridge built by the English and still (they say) visible at low water: otherwise there are only narrow gorges below the dams and lochs twenty miles long above them. But south of St Flour there is a man-made curiosity at the superb, fir-surrounded château of Alleuze close to the most intriguing church of Villedieu—the most romantic ruins in the whole Auvergne, they say, built on a site so impregnable that France had to destroy the castle to cast out England—and a natural one in the *cirque* (which word usually means an abandoned ox-bow, a dry but still green river meander, but may also mean a glacial cut) of Mallet.

Then, where the 121 comes down from St Flour past the ancient church of les Ternes, there is the village of Neuvéglise on its promontory. And further south, close to the departmental edge, stands the remarkable town of Chaudes-Aigues.

*

One curiosity of Chaudes-Aigues is the series of saints' images which sit in their lanterns at almost every street corner in this small town of a thousand or two inhabitants. If they all represented Our Lady or other popular saints they would hardly be noticed, for though of

Illustration 22

some antiquity they have no remarkable beauty. But *these* are the emblems of the little *faubourgs* of the town, each comprising only a few streets: *these* are still borne in procession though their names and acts are obscure and their churches have vanished save for the rather undistinguished parish one on the hillside: *these* are a unique survival of the ultra-local loyalties of the middle ages. They still seem quite in place in roads where the town-crier goes round announcing the latest arrival of greengroceries with a drum-roll.

For these statues alone Chaudes-Aigues would be a halting-place. It is also a bright and pleasant township, with a gracious gardened stream-frontage and the right chaos of lichened roofs: to find so charming a spot a day's march—or an hour by car—south from St Flour seems almost too much. It is certainly too much when one remembers the great attraction of the town.

Chaudes-Aigues has hot water.

This would be remarkable enough in itself, in France. But it is natural volcanic hot water which gushes at 82 degrees centigrade from the spring of Par at the top of the spacious town square, steams out of faucets at those imaged corners whilst still hot enough to scald, and is so plentiful (for there are dozens of places, like Dax, which have a *bit* of natural heat) that it is piped to two thirds of the town's houses through oaken or leaden or stone conduits of venerable artifice. It is strange that after all this a bath is no easier to get in Chaudes-Aigues than elsewhere in France.

I do not know how these statistics measure up against Reykjavik or Rotorua: it is striking enough that a township so near to the busy world should have so strange a natural curiosity. If only they had left the waters to their task of warming—one thinks—if only they hadn't wanted them *healing too....*

But already Chaudes-Aigues boasts a thermal establishment where one stews in little boxes and a faint smell of burned fireworks; and now it wants to be a real spa, a tinpot Mont Dore. Already the familiar words are abroad—'*les eaux excitantes, radioactives, stimulantes, limpides, presque insipides ... pour une paralysie rheumatismale, les engorgements, les laxations, fractures et blessures de guerre* and Lord knows what other wicked witchcraft. The chamber of commerce has induced Clermont's Institute of Hydrology to put its hands on its heart and swear that millions are dying in agony for

167

Illustration 15

want of the water of Chaudes-Aigues—which, in the great carve-up, only got the joints and the peripheral nervous system anyway. The cardinal point—and it would be comic were it not for the evil imposition on those suffering from the natural ageing of the flesh—is that not even a French doctor has seriously claimed that the waters have any other virtue than mere warmth.

The attempt to sophisticate Chaudes-Aigues—to slick it up and rebuild it—must fail. It will fail for lack of transport, for they never cut even a narrow-gauge line to Chaudes-Aigues and today it depends on an every-other-day-if-you-are-lucky bus service from St Flour. It will fail for lack of money: one has little faith in the scheme to finance the building of a casino by digging oil wells in Chaudes-Aigues, though it sheds a very quaint light on the Swiftian projector-ship of French mayors. And it will fail because the world is growing weary of this imposition on the credulity of the sick and the aged.

*

Beyond Chaudes-Aigues, close to the templars' church at Jabrun, ended the ancient bishopric. Today Cantal ends there, for departmental boundaries are never quite as artificial as they look. And here too, as the 122 road moves southwards, ends a chapter.

For south of Chaudes-Aigues the broom-covered hills climb through deepening greens of birch and ash and pine. Somewhere thereabouts you may find an open space, and from it look, before returning north, through those gaps and valleys ranged like the back of a hand, over the pent duckponds and the headwater streams, and beyond to a blue and white haze south-westward which might be cloud and might be the Pyrenees.

The Roof of France

So often in the structure of France does there emerge a land-scape in the shape of an aureole that one feels her face is that of an heraldic field, lozengy of or and azure, or like that re-flected off an engine-turned surface with the rings of the departments intersecting to form mandolae. These figures may sometimes, as in the Livradois, correspond to a simple range. But they may also cut across many contours and frontiers and still be integral.

Such is the area of this chapter. It has no particular name, and though it is a component of the great central watershed of France it is *only* a component. Its peaks are no higher than, if as high as, the surrounding crests, though the general table is so consistently high as to justify the above much-used and much-abused title. And yet this land is an epitome of the whole Massif, not least in that it touches as many parts of the Auvergne as the Auvergne touches parts of France, and yet is as little travelled as any.

This is so despite the fact that the northern half of the lozenge lies between the two branches of the great longitude of the Massif—the 9–Beziers line–Allagnon valley to the west and the 102–Nimes line–Allier valley to the east. The little turntable where all meet has already been mentioned in more than one chapter of this book, for it is the region of Ardes and Arvant, Auzon and Lempdes. But its leading town has not been mentioned; for it stands at the northern point of this heartland and of the department of Haute-Loire.

*

Brioude, however, need not rely on any topographer's trick: it is in its own right one of the cardinal towns of central France. Not quite at the road or rail junction, not quite at the confluence of the

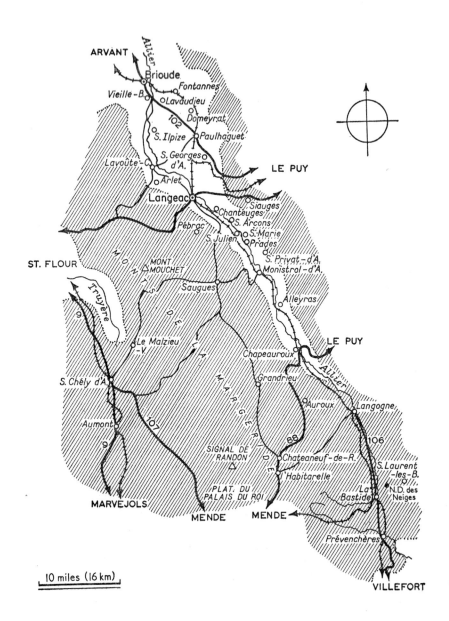

ARVANT

Brioude

Fontannes

Vieille-B.

Lavaudieu

Domeyrat

S. Ilpize

Paulhaguet

S. Georges
d'A.

Lavoûte-C.

Arlet

LE PUY

Langeac

Siauges

Chanteuges

S. Arcons

Pébrac

S. Marie

S. Julien

Prades

S. Privat-d'A.

ST. FLOUR

Monistrol-d'A.

MONT
MOUCHET

Sauges

Alleyras

Truyère

9

Le Malzieu
-V.

Chapeauroux

LE PUY

MARGERIDE

S. Chély d'A.

Grandrieu

Allier

Aumont

107

Auroux

Langogne

9

88

106

SIGNAL DE
RANDON

Chateauneuf-de-R.

S. Laurent
-les-B.

l'Habitarelle

9

La
Bastide

N.D. des
Neiges

PLAT. DU
PALAIS DU ROI

MARVEJOLS

MENDE

MENDE

Prévenchères

10 miles (16 km)

VILLEFORT

Allagnon and Allier, not very high or very large, Brioude still has an air which reminds you that this amiable market-town and *sous-préfecture* of about 6,000 inhabitants has for 700 years been quietly sharing with Aurillac and St Flour the capitalate of the High Auvergne—quite apart from the times when it stood as an independent Berwick between the two Auvergnes.

It lost the bishopric, of course; but it still has the best church of these three cities. Founded about a proto-Christian tomb, it is essentially a romanesque building which has suffered from a certain amount of ill-informed monkeying. Architecturally and spatially it does not come knee-high to the great four of the Clermont ring and is usually awarded a *senior optime*, bracketed with Châtel-Montagne, by the ecclesiologists' examining board. But it is the heart of a most lively cult.

St Julien's church—which drew in Brioude's little wealth and whose canon-counts wore the violet soutane of aristocracy—is hemmed in by the town. Even to a layman it appears at once a part of, and a deviation from, the basic Auvergnat school. The intersecting chevet is there; but the porches are far less classic in form. One's exterior impression is of polychrome stone, random of pink and brown and cream and white. Inside are porches, rebuilt in the sixteenth century, which provide the chief interest; for one can clamber up through their chapels into a world of capital-levels (the capitals are *very* good) and of bird's-eye vistas commoner in Gloucestershire or Suffolk than in Haute-Loire.

The detail of St Julien comprises frescoes of various dates and states, ancient door-knockers, and some very lively recent *zinguerie* in the same spirit. The detail of Brioude itself comprises Volvic fountains which remind you that you are still where men look to Clermont, old houses, and a Hôtel de Ville whose terrace looks out —as so often in this area—across a valley momentarily so wide that men speak of the 'Limagne de l'Allier', the village of Fontannes a pleasant evening's stroll away, and the dim hills beyond where they mine antimony. This is not one of the great cities of Europe, but it is one of the good towns of France. The inn is satisfactory, even when it does not serve what are claimed to be the kings of all the salmon of the Auvergne.

*

171

A little south—beyond a bridge-town of the Allier intriguingly called Vieille-Brioude and on the way to the pretty castle of Domey-rat—there is another small ecclesiological treasure at Lavaudieu. This has preserved an octagonal tower, some frescoes and the cloister from its benedictine abbey; and even though it has only preserved them with diligent help from the nineteenth century there is always a peculiar charm to a cloister not too scraped, varied in sculpture and with timber upperworks—especially in a rural setting. Cambridge, Rouen, Arles . . . in cities like these I have lain on July afternoons and stared beyond cream stone and brown oak at a deep sky hazed by cloud and wine. Lavaudieu belongs in this enchanted company.

Westward the land shelves lazily beyond the valley to my boundary. Eastward there is some shaggy, woody country. And southish, in the Allier valley, there are several pleasant little places. Arlet and St Ilpize are good, but Lavoûte-Chilhac with its gothic church, old bridge and hotels is better. Near are the centres of Paulhaguet in its strangely-named combe (which was and may still be the site of one of those penitential processions typical of Haute-Loire and which certainly retains some artificial caves nearby) and Langeac beyond the rail junction of St Georges-d'Aurac.

The 102 road has now left eastward for the heights of Velay; and though there is another cross-country highroad a little further south only the Nimes railway closes in on the Allier here, in an embrace which will last for nearly 100 miles. A last half-lowland halt before the real hills, Langeac is a sleepy old place of Cotswold-like stone, quite large and with plenty of good streets. There is a welcoming sort of church with good furniture, and an ursuline chapel where the unofficial local saint, Mother Agnes, is buried. (To those who pray to her she offers only the way of the cross for salvation: few pray.) There is not much to remind one that coal was worked hereabouts, though. If only it could forget its associations with Lafayette, Langeac would be one of my favourite *relais*.

The next few miles of the Allier are rich ones, and it is merciful that the railway—over what Baring-Gould regarded as the most daringly engineered trace in France—provides a good enough service to allow exploration. First comes Chanteuges, the red-capped romanesque abbey (but with a fine gothic window too) on the basalt bluff, where once the monks carried the ideal of Theleme a bit too far and

172

Illustration 29

became open brigands: until recently it was the site of a very rowdy Whitsun bun-fight. Then follow St Arcons (with Pébrac to the west and worth a visit), the villages of St Julien and Prades, and the chapel of Ste Marie, all on their own peaks; and then some pure scenery as the line cuts through tunnels and galleries up what may not be the most spectacular valley in France but which is as noble as any, up through the lava and the gneiss, up to Monistrol-d'Allier.

There is not much to record of Monistrol or of those towns with the similar names, Siaugues to the north and Saugues to the west—not much, that is, except on Maundy Thursday when the latter's old church and tower, empty tomb and streets are the setting for a penitential procession of scarlet and white which *sounds* magnificent. For those who like celtic legends, Baring-Gould collected a fascinating one in its neighbourhood; but for the rest there are just holiday villages. Still, Monistrol and its basin (which takes in two other villages of infinitesimal note in St Privat-d'Allier where the bones of a Roman doctor were unearthed and Alleyras under its crag) have a topographical significance as the first landing on the climbing river. It mounts 2,050 feet, as against Langeac's 1,675.

As far beyond again, the bridge and the curve of the railway at Chapeauroux mark the second landing and the end of the gorges. This bridge is that of an important road, the 88 coming down from St Etienne. And that narrow road winds and snakes up, west of the Allier, through the resort of Auroux into the ringing country which truly deserves the title of this chapter—the forest, or mountains, of the Margeride.

*

The northern point of the famous Margeride (for the name *as* a name is almost as common as 'Limagne') is on a latitude with Langeac. A little further south, the 4,850-foot crest of Mont Mouchet sustains a monument to all the fallen maquisards of France, raised on a site where 15,000 partisans fought and 1,000 were killed in their greatest battle of all. (For despite the essential conservatism and catholicism of its men this was ever a battleground of *francs-tireurs*, and the accounts of the St Florines' forays and sackings and ambuscades and counter-attacks, *c* 1944, read much like the disagreements of six centuries before.) And back from that prowhead, the meeting-

Illustration 28

place of Cantal, Haute-Loire and Lozère, the Margeride runs south and a little east in a single granite ridge some thirty miles long, ten wide, and steadily between 4,000 and 5,500 feet up—the loneliest part of France, for its population density of six per square mile is a bare fifth of the national average.

To the west the Margeride shades down to the *planèze* of St Flour, the 9 road and its branch the 107, and the Beziers line: southward it leads to rolling hills and flat valley-floors. There are places of some substance here on the Lozère flank—le Malzieu-Ville, a resort and former Merle stronghold where the Truyère shrinks from a river to a stream, and on the great axis itself belfried St Chély-d'Apcher (more than 3,000 feet up and claiming, with its two months' summer, the odd honour of being the coldest place in France) and Aumont. Not even the local guides find much in particular to say about these northern fortresses of the Gévaudan, though in general they are attractive towns with main-road hotels and tight-packed houses built in that same Somerset-looking stone as characterizes the Allier valley. But *that* lies thirty miles to the east, and between rises the highest, southernmost and most fascinating part of the Margeride—the plateau of the Palais du Roi below the peak, nearly 5,000 feet up, of the Signal de Randon.

This is the veriest high-headwater country, a moor and peat-marsh broken only by granite outcrops not yet eroded, by icy rivulets and desperate drystone walls where the woods of pine, scattered oak and beech of the northern Margeride have thinned to thickets. The names of the townlets like Grandrieu sound like the echoes of hurricanes, and the whole upland area of brown oxen and blazing narcissi is soaked in a sense of the battles of man against man, man against nature, as in a mountain mist.

This history is particularly present in the one main-road centre which the area supports—Châteauneuf-de-Randon, otherwise just a big grey village of about 600 inhabitants, set up on a 400-foot bluff, which comes to life only at its great cattle-fairs. For it was under the walls of Châteauneuf that du Guesclin died.

*

Un peu d'histoire. In the spring of 1380, when this land was the chequer-board on which the States, the British and the brigands took and retook towns like chessmen, the great constable was charged by his great king, Charles V, to drive westward and recapture the countryside at least as far as Aurillac. In August he left le Puy and invested Châteauneuf, a stronghold of the British: he drank from one of the Margeride's thousand trickling streams: he caught a cold, pneumonia, or something referred to as a *congestion pulmoni-aire*: and on the quatorze juillet (or, maybe, the thirteenth) he accepted the British surrender and then expired.

There is a mystery here, for in high summer even the springs of the Margeride are not (as the accounts claim) exactly *glacée*. But still the waters of the Auvergne, which cured nobody, did kill a gallant, courteous and much-loved man who—whatever his capabilities as a general—was the greatest Frank after Charlemagne and the greatest Celt after Arthur. And if there is an inappropriateness in du Guesclin's end, there is something worse, a grisly *opéra bouffe*, in the story of the disposal of the remains of one of whom all that is surely recorded is to the good.

The middle ages had a love—part patriotic, part pious but mostly commercial—for *membra disjecta*: it must have clashed with a stronger faith than ours in the physical resurrection of the body. Furthermore, the constable had himself expressed a dying wish to lie in Brittany. From Châteauneuf to Dinan is 500 miles; so first they took the body—with the keys of Châteauneuf laid upon it—to le Puy for embalming, and left the entrails there. Le Puy messed up the job and made a Lenin of the cadaver: it was summer and they were running out of ice: and at Clermont it was clear that cremation would be the only solution.

So the ashes remained at Montferrand and only the heart and skeleton went on—bumping over dusty roads, gliding down rivers, week upon week across half France. And then, at le Mans, the cortege heard that Paris had demanded the bones to lie between the kings and those cold women who were the mothers and makers of kings in the great nave of St Denis. Only the heart reached the Breton orchard.

Rather than this grisly history I prefer to remember the crossroads of the Habitarelle below Châteauneuf. There is a monument there, of which the canopy is shiny and new but the effigy looks far older. How *much* older it is I do not know; for the weather has eaten and lichened it until it is as unrecognizable as those terrible blind images of Crowland in Northamptonshire. But at the foot of the bluff, where the once-a-day bus stops for a moment, it stares out from the place where du Guesclin died, down the emerald slopes of the Margeride, towards Langogne which is back in the Allier valley but some forty miles south of Langeac.

*

Well above the 3,000-foot contour and just under the keel of Haute-Loire, Langogne is the penultimate landing: here the Allier (a mere day's march from the Loire, as Stevenson marvelled) is only a stream wandering attractively if sometimes malodorously through gardens and allotments and little stone quays and bridges at the back of the town. This was itself once a great crossroads and cattle-market, and is still a surprisingly large, busy and metropolitan place for these parts; and in addition to having a turntable situation, it is not without character. Once more, though, there is no great attraction, and the sacked eleventh-century church is a wild muddle of Victoriana. Langogne claims to be a ski-resort (which means that it should be pleasantest in summer); but at any time of year its hotels are rather sleepy, hidden and indifferent.

To find a smaller place which *has* put itself on the map one must climb through lonely country on the comparatively minor 106 road to the last landing and la Bastide. This is 3,400 feet up on the edge of the new department of Ardèche and—as near as makes no difference—at the crest of the Nimes railway. As the express pants up those last long gradients, double-headed by two 8-coupled engines whose fires flare through tunnel after tunnel or drench the green sunsets of pine country, the sense strengthens that one is approaching the highest main-line railway station in all France.

The station itself (and it is a junction, whence a spur leaves for the Lot country to the west) is wood-shingled and wide-platformed; it has a far more alpine look than any I know in the French Alps themselves. The temperature will be ten degrees lower than in the surrounding area. The town is all white walls and steep gables, bridge-parties and sawmills by the Allier headwaters, the smell of pines and of bacon-and-eggs. But it has two really good hotels which realize that one puts oneself on the map through service and not through boards at the roadside. La Bastide is to my mind a far, far

176

The faith of the central mountains still finds expression in the penitence of Saugues (*above*) as it once found it in the peace of Lavaudieu (*below*).

30

God's House—the distant view (*above*) and a detail from the frescoes
within (*below*).

31

better place than its increasing number of rivals for anyone who wants to go Swiss in the heart of France. And it has two other claims to fame, of which the first is Robert Louis Stevenson. . . .

It was a long ass-back trek, and most of it belongs to other chapters of this book. But neither in Velay nor away to the south is RLS remembered as here at the watershed of his route. It is typical of the still-untravelled solitude of this region that, for all the sophistication of la Bastide itself, an *écrivain anglais* is regarded precisely as he was when the first pages of that book were written. He is a kind of comet—a portent from outer space, sweeping through the skies at unexpected intervals with or without a beast in train. And all this is so despite the fact that two recent attempts to emulate the *Travels With a Donkey* have proved little short of disastrous.

There was, for instance, the case of the bitter little brunette from Birmingham. Her name was that of the makers of a domestic device as well-known in France as in Britain, which led to her being called the *machine à coudre* when not plain 'Miss'. She turned up at the tourist office in le Puy asking for a donkey—not, she explained, to ride, nor even as the original pack-beast, but for company. Enterprisingly, they gave her one, under the misapprehension that she was some kind of representative of the sewing-machine company. And from there on the file becomes a fascinating essay in Franco-British misunderstanding.

Miss was given the full PR treatment. Miss was the excuse for a fête in every variety-starved village through which she passed. Miss was offered sticky vermouth and caporals, both of which she detested. Miss was subjected to mayoral harangues and soccer-matches, neither of which she understood. Miss, in fact, protested that she had escaped from Brum because she hated football: she wanted to commune with Nature and talk about existentialism to the artistically- and politically-conscious French. The Auvergnats, muttering '*Sale type de St Germain-des-Prés*,' slunk away to fill in their pools.

At last The Sewing-machine found a kindred spirit—and stuck, eating him out of house and home. She disappears from the local newspapers; but in those documents which always seem to get clipped to the file I met the deepening *cris-de-coeur* of *effroyable . . . insupportable . . . vraiment impossible*, until the whole land seemed to be crying 'Get Miss S out of town.'

Later came two delicate flowers of Portland Place, combining business with pleasure on a BBC stringer. But rain and the ways of donkeys got them down, and RLS's route has not yet been duplicated. Give me a docile Modestine, my x's, a favourable met report and the second serial rights in the republic of the Philippines, and I will have a shot.

*

La Bastide is a peak and prow and pivot of the whole Auvergne: its very name, of course, means bastion, *bastille*, fortress. High for a centre of habitation (though far below the crests which rise above even these topmost valleys), and within a day's march of Channel, Biscay and Mediterranean rivers, it is at once a centre and an end, perched potently on the relief map. This, the literary association, and the *different* quality of the town itself would all give one good enough reason to end a chapter here, before the Allier dies to the west and southward Lozère slopes steeply down to the romanesque-cum-gothic village church of Prévenchères.

But la Bastide has a last diamond in its crown. A few easy miles away (so few and so easy that the place is not a real *hospice*), only a hundred feet or so higher, is that small but famed monastery whose name has the high and windy ring of la Bastide itself—Notre-Dame-des-Neiges. Here Stevenson—though not his capitalizers—slept and worshipped. The latter claimed to have been deflected by the reasonable assumption that a trappist house is not likely to entertain visitors in general and women in particular. But they were wrong. Our Lady of the Snows is a far more hospitable house than—say—that beastly Grande Chartreuse where the coach-trippers have to peer over the monastery wall like peeping Toms at a nudist camp. It is true that only some particular magic enables my adored St Peter Damian of Assisi to fling open its doors to hordes of rubbernecks yet strike a bell of silence in every heart. But of the lesser places Notre-Dame-des-Neiges, like St Cross outside Winchester, is elusive enough to be able to maintain a medieval approach to its guests.

It offers no architectural attractions of the kind which get into the guide-books, for it is essentially only a collection of farm-buildings for work, an enclosed dormitory block for study, and a plain, timeless church for worship. Even the site is not the mountain peak one would expect: the monastery nestles, sheltered by the quite gentle contours east of the Allier, on the way to a minute spa called St Laurent-les-Bains. But it is a gracious, dreamy place to meet at the end of a lane in summer, whatever the austerities of winter's midnight offices. And it offers two things which I care for and which you will not find bettered in the whole Auvergne—its wine and its Mass.

Wine *is* a surprise. The French suffer from a misapprehension in believing that you cannot grow good grapes above the 1,400-foot contour—though everywhere in the plateau you can see men growing bad ones in impossibly sunless gorges. But certainly not even Austria grows them at more than three times that height, and what one would expect to flow from these breasts would be some sticky liqueur tasting of pine-needles or else a quinine-doped tonic. However, the brethren who traditionally advise the government on local agriculture—and who helped Pasteur to save the worms in the days when silk was important locally—import their grapes from the valleys to the south (where men produce a foul enough brew from such vines as they troubled to replant after the phylloxera) and ferment them in the mountain air. The fact that one can produce anything palatable this way is a bewilderment to the comic *tastevin*-ers of France and their English sycophants, with their interminable discussions about the merits of this or that muddy Bordeaux brew. The fact that one can produce anything as delicious as the white *Fleurs des Neiges* is as good an argument as any for divine providence. Nobody catalogues these *crus*, which are as clear and cool and sweet and innocent as a mountain stream, and in any case upland wines are much of a muchness. I should not like to have to distinguish *this* from the hundred *-burgers* and *-bergers* of the Tirol, for instance; I only know that you will find nothing else as lovely, clean, cheap and unknown until you reach Grenoble, which is almost Italy anyway. With the reds of the Clermont ring, *Fleurs des Neiges* is the worthwhile vinous experience of the Auvergne: you will not find it far afield, and if you are crazy enough to want to spend a ski-ing holiday in the Auvergne it would provide one more reason to make la Bastide your centre.

*

But I have heard my Mass here too, shut behind a grille in that simple whitewashed church. Watching the novices in their brown habits, the regulars in their white and the three celebrants in liturgical colours weave and cross like performers in some May ribbon-dance or leave and proceed and return through the blue incense-haze; listening to the long chant which runs unbroken even through the consecration and is interrupted by no tintinnabulum but only the quiet insistent striking of a table-clock; there I have sensed the true conventual gift of a perpetual intercession which is directed to God and not to men. Notre-Dame-des-Neiges is not very high as the land lies, not very remote as the Auvergne stands, and not unapproachable at all. But it has some secret shared only, perhaps, with the monasteries of Asia Minor; and that secret is older even than the Faith.

It is the last of la Bastide and its area.

II

Velay & Vivarais

Just at the southern tip of Puy-de-Dôme, just on the northern edge of map sheet 76, just off the 106 road and just holding on to its cliff above the dizzy headwaters of the Dore, *St Sauveur vous invite*. Delightfully-perched miniature resort though it is, St Sauveur's real importance is that (together with St Alyre) it holds the frontier south of Arlanc which leads into Haute-Loire. And at the northernmost part of that department, as the road straightens out from its last hairpin amid dense woodlands where the beech fruits only every four years and the oak every six, where the railway climbs on to the heights at something like 3,500 feet, stands the city which epitomizes all this land. It is the city of la Chaise Dieu.

'Its sheer blanks of wall confront time.... They are very dark; and their simplicity is more than austere, for it has about it something of doom.... If ever too great a title might be excused it is here.' So Hilaire Belloc, writing thirty or more years ago of this great and lonely abbey of St Robert and of the little village which surrounds it. And there is much more which he says better than I concerning its battered collegial, its tunnel-dark gateway, and of how 'its proportion and assize have withstood the hurricanes of winter on these Auvergnian summits, their long depths of snow and their frosts so near the stars, and the brazen heat of their summers on the bare uplands', as well as of all this land between 'endless, level and high, the blue ridge of the Margeride' and the 'indigo edge of lump and peak of the wilder hills to the east'.

In Belloc's day, when neither the motor traffic on the 106 nor the machinations of tourist offices had reached their present intensity, the solitude of the Chaise Dieu must have been as overpowering as his essay. Now Lord knows how many coaches pull up on a sum-

181

Illustrations 30, 31

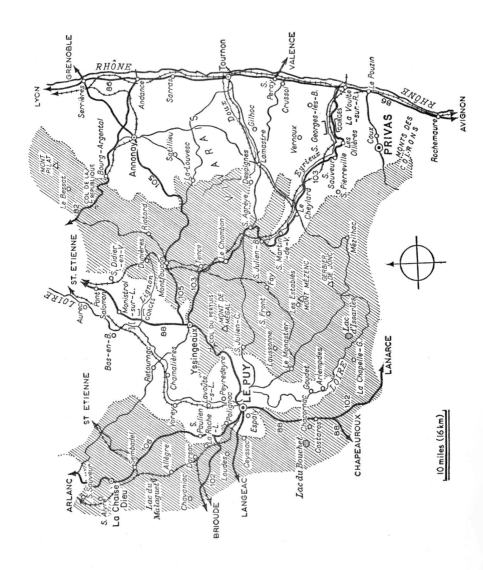

mer's day, how many conducted parties have climbed the great stairs
to the abbey's west front and worn down its flagstones and learned
its history—how Robert the seigneur and two disciples built a log
church here: how the pilgrim trade grew with no apparent reason:
how Aquitaine and Auvergne contested the site and between them
begat the cluniac order: how a norman church grew and was followed by the present fourteenth-century one (*achevé* by a brace of
popes, father and nephew. . . .): how the huguenot raids turned the
place into a fortress: and how the last dissolution came after the
abbey had become an exile for over-proud prelates and turbulent
priests, even though its three hundred monks could still look down
from the Clementine tower on the fifteen churches (of which only
one remains of interest) and three manors which they ruled, and
count their domains from Italy round to Spain. Lord knows, too,
how many have gazed up at the ogival *jubé* and the low vaulted
roof which spans this stark apsed basilica: how many have gaped
at the superb Arras tapestries, and the woodwork, and the wonderful fifteenth-century *danse macabre* fresco—and at the probably apocryphal report that the echo remaining in the two galleries of the
cloisters was used for confessing lepers. Almost every tourist who
enters the Auvergne today will learn that 'Chaise Dieu' means the
house (*casa*, *hasa*), rather than the seat, of God.

And yet this business remains one of day-trippers. There are few
trinket shops or camping-grounds in this mountain village: the inns
are still small and ill-frequented: and at night the place is yours. The
silence returns, enriched and ennobled by the majesty of the past.
And in the twilight you can hear, like bats' wings, the beating of
those mighty names—Anselm and Rufus and Edward the Confessor
from our own land alone—which hover between truth and legend
here.

Belloc believed that in a century or two the Chaise Dieu would
become again a living place. As yet, even the prosaic and rose-tinted
Michelin guide can only confess that '*elle est demeurée dans l'abandon d'où la tirent seulement les archéologues et les touristes*', And
over all our predictions and our judgments the great grey church on
the height broods—forsaken and alone, infinitely sad, but not, I
think, not dead.

*

A couple of miles up the 106 from God's House is the rail junction of Sembadel to which I once came sweating from the south-western tip of the Livradois: and further beyond one comes to St Paulien, the ancient capital of the Velay tribe. This has a distinguished roman-esque church, a museum, some roman fragments and a very curious pyramidal monument in its square of which the plinth is said to be the fifth-century bishop's altar. St Paulien is in itself a much-sacked and rather dull town; but in addition to the above features it was the birthplace of a shepherd-sculptor called Julien.

The railway bows westward; and *its* town, past the lake of Mala-guet, is Allègre. There may be no striking *allegro* quality about this place, though it has left its little mark on history; it is rather domi-nated by a strange ruin of tumbled stone and weed, of which all that the centuries have spared stands in the terrible form of a gibbet. But the whole of this western half of the volcanic Velay hills, which roll between the headwaters of the Allier and the Loire at about the 2,000-foot contour, is a noble land.

Take a day's walk here. Stumble up and down the stream-enclos-ing slopes, work out the *correspondences* between the two buses and the three trains, lie in the sun a little and outline the blue-rimmed horizons, or drink too much wine in one of those village-towns whose roads are paved with the droppings of hay-wains and their oxen. You will end up tired enough, but with the certainty that this is one of the inexhaustible quarters of the high plateau.

*

For those who collect them there are innumerable castles and ruined abbeys hereabouts. La Roche Lambert, which George Sand im-mortalized, is the most famous; and a fine place it still is, though the castle hammered against the hill has become a rather dull museum. But I prefer the dimmer ones—the long, narrow, brown *Schlösser* which cling against the hillside, damp and abandoned behind their rusted gates, shuttered and half seen at the end of a cypress-ride. The only town of the area which I cannot love is the tourist-famed little place which stands up in the hills where the 102 cuts eastward from Brioude, the town of Chavaniac-Lafayette.

The château here is typical of the less attractive idiom of the region, with its long barrack elevations linked by round towers and

184

its ribbed-tile roofs: it would be easy to dismiss it as an early Worm-
wood Scrubs, did not such thoughts lead one into all the complex inter-
relations of architecture, landscape, climate and association. In any case,
nobody comes here for any other reason than that they are Americans
directed by the local *syndicat* to the birthplace of a compulsory hero.

The other year, which was some centenary of this horrid little
general, they even smothered a dirt-track in roses and called it the
'Lafayette Road'. There was in fact, a truly great military family
based on these parts, the Polignacs whose name comes up as often
in Auvergnat history as does that of the Estaings and who were the
ancestors of the Rainiers of Monaco. But they did not achieve the
kind of blighting notoriety which Lafayette casts on this land, as
Cromwell casts one on East Anglia.

*

Like moth to flame—or any other corny simile you like—the ways approach that city which must dominate this chapter as it dominates half
Auvergne. But before proceeding one should consider another route
south, that which comes down from St Etienne beside the Loire.

The 88 leaves the coalfields behind and enters Haute-Loire at Pont
Salomon. This is an odd name: just as odd is the fact that its bridge
is not one of the Loire, for the road keeps to the uplands of eastern
Velay at something over 2,000 feet. It is a fine and rolling road, but
in its forty-odd miles south-westward it passes through only two
towns of note, Monistrol-sur-Loire and Yssingeaux. The former is
quiet enough, but Yssingeaux is the *sous-préfecture* and tourist centre
for the local mountain of Mégal (4,500 feet) and the gorges of the
high Loire's outstanding tributary, the Lignon. This lends it a certain
presence; but an air of sun-scalded decay hangs over even Yssingeaux's one architectural possession, the Italianate *hôtel-de-ville*. The
town is typical of the Velay and has a hotel or two out to make the
most of the area's limited contributions to gastronomy. But it does
not live up to the promise of its golden name.

The railway quite faithfully follows the Loire gorges even where
no path does, and as so often in the Auvergne affords a complemen-
tary, upward-looking landscape to that of the highroads' downward
scan. Its villages also are the reverse of those along the 88: they are
small, but surprisingly clean and bright and prosperous, centres for

campers and fishermen. And if only for the benefit of such folk the winding track of this great river—perhaps as fascinating a trace as all Europe can show—is worth following up its penultimate reach.

The course of the Loire enters the department at Aurec, then: it swings under the great rock of Bas-en-Basset: and beyond some stony gorges it finds Retournac. This is in itself a town of standing, a fine, balconied self-contained place with a simple and impressive norman church; but if you are looking for the romanesque you will do better at the quarry-town of Chamalières on its rock-crest a mile or two on. Then comes the resort of Vorey with its legend of a local leper-saint. And after that, where the cliffs tower to nearly 2,000-feet—a blend of all the impregnable, ruined hilltop castles and accessible lowland manors which follow along the stream—the great renaissance house of the Polignacs at Lavoûte-sur-Loire closes this green corridor.

It closes it. There are ten miles or more of this still half-northern reach to go, past the mighty rocks of Peyredeyre. But at Lavoûte, as at St Paulien or Yssingeaux or at Loudes away to the west, the whole air begins to tremble with the proximity of something rich and strange. For beyond this land where a volcano buried many men in its ultimate explosion stands the city of le Puy.

And what on earth new can one say of that?

*

Le Puy is the *préfecture* of Haute-Loire, a place of some 25,000 inhabitants. Its commercial prosperity was knotted out of the Vellavian lace whose often-told drama is itself a fascinating one in three acts even though in no account which I have read do the dates make sense. First there is the tableau of whole mountain communities knitting through snowbound medieval winters into an over-production which led to a lack of girls available for hussifry, to peasants dressing like noblemen, and so to the edict of 1640 (or, as the scholars say, 1547) which almost outlawed this luxury. Then the great jesuit priest François Régis (who in his lifetime combined the jobs of welfare officer for the lacemakers, political lobbyist for the repeal of the law, and general export agent so successfully that he now represents the *dentelle* business in paradise) had the edict repealed because it was leading to huguenotism. And finally hand-made lace declined to a

186

tourist curiosity, though even at the date of the Chicago Fair there were more lace-makers in le Puy than in all Belgium.

The most characteristic industry of the city today is the making of pleasant liqueurs of a Chartreuse type from verbena and suchlike local herbs: these also enter into the *infusions* favoured by those French who believe in a cup which cheers as little as it inebriates. But who cares for industries here? Who remembers even the curious sidelight of the history of le Puy—the splendours of its courts of troubadours, or those dark twelfth-century days when various Ku-Klux-Klan-hooded freebooters were chasing each other round the valleys and changing sides on divine inspiration but in a very confusing way? Who can bear in mind the complex geological plan which helped to make le Puy—that alluvial plain which is comparable in structure to the Limagne and in strategic force to the Belfort gap, yet which is a completely enclosed basin save where the Loire enters as a stream from the south through comparatively gentle clay-country and leaves northward through a granite gate? Who works out all those details of erosion, and counts the circum-ringing volcanic towers of every type, when the staggering fact is that from the heart of the city the sky is lanced by two peaks of lava which would be a *stupor mundi* in even an isolated site?

*

Anybody who has entered a tourist office in New York or Nagasaki knows the profile of these needles. The higher, the rock of Corneille, supports nothing but a 100-ton statue of Our Lady made from cannon captured at Sebastopol. This provides innocent exercise. But more awaits at the crest of the *aiguille* (or *dyke*) of St Michael, where each of 267 or so steps takes you nearly a foot more above the plain towards a dizzy chapel once called Séguret or the secure refuge. Formerly men climbed these from piety and on their knees: those who today follow from curiosity should not, once they have recovered breath, be disappointed. With its mosaics and arabesques of polychromatic stone, its slim minaret and its lobed portal arches, this tenth-to-twelfth-century chapel has an oriental note which overrides the charming and christian little lava capitals. It would be a unique building, even were it not so strangely and even weirdly sited between earth and sky.

But the heart of le Puy is a lower rock—the shoulder of the Roche Anis which is now called the Roche Corneille, the black bluff which supports the Ville Sainte (which should *not* be translated, as in the local guide, as 'Holly City') and the cathedral itself.

Up the stairway-street of the town, up the steps which still lead into the church itself and which once led straight to the high altar and vanished black Virgin of St Louis, climbed the pilgrims who made le Puy rich. Today countless sightseers follow; for the history of the whole city is that of St Michael's needle. How, in such a place, can one distinguish religious veneration from architectural and scenic appreciation, or either from sheer rubbernecking?

I think that the many-coloured Our Lady of le Puy is a genuinely great—if not a beautiful—cathedral. Its repute would endure without the legends of druidic and roman sanctity, without the revived pilgrimages and processions, without the setting and curious plan and sense of being built on air which the site imposes, without that same oriental (or at least Iberian) accent which distinguishes St Michael. It is certainly a fabulously rich church, packed with every kind of ecclesiastical treasure—including an eighth-century bible—and accreted with chapels, a very ancient baptistry, towers, and a most lovely cloister which also wears a mosque-like air despite its carolingian capitals. France has greater cathedrals than this, just as England has greater than Lincoln. But the heart takes more hold of these rambling complexes of stone than of the simple *thereness* of an Amiens or a Salisbury.

*

One can explore this domed and zebra-striped cathedral, even in high season, curiously undisturbed. This is not true of the rest of le Puy. The old town (with only a few other and minor antiquities to its credit) preserves the worst of medieval tawdriness with its scrofulous and pustulant beggars, and adds a modern phoniness with tourist-baiting lace, 'dainty objects for the pencil', and sticky liqueurs done up in fancy bottles. The new town is museums (mostly of lace and local painting), pricey shops, and car-parks. But further out, beyond the last remnant of the city's eighteen gates and on the way to the old bridge, the gothic church of St Laurence which enshrines Du Guesclin's organs looks on a very gracious and quite unrenowned boulevard. I prefer to linger there: or in Espaly of the basalt *orgues*, the suburb where the bishops of Puy took their vows before entering the holy walls and where a few stones remain of a castle eight times taken: or perhaps still further out, beyond the rich men's suburbs, in a village like Ceyssac with its church carved from the rock: or the one named Polignac itself, with its distinguished romanesque church and superb fourteenth-century ruined castle which once housed a thousand men and gave France many of her giants. Here, church, castle and hollowed cliff (*did* it once support a temple and fraudulent oracle of Apollo and so give the place its name?) all epitomize the spirit of this wind-stung basin of volcanic needles and sacred lakes which was long ago one vast flood-plain of the Loire and which is now—like the *limagnes*—fertile from volcanic soil.

From such a spot, where the towers of nature and man lift above nature's mist and man's smoke, it is possible to recapture one's first rapture. Of course the city is all that the guide-books say of it, often in as many words as would fill this volume. Of course it is unforgettable, overpowering, unique in the world for its site and its history and its monuments. It is only when one stays in it that one is oppressed by the fact that since the Revolution—and perhaps since the days of the League—le Puy has been out to get your money and to get it without finesse.

The hotels are drab and still counting, as in Biarritz, their lost crowned heads. The gastronomic speciality is lentils. And such of the history as is not of murders has a pervading theme—which the tourist office perfectly preserves—of tottering between chicanery and bungling. Le Puy's most famous house is the House of Cuckolds. It shared with Rome about the most sickening instance of simony which even the eleventh century witnessed; and after having given christendom five very obscure saints went on to present it with a host of episcopal villains. Ponce the murderer, Bertrand de Chalenson who killed innocent and guilty on the principle that God would know his own, the lecherous bailiff de Rochebaron who was butchered by the butchers of le Puy, Durant de St Pourçain who burned the lepers alive, the hangman Antoine de St Nectaire (brother of the lovely and terrible calvinist Madeleine of St Nectaire): these are a few of the catholics, and the huguenots were far worse. It botched the embalming of du Guesclin. It merited Mrs Edwards' scorn, as it merits mine. And it gave Miss Sewing-Machine a donkey when she really wanted a donkey-ess.

*

This is, however, a city which can afford to many what they love most. And, since I particularly love forgotten railways, it is good to find two which lead from Le Puy into other lands.

The railway situation of Le Puy itself is still as curious as Baring-Gould noted half a century ago. For though the once-a-day through-car link with Paris runs *via* St Etienne there are three other means of access from the north—from the Thiers region *via* Ambert, from the Forez *via* Sembadel, and most beautifully of all from the Allier *via* St Georges d'Aurac—all these finally joining up at a junction called Darsac near the 102. Only the way to Langogne in the south has been abandoned. But more exciting than any lost lines here is the line they never built.

It set out from Le Puy about 1926, in the last flush of the French railway age, heading south-east across an impossible watershed. By 1939 tunnels had been opened, stupendous viaducts built, even impressive stations erected and the ballast laid. But not an inch of steel was down. At war's end the project was formally abandoned (though the maps of the period still mark *voie en construction*), partly because the highlands were now earmarked for hydro-electric works but more because France had lost faith in railways. But still the trace sprawls across the map like the Surrey Heights line; and still the great *ouvrages* soar as if it were yesterday, rather than twenty or thirty years back, that the last shot was fired and the last mason's saw whined still.

All this activity ended in the middle of nowhere. But it ended *near* to a town as remarkable as it is unregarded, le Monastier. Even for historic reasons one would expect some signposts here, for it was at le Monastier—a drunken, God-damning, disputatious place as *he* found it—that Stevenson saddled Modestine. But today things have quietened down, and it is as fine and as forgotten as St Bonnet —which is almost on the same longitude but three times farther north of Le Puy than le Monastier is south. The place is steep and splendid. Its abbatical church—polychrome but mostly dark brown, transitional in style, low in height and memorable in impact—enshrines an exquisite seventeenth-century Virgin. And I would not be surprised if in it you could not still find the house of the *béatre* marked by a bell-cote—the chapel, school, lace-making seminary, assembly hall, crèche, funeral parlour and citizens' advice bureau of those days, extending into the present century, when in winter every Vellavian hamlet was isolated.

Obscurity has settled on le Monastier, and indeed on the castles of the nearby headwaters of the Loire like Goudet and Arlempdes—as noble a ruin as you will find. But it is a place where every prospect pleases, though my favourite picture-postcard of it is of the station in the middle of the fields—that big clean white station which never heard a train.

*

Le Monastier is on the extreme eastern edge of the historic Auvergne, to which le Puy itself was never more than a gateway. But the department of Haute-Loire climbs a little further to the east and south, and the tourist circuits which rely on le Puy trespass even into Ardèche to net-in the mixed bag of sites and sights which stand in an arc around the departmental boundary.

In the north there is first St Julien-Chapteuil with its scraped, white, many-gabled church up amid the rocks and then three resort-villages—Laussonne, St Front (which has a church, a lake, and nearby mill once famous for its poltergeists) and Fay of the volcanic needle, formerly suffixed -le-Froid. Further south, above straggling les Estables—in Baring-Gould's time 'a poor and dirty place where the natives shiver through half the year', but now capitalizing on its isolation in an attempt to become a winter-sports centre—comes Mt Mézenc on the border itself, a peak of lava nearly 6,000 feet up at the crest of all the Velay. And south again rises a crest which is nearly 1,000 feet lower (*more* nearly since a landslide in 1871) but rather more famous. This is Gerbier de Jonc or des Joncs.

The name means, roughly, 'stook'. It is, however, misleading, for the shape of this craggy clinkstone mound—which rises no higher above the plateau than the energetic can climb while the coach parks amid the tourist chalets—is more that of a pine-cone or sugar-loaf. But the Gerbier's greatest fame is that in a farmhouse below it rises the Loire.

191

Illustration 35

This is, you are assured, the source *géographique et authentique*; for it is easy to lose sight of the stream amid the tributaries which vein the map south of Le Puy, and easy to raise an eyebrow at finding that even this extraordinary river begins by flowing south. It is easy, too, to make mock of this grubby steading against the rock where France's greatest river issues from a pipe stuck in the wall and escapes, *via* the kitchen sink, as a tired peasant holds out her hand for a few francs for the privilege of watching it and hopes you will buy a postcard. And yet... A sense of reverence at the rising of great rivers is part of our classic heritage, and perhaps we who come from a land where water more often emerges vaguely from buttercup meadows than comes icily foaming out of the cleft rock should more often honour such things.

But if these crests of Velay are nothing like England they are considerably like Scotland, for the land is covered with heather and harebell and gorse and occasionally a soft mist, punctuated with white thatched crofts and rowan trees, and not at all the dismal tableland which most of the guide-books dismiss it as. It is also a bee-loud spot: from these honey-coloured heights (which are statistically the dryest and coldest in France) still comes a fair proportion of the country's honey, as once the violets and fragrant herbs came too. It is, in fact, a pleasant land to watch from the windows of bus or car as the by-roads bend back past the deep, undrained lake of Issarlès.

This is not much as lakes go, though surrounded by some intriguing cave-houses. But it is brighter than the dreary puddle of Bouchet away to the west, past la Chapelle-Graillouse which Stevenson failed to reach on his first night but which I reached all too soon, with two hours in hand to stare at waters which looked no more exciting for being 100 feet deep and lying in the gap left by a bursting bubble of lava. The other sight of this area is Chacornac, where there are some artificial caves: legend associates them and their hauntings with the historical figure of Mandrin, a brilliant forger and *faux-monnayeur* broken on the wheel in 1755. Costaros on the 88 road south of Le Puy serves as centre for both of these. But by bus or car it will have to be; for even the last hope of the le Monastier line gave up at the departmental frontier.

To find a stranger line which has not yet quite given up one must

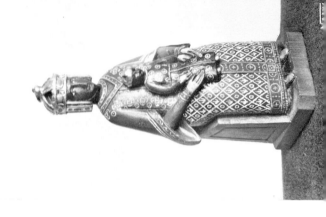

Le Puy, the most famous city of all the plateau. Not only tourists, but pilgrims (*left*) still flock to admire its treasures (*below, left*) and adore its relics (*below, right*).

33

34

Two rivers of the Massif. In the photograph (*left*) the Gerbier de Jonc guards the head-waters of the greatest river of France. *Right* is a typical narrows in the gorges of the Tarn.

begin with a return, north and a little east, past le Puy and almost to the far edge of the department.

*

From the abominable Firminy a branch railway leaves the Loire valley, climbs up beside the 88 for a while, wanders away near a sizeable town called St Didier-en-Velay, and after a few more plea-sant and unexpected miles ends up at Dunières. There is nothing but a church of minor note here, nor in its neighbour Riotord, nor yet in the fact that the SNCF passenger service gives up at Dunières: the surprising thing is that it gets so far. And the *staggering* thing is that one can still go on on the narrow gauge.

I have twice before written of the private Réseau du Vivarais; and there is a limit to one's expressions of love, especially in a book which is not about railways at all. But to take the little railcar out of Dunières—to sell your car and *take* it—is to begin an unforgettable journey in which, for six hours, you will be an angel soaring over the hills and valleys. The old PLM, envying it, used to admit 'very inter-esting travelling': today one of the holiday resorts along it, asked for the name of its station, says just 'local line'.

For thirty or forty miles the metric tracks run generally southward. They cross the 105 cross-country road at Montfaucon above the 3,000-feet contour, from which there was once a branch-line which led west over magnificent viaducts to Yssingeaux and so on down to the Loire at Lavoûte. They dip down to Tence. And then they climb again, around and about the 103 road now, to le Chambon and St Agrève where the altitude plate again translates as well over 3,000 feet.

There is nothing of architectural or topographical significance in any of these towns: even their history is only one of the tired out-rages, the routine brutality, of the wars of religion. They simply follow each other along a corridor which has become a country for unmechanized (and rather uncertain) ski-ing in winter, and in summer for the *cure d'air, de repos,* or simply *d'altitude* which supports some surprisingly satisfying (and correspondingly expensive) hotels and restaurants. Prowl round in the country and you will find castles and manors of note. But its glory is in the land itself—the wild tangled contours of the hills, the gorges of the Lignon (which is here so steep that it supports three hydro-electric plants) and the dusty white roads and heroic little railway lacing it all.

*

St Agrève, when you come to it, is one of those great crest-points of the plateau. The ridge here marks the division between Haute-Loire and Ardèche, as it formerly marked that between Velay and the Vivarais—which was *never* part of the Auvergne. For these are political and not geographic terms, countrysides rather than ranges, separated by a watershed and not a river.

The line's entry into the Vivarais is precipitate: the vast upland horizons become glimpses only as it drops on—still south, over the crease of the map—to St Julien-Boutières, St Martin-de-Valamas (the place-names can chime very sweetly hereabouts) and le Cheylard—which is itself a dull nineteenth-century place. And after this loss of 2,000 feet in little more than fifteen miles, under the hill and comfortably in Ardèche, it is time once more to take stock.

For here the train halts, here the tracks divide. One way follows the Eyrieux, heading south of west: the other returns northwest, over a quite easy shelf, to pick up the Doux at Lamastre.

There is a quite large and castled town here, with the distinction of being a gastronomic centre: its main hotel offers a table of six unchanging specialities classic enough to draw a millionaire-gastronome through three departments—and as usual has dragged-up its rivals to a sophistication staggering for Ardèche. For the rich, indeed, Lamastre must be the best of all the resorts of the eastern hills, though scenically it has nothing as spectacular as the ramparts of Desaignes a few miles upstream.

But both tracks of the Vivarais lead down (as so many ways mentioned and abandoned earlier in this chapter lead down) to the mighy Rhone. And so it is time to travel north once more—back to the latitude of St Etienne, from which the sunrise shelf of the Massif strikes southward in a single edge for sixty or more miles and for every inch is bordered by a single river, a single departmental frontier, and a single map.

*

The Michelin sheet 76 is unique. It includes the whole of Cantal and

Illustration 5

Haute-Loire, large parts of three other departments of the Massif, and fragments of three more. Its western edge drops roughly from Meymac in Corrèze to Figeac: its northern runs north of Bort, Lempdes, Arlanc, St Bonnet and St Etienne itself: its southern leads into desert lands, as yet unexplored, where the lizards come larger and the cicadas noisier than on the hottest rocks of Ardèche. And down its eastern edge—almost straight down, one rule of blue—thunders the Rhone, with beyond it a token corridor of the Dauphiné and then Provence. To open this map is like opening the window in a souvenir postcard: a dozen views tumble out, different but linked. And men who love highlands go through the *soixante-seize* as they go through their mountain boots.

Close to the top right of the sheet, half way between St Etienne and the Rhone, not much further from the Loire river and indeed still in the department of Loire, there rises above the tourist village of le Bessat a cone of earth called Mont Pilat. At less than 5,000 feet it is not even one of the sky-scrapers of the Auvergne; and, of course, it would come barely knee-high to that Swiss namesake which also associates a dutiful and humane Roman civil servant with legends of towering heights and catastrophic sin. But it, and its sister-crests, and the Col de la République (*ou du Grand Bois*) over on the 82 road, are part of that east-thrusting upheaval which forms one of the most dramatic and cardinal bastions of all the plateau. For, only ten miles beyond them, the Rhone flows into Ardèche above the quayside town of Serrières.

To come down from the granite hills to such a place is a fore-taste of an experience which recurs and recurs along the mighty valley, and is always staggering. After the hairpin bends, the familiar dusty villages, are that look of Mediterranean animation and that sense that even a hundred miles north of Avignon one is nearer to Provence than Burgundy more than an illusion? After the tight gorges, the swirling brown streams, can any river be so glacial, grey and majestic? After those rolling and carpeted hills, are those bare classic peaks a hand's-touch away more than a mirage of cloud, are they indeed the southern Alps?

The answer to all these questions, of course, is 'Yes'. This *is* the Rhone, approached in the only way which can develop its grandeurs; and the paper-thin strip of Ardèche which runs down its right bank is utterly different from all the rest. Across the river—three miles away at the most and usually less than one mile—the *nationale sept* and the great PLM railroad scald south, south, south through St Louis' land: as near on the landward side the shelf of the plateau presses against the road which comes down from the polychrome towns, the beehive-wells, the silkmill villages and dyeworks dependent on Lyons, and the vineyards of the Côte Rôtie.

They number this right-bank artery 86: and there is a railway beside *it* too. Nowhere else in France—nowhere else in Europe, or perhaps in the world except along the Rhine—is there such a duplication of highways for mile upon mile. But there is a profound difference between the two banks. No *wagon-lits* expresses hammer the Ardèche shore, but only three sleepy locals a day: and little enough long-distance road traffic takes to the 86. There is no technical reason for this, for it is on the whole a better road than the overglamorized *Route Bleue*: away to the north, indeed, *ponts et chaussées* road-signs try to attract drivers over the river as ardently as do the viticulturers of the Côtes du Rhône. But despite the finer scenery and the kinder towns on that side they fail. It is as if some miasma blows down from the heights to battle with the sweeping mistrals: as if even the shoulder of the thunder-capped purple hills rising over their own shoulders give men an *on ne passe pas*.

*

So it is that, a quarter of a pint of petrol west of Serrières on the long, lonely 105 which leads back to Montfaucon, and up an entry as gentle as a Bournemouth chine, the silence of the Auvergne returns. And this is despite the fact that only a few miles into the hills stands Annonay, with its population of over 15,000. It gets into the guide-books on the strength of its museum and its fishing—and into the history-books because it was here that the Montgolfiers made their first balloon ascent and Séguin devised his bridges. But the fact that any description must stop there, despite Annonay's obvious size and importance and the small industries which survive in the wake of this latter inventive genius, is perhaps enough in itself to signify a town of Ardèche.

Annonay is just off the traffic crossroads of the 82 and the 105. It also has a station: and once a week a mixed train grinds up to it from the Rhone and then on again, over the crest close to the triple point with the two Loire departments, and down into Bourg-Argental. This is one of the pleasanter forgotten towns of France, though all it offers of formal note is a decent medieval church. But—again—look at the map.

Just before Bourg-Argental the branch-railway makes a full loop, half in a tunnel and half out of it; and the SNCF map exaggerates this to the scale of an approach to the St Gotthard. In fact it is a more humble affair; but it *is* almost its only corkscrew track in the whole of France, except for a frontier affair in the Pyrenees, and I am proud that the Massif and not the Alps should have it. What I am sad about is that even the hebdominal passenger service ends halfway up the spiral: only freight-cars edge on, back through the tunnels and tangled watershed, back to Dunières. . . .

That is one link between the west and the east of the Vivarais. There is a triangle of land, bordered by the Rhone, the 105 road, and nothing in particular, before you come to another—a great green triangle where it seems a man could get thoroughly lost were it not for the tourist and skiers' villages of Satillieu and (does the Michelin really recommend a nineteenth-century church here because of its pilgrimage?) la Louvesc. And even on the boundary-river itself there are only one-hotel, main-road villages like Andance of the barges and Sarras, to halt the motorist.

Still, halt a moment and smell the land. It is mid-afternoon and men are away in their fields watching a few lean beasts. The women are sewing or stringing beans in their doorways and the brown children playing bored, secret games in the half-abandoned station square. The bead-curtains across the door of the railway hotel will not be disturbed till six, the aperitif hour: at six-thirty the bus will come in: by eight, all will be silent and shuttered again. Perhaps next month there will be a fair—or a *crime passionnel* to blast the pages of *France-Soir/Paris-Presse*. Until then there is only work and sleep. Smell this—and then drive on to the south-eastern tip of the triangle at Tournon.

*

Pimpante is the word they give to Tournon against the scarred granite, which bears a last hint of Burgundy and was indeed a major wine town before the phylloxera upset the economy of the *côtes*. And it is a bright, gracious enough little *sous-préfecture* whose pale stone is here and there crystallized into an attractive building like the renaissance chapel or (which is remarkable for France) a grammar school of the eighteenth century. Behind it, the northern spur of the Réseau du Vivarais comes down from Lamastre along the Doux— a dizzy enough journey, for this little tributary of the Rhone has been grossly under-starred and, to my mind, flows through as continuously exciting a cleft as you will find in the whole plateau.

No main road follows the Doux, nor does one descend from the hills until St Péray (an unfashionable sister of Valence, though still something of a viticultural centre) and the huge castle of Crussol with its grey ruins atop a grey rock. Tiny resorts like Gilhac and St Georges-les-Bains are scattered about the towny, abrupt hills here, however, and there is a real town in Vernoux. The main interest of this is that it was—and to some extent still is—the centre of the protestant intolerance of these hills. Baring-Gould tells the pleasant story of the lady who went to sleep in the meeting-house during the sermon, got locked in and rang the bell for help. None came: she had to climb down the bell-rope: and then she found the town barricaded, it having mistaken the sound of the bell for a tocsin announcing a new St Bartholomew's Eve. But it is the centre for a fine collection of lonely castles and natural sites.

Further south again are St Pierreville and then, up on the watershed under the Gerbier de Jonc and boasting a well-known little waterfall, Mézilhac. In any of these places a man could drink his fill of mountain solitude. But for me this centre-land of Ardèche is dominated by the gorges of the gold-laden Eyrieux—sometimes a narrow stream and sometimes a torrent carrying more water than the Seine at Paris —and by the last limb of the Réseau de Vivarais which follows them down for thirty miles.

Again, I have spoken elsewhere of this journey with its countless bridges and viaducts, its leaps high over road and river, and nothing of a town except the fishermen's villages of St Sauveur-de-Montagut and les Ollières. (The line misses, for instance, a village where the last of the elms which were planted all over France to celebrate Henry IV's conversion may still survive: these are called 'Sully' trees, through the great minister's name is more closely connected

198

with the worm-feeding mulberry.) But what, perhaps, I did not do justice to was the riverhead town of la Voulte-sur-Rhône—which is, as the eagle soars, just about fifty miles east and south from the Vivarais' abandoned terminal of Lavoûte-sur-Loire.

It was indeed this coincidence of names—this expression of the contrast between the Loire above le Puy with its last hint of the meadowy, tree-shaded north and of the Rhone as it accepts the waters of the Durance and becomes yet vaster, more glacial, tempestuous and alpine and southern-seeking, which at first seemed to me the one distinction of la Voulte. But now I have come to know what a Victorian writer called 'this picturesque congeries' as an expression also of the ambivalence of this reach of the river. Above it stands an eyeless despoiled Ventadour château, a perfect witness of the steeps. Before it flows the river. The town itself is split between high old tumbledown streets (which knew just two decades of prosperity when iron was mined here) and a straggle of roadhouses along the 86. And its railway system, too, looks both ways.

For whilst the narrow-gauge ends here after its long experience of the sun-tired spaces, something almost as odd *leaves* la Voulte. The SNCF has recently—and largely to provide a link from off the Vivarais—pulled back into use a spur which crosses the Rhone here; and over it one or two trains set off daily at impossible hours with their eyes set on places like Valence. But so strange is the configuration of the cruciform station, and so sharp is the edge of the plateau, that they must dive into a long curving tunnel under the cliffs of the Vivarais before they seek the crystal peaks of Savoy.

*

A little below la Voulte, at a place called le Pouzin, there was once yet another railway entry into the hills. The brief spur whose cosiness struck Baring-Gould offered the same experience as its sisters, the experience of a violent geographic and cultural change in its first mile; but it is now abandoned. And not much traffic takes even the by-road up to the préfecture of Ardèche.

I do not know why Privas has that honour, for with its population of a mere 7,000 it is not the largest town even in that under-populated department and is less than half the size of its similarly situated sister Annonay. It is roughly on the waist of the department, but far over

199

Illustration 51

to its east side, since less than ten miles from the Rhone but more than fifty from the Allier frontier at Langogne. But still, it *is* the county town, and has for Ardèche almost a metropolitan note.

Heavens knows, that note is muted. All French towns which have lost their railways wear a slightly dispirited air, and Privas is a local joke for having absent-mindedly lost most of its hotels too. (The *gendarmes*, for instance, are very helpful in getting benighted tourists out of town.) I have elsewhere—at Guéret and at Tulle—reflected on the dimness of the *préfectures* of the Massif: Privas is no exception.

In fairness, one should add that it is a gracious-looking place, most beautifully-sited, friendly and *sympathique*: Diane de Poitiers, who was its baroness, missed something by never visiting it. But it leaves no striking impression: not so striking a one, even, as its little suburb of Coux which straggles along a promontory in white-walled and red ridge-tiled cottages which are half Mediterranean in look though wholly Auvergnat in drowsiness.

*

Stand here for a moment. Behind you tower twelve peaks higher than Ben Nevis, including the three-fanged Mézenc itself. But away to the south there is a range of hills more twisted, more coloured and barer—rocks striped like Alum Bay sands arranged in a test-tube, rocks twisted like Les Baux or covered by mud landslides and ironstone outcrops though their substructure is volcanic. These make up the jagged, chestnut-studded, and geologically-fascinating Monts des Coirons, which thrust out to meet the Rhone at the ruined castle of Rochemaure. And the Coirons, where the skeletons of early men have been found in the lava and where there was a violent earthquake, if not an actual eruption, in the fifth century and possibly the eighteenth also—the Coirons are separate from the Vivarais proper.

Other changes are near. The escarpment is pulling back a little from the river to make way for the true, great delta of Provence: the next Rhoneside landmark will be Montélimar, a latin town at the tip of the map. And so, barely halfway down Ardèche, one must return westward the full breadth of that astounding sheet 76 and begin another long traverse from Figeac.

Red Rock Country

The Marche and the Limousin, Perigord and Quercy and Aquitaine: in its swinging arc from la Souterraine to Figeac the western edge of the plateau has passed through, bordered on or at least overlooked all these ancient provinces which lie tangled together, similar and yet distinguishable, under the gold south-western sun. Now it meets another. Away to the south-east of Figeac, not much larger than (but once as puissant as) the Bourbon-nais, lies the land which remembers, though the world forgets, the name of Rouergue. Virtually all of it is now included in the most south-western department which is wholly of the plateau. This starts a new belt of limestone mountains, stretching eastward halfway across France, where the sun is higher, the men darker-skinned and even the rocks wilder than one has met before. It is Aveyron.

*

If you start looking for Aveyron by train, there is a little difficulty before you as you are ten minutes out of Figeac and away from the great green forest to the north. It is called Capdenac-Gare (there *is* an old village named Capdenac across the Lot); and it stands precisely and symbolically on the border of Aveyron, holding a sword which is not so much two- as five-edged. For more branch-lines than one would have believed possible in rural France meet here, and you will have to change, and while you are changing the train will change itself and steal up behind you on another track, and before you know it you will be back in Mauriac and Aurillac and all the *-ac's* of Cantal, or up in Brive, or even over in Cahors or down in Toulouse.

Even down in Toulouse. . . ? That, in fact, is the way one should

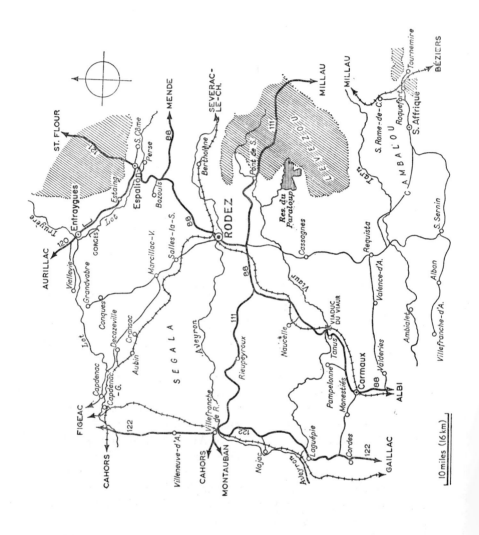

10 miles (16 km)

move in order to find the western edge of Quercy and the eastern one of the Rouergue and Aveyron. For most of the height of a Michelin sheet (and near to its edge) this cardinal branch-line drops on like a plummet through the bulge of Aveyron and out again. The 122 road which parallels it is even truer, but not quite as scenic.

From the Lot crossings downwards for a matter of twenty miles there is extraordinarily little of note. Road and rail here are continuations, farther west, of the road and rail from Bort; and perhaps they are less spectacular here than they were in Corrèze and Cantal. There is, of course, the wide and wonderful panorama of Gascony to the right, the sudden glimpse of great hills when the escarpment to the left falls away. But one has seen all this before—twenty miles before—and even the church of Villeneuve-d'Aveyron is failing to break the monotony when suddenly all the boards say Villefranche; Villefranche de Rouergue.

*

The very foundation of the place was unusual, and linked to a little-known enterprise of the middle ages. In the middle of the thirteenth century—some forty years after New Sarum was new—a brother of St Louis called Alphonso de Poitiers found himself count of the Rouergue but without a capital to be a count in. Accordingly he built one in virgin country—an enterprise which took a mere year, which is better than you would do in our age of concrete and restrictive practices.

Certain privileges—such as that of rule by elected consuls—were granted to those who settled in Villefranche; and despite the anger of the bishop of Rodez the whole thing was so wildly successful that every baron of Aquitaine decided to have his own *bastide* or free city —and the liege lord, Edward I of England, to have many. Never was there such a frenzy of building artificial towns until in the eighteenth century the Palatine cities rose along the Rhone—or, perhaps, until the age of Crawley and Hemel Hempstead. Their rate of foundation approached one per year for thirty years.

When truly new, all these Villefranches and Villeneuves must have been as monotonous aggregations of gridiron streets and squares, terraces and even semi-detached's, as their modern equivalents. Time has done little to mellow the most perfect of the *bastides*,

Montpazier in Perigord, for instance—nor yet its far later copy, Richelieu outside Chinon. But Villefranche grew and changed; a softer flesh clothed its classic bones; and now it is a golden place.

One can have three relationships to a beautiful city, as to a woman. One can never have loved at all, in which case it is easy—whatever her admitted charms—to be bright and brief. One can have loved and lost, in which case the note becomes brittle and bitchy. Or one can have loved and gone on loving. These cities, these women, are the hardest to describe. And that is how I feel about what is, for me, the *only* Villefranche out of the hundred so-christened in France.

When I first came there (and *that* was twelve years ago) it was on a summer evening when the sky was veined and skeined and grained, a western sky. I went down to that arcaded, unphotographable and almost un-drawable square, caught my breath at the tower of the church of Our Lady, and went in to hear benediction with the nuns.

Turris Davidica, ora pro nobis. The church of Notre-Dame-de-Villefranche keeps vigilance on its square like a leopardess: powerful, proud and poised, but at peace. The great buttresses stride forward like paws, each ten yards wide, into the busy market; but they rest there, the claws drawn back in grace. 'Pillar of strength and tower of ivory': I walked back when it was night, and even then there was light behind the pointed windows of the little charter-house and the sound of monks at vespers, complines or some such office. So was enchantment born.

*

Daylight shows the details of the church—the three lancet windows, marvellous and high, the woodwork in the retrochoir, the carillon which plays a number of tunes including (and it is a strange sensation to hear it hammered out under an indigo night in what was once English land) *God Save the Queen.* It also, I am afraid, shows that the church has been heavily scoured and repointed. But nothing can destroy the magnificent proportions of this building, not even the memory of Chartres or Keble chapel. It was built, like the town itself, at one *coup de poing* and the very apex of the gothic. There is no parish church in France, not even Royat, nobler than this.

To make such a building and beautify such a city, of course, demanded the old folding stuff. Villefranche had it before the stuff started folding, in the great days from the late thirteenth to the early sixteenth century when it stood like a little Venice guarding the passes and the plain. That sense of late-gothic richness continues, and Villefranche de Rouergue—a *sous-préfecture* of Aveyron, population 9,000—is no ghost city today. They are building a modern chapel in a dusty backstreet, and it is the most confident, the most faith-filled—and, incidentally, the most beautiful—thing of its type I have seen in France.

*

Such is the Villefranche of my enchantments; but whatever is the Rouergue? I have mentioned that it was the ancient province which made up most of what is today called Aveyron (so that Villefranche was always near its western edge), but it was more than that. It is even today a recognizable topographical entity whose trademark seems expressed in a name in fact derived from the old tribe of the Ruthenes. For everything in the Rouergue is *rouge*, or *rougi*, or at least *rougeâtre*. Ferruginous limestones and sandstones wear down to a Devon-coloured clay in the valleys: houses of ruddy brick or stone are plastered pink on top: creepers turn russet with autumn, the rivers are encarnadined, and even sunsets seem to flush deeper than elsewhere. It is a gateway to red-brick Albi with its Battersea-power-station cathedral, to the English-midland grime of Toulouse, even to the Roussillon and the *côte vermeille*.

With so much red, it is not surprising that one thing which would normally be red is almost black—the local wine which turns the teeth violet and the tongue purple and which tastes bitterly of iron. It *should* have a tonic quality; but I prefer to drink Gaillac, that much-publicized brew, from a countryside which also specializes in fungi, which is popular far up into the hills and is indeed the one major penetration of things Mediterranean north-east of Villefranche.

*

A river runs through the middle of Villefranche; and it is the Aveyron itself. It has here abandoned the white hills from which it came and is resolved on a little experiment—to flow due south for a few miles. The experiment is abandoned after about fifteen miles as the crow flies and thirty as the river runs, but while it lasts it aids the railway and allows travellers thereon a sight of Najac with its dizzy hilltop town and castle.

The 122 *route nationale* avoids this altogether. But it, and the railway, and the river, suddenly unite in the town of Laguépie.

This is a frontier spot if the whole Massif can show one. Just as the Aveyron has pulled first the railway, then the departmental border and finally the road beside it, it makes a right-angled bend westward and leaves this book like a rather abrupt guest at a dinnerparty. But its excuse is that it had to go with a friend, this friend being a tributary called the Viaur. Through an odd neck of the boundary, Laguépie is technically in Tarn-et-Garonne—a department which will not make any further appearances here. But the Viaur brings in the border of another department, that of Tarn (*nature*); and though the edge of the plateau begins to shelve back very steeply south of the Aveyron, some few of the towns of Tarn do, I think, belong here. Cordes, for instance, is only a few miles due south of Laguépie. But it is nearly a thousand feet up in the limestone cliffs which are here as white as downland chalk.

How little, though, such figures express the effect of a town on the eye. Fifteen or twenty miles inland from Cordes, a place a mere thousand feet up would lie deep in a combe. But Cordes itself—as almost everyone knows—is perched on a dizzy promontory which makes it one of the most fabulously-sited little places in France.

The 122 skirts it, as main roads skirt so many such splendid places: the plan of Cordes, for instance, is almost a miniature replica of that of my lovely Sémur-en-Auxois, or of Langres far away in a greener land. Only a village, it harbours no individual building of great distinction, though its church is tiny, odd and (of course) precariously set. But the general *ensemble* of old houses leaning over narrow streets is wonderfully picturesque and a delight for amateur artists.

A little east of Cordes there are several villages of note, the most noted being Monesties of the *trois églises*. These are the retinue of its lord mayor's show. But after them all comes the dung-cart: the dung-cart of Carmaux.

This is not a continuation-town down the 122 which goes on, still southward, out of this book to Gaillac. It is not even on its inland

Illustration 39

spur which heads for Albi. Both these Tarn-towns are splendid ones, but their respective altitudes of 460 and 550 feet do not get them into the first heat of the junior high jump so far as the plateau is concerned. Carmaux, a few miles due east of Cordes, makes 800; so Carmaux it has to be.

Carmaux is in Tarn. It has a population of over 10,000. It is a mining town, an industrial town, which means that the girls are smartly dressed and you can get a drink after 9.30. It is an unrelieved industrial town and very sleazy indeed: if Toulouse is Rugby, then this is West Bromwich. The sunset shines sweetly on the gas-holders. Want to know any more?

*

Behind Carmaux, from the Viaur south to the Tarn and past it, this northern edge of a department climbs to the great 1,500-feet frontier. It climbs quite slowly—but it climbs through an utter vacuity far more evocative of the Massif than of the soft south-west. Villefranche-d'Albigeois, Alban, Ambialet, Valderies, Valence-d'Albigeois, Pampelonne . . . These names, in the type which means that they are villages rather than hamlets, fill two full folds of the map, an area of perhaps three hundred square miles with little to inhabit it save thin sheep. And the Michelin cannot find a single thing to say of any of them except that one has a hotel and another a garage.

Perhaps it is right. But I cannot believe that a dedicated soul on a motor-scooter would not discover something of merit in this land which looks—again on the map—as white as a slice of Andalusia; until it reaches the minor road which runs down through Cassagnes and Requista to the old-bridged town of St Sernin in its dizzy valley beyond the Tarn where earth and sky seem intermingled and the car soars higher than an aircraft. It is not a savage land, for on this edge of Aveyron even the mountains seem trim and park-like. But it is a very unexplored one, and it will get the taste of the steelworks (and the local *rouge*) out of the mouth before it is put back there again.

For all round the edge of the plateau—though never in its heart—are dotted these little pockets of coal-mining and its associated arts. The necessary return northward from Carmaux and its terraced back-lawn skims over sixty miles of a solitude whose only landmarks are a few secondary roads, the obscure branch railway inland from

Albi which crosses the third highest (and perhaps most graceful) viaduct in the Massif where it meets the Viaur, and the village of Rieupeyroux. The only other towns within hailing distance of the 111 and 88 roads here are Naucelle and Tanus: these have appointed themselves the tourist centres for all these five hundred square miles of a plain with the old name of the Ségala. Heavens knows, though, there is not much to do in either but go out and look at the viaduct.

So, coming back north up all this borderland of Aveyron, crossing the eponymous river at some spot so lonely that the map marks its course by a vague wiggle (does it, one wonders, go *underground*? ... No, there would be a tourist café if it did), one comes back to habitation.

*

How green was my valley? The overtones of the phrase ring, like an amateur brass-band, as stridently in western Aveyron as in Glamorgan. The belt of green which straggles eastward on the map from the Figeac-Capdenac basin tells the same tale as the belts straggling northward from Cardiff. Here, beside unimportant rivers, were charcoal-forests for the eighteenth-century iron-masters: here, in the nineteenth, coal was exploited. And if Merthyr Tydfil is not yet paired with a French city, it should surely choose Decazeville.

For there is the same sensation of looking down from the crests to see the vents and chimneys tall, the slagtips taller, but you tallest of all. There are almost the same trains working over, each eight-hour shift, to the junction in the next valley near Aubin and Cransac where Baring-Gould gave a graphic account of spontaneously-burning mountains such as *I* have never seen. What France adds is black, brawny women who *look* as if they work hand-mills, a Nord-Simenonesque atmosphere of throbbing stoves and zinc counters aswill with cheap wine, and a far more violent contrast with the wilderness behind.

For only fifteen miles from mineral-stained, sulphurous Decazeville—and at 830 feet barely higher, though you must pass through some snaking gorges to reach it—is the village of Conques.

*

Village? Yes: Conques has barely 500 inhabitants. Today it is a

Conques, and an example of its treasure.

38

39

40

Cordes (*left*) — a dependant of Rodez, whose cathedral (see frontispiece) enshrines such monuments as this entombment (*right*).

name across the world, but that is entirely due to one building and one man. The man, rather unexpectedly, was Prosper Mérimée, one of the few great *littérateurs* to have escaped from the hothouse of the *académie* and done a job of work. Mérimée was, in fact, of the same anglo-saxon type as Chaucer, Pepys, Matthew Arnold or T S Eliot. He combined creative with administrative ability: he was quite a dutiful civil servant too.

As curator of ancient and historic monuments, or something, Mérimée did a lot of good all round. But he was at heart an Auvergnat, and his greatest work of all was discovering Conques. *Discovering*—for only a century ago this hillside hamlet was as forest-buried as an Inca temple

Conques *is* its church. Begun in the tenth century, though mostly of the twelfth, this ranks with the great basilicas of the Auvergne proper though it does not surpass them. Its starred attraction—especially at sunset—is the tympanum of the last judgment. Whether or not this is a copy of one at Toulouse, it seems to me grossly over-rated and out of proportion to the great west front. Trace out with the guidebook its iconography of heaven and hell and Charlemagne if you like. But it all remains a curiosity as historically fascinating, and as aesthetically worthless, as Alfred's Jewel. I am writing these words in Autun; and I remember little Kilpeck.

But though this detail—and perhaps the ironwork and frescoes too—has been over highly praised, the church as a church has remained almost as forgotten as it was through the centuries after warfare had swept away its convent but left the building (which is modelled, with historical cause, on the old St Martin of Tours) without scraping the paint from its capitals. I remember the towering clerestory which barely reaches the level of the mountain-road beside it; and the crossing which does; and a bird trapped in that space like the bird of Boethius, who must have been a contemporary of the first church on this site—a bird which flew for a little from darkness into light.

It is a great building in itself. It is greater in its situation, for no parish church in central France—none, perhaps, in Europe with the exception of Malvern—has such a combination of Lhasa-like site and intrinsic majesty. And it is far from negligible in its accoutrements.

*

In half the churches of France you will be asked to pay to see the

Illustrations 37, 38

treasure. Resist: it is usually very dull. But it is well worth-while in Conques, with its glittering crucifixes, its Felletin tapestries and its continuous accumulation from the ninth to the sixteenth century. And one does not have to tip a monk, however garrulous.

This is the first adjunct to the church of Ste Foy. The second is its dedication, for Ste Foy was one of the few martyrs of the plateau to achieve a wider fame. She was put to the sword by Diocletian, at the end of the fourth century and in the town of Agen away to the west, after having escaped an earlier fate by angelic intervention but after (I hope) having *not* written the smug verses attributed to her.

For five hundred years her cult thrived there, while Conques itself became a religious centre. Then a patient and ingenious monk of Conques stole (and there is no other word for it) her bones from Agen. But the martyr seemed happy in the new shrine so far from her *pays,* and by the eleventh century her miracles had acquired a european fame. Wealth showered on Conques, not least since it made a convenient relay on the road to Compostela. The cult—vulgarly called 'Ste Foy's fun and games'—spread from Bamberg to the Pyrenees and from Genoa to the Yorkshire wolds: in England alone a dozen churches were dedicated to Ste Foy of Conques, and are still to be found in such unexpected places as Havant and Newton-le-Willows.

The religious wars ended this pilgrim trade as surely as in Walsingham; and when the faith awoke again it was generally to the tinsel tawdries of Lourdes and Lisieux. There are few cities in Europe—outside Spain and perhaps Italy—with an unbroken record of devotion: but that breaking has at least left little Conques unspoiled by gimcrack souvenir stalls.

It consists today only of a few timbered streets which are picturesque and something more, an excellent inn which I am afraid to call half-vernacular lest next season it becomes wholly touristic, some rather bad wine which they are unreasonably proud of, and that church—that great church with the sparrow soaring through it from light into darkness. The Michelin guide makes a special bend to include Conques in the Auvergne. I am not going to cheat: *that* region ended fifty miles north-west. But Conques is at least wholly of the plateau—and wholly of Aveyron.

And now it is time to *look* at Aveyron.

*

More than most departments, this has a distinct personality. It arises partly from its colour (for the red spreads far inland from the Rouergue marches) and partly from its form. For Aveyron is shaped not unlike a lemon-squeezer or the crown of a chess-queen, with a high, ragged limestone centre 3,000 feet or more up, ringed by a castle-moat of lower, fertile land, with that in turn encircled by a jagged enceinte of hills whose passes are rarely much below 2,000 feet except at the sunset edge where four great rivers—Lot, Aveyron, Viaur and Tarn—escape.

This terrible rim gives to Aveyron—especially when approached from an easier land—a sense of unattainable remoteness. I remember, for instance, one journey up from the west, from the soft and rain-soaked Albigeois. As we climbed and climbed towards the departmental confines the mist deepened until one could barely distinguish the hump-backed tumuli from the thin sheep. But even there the red struck through—through from the sandstone and the inch or so of clay which covered it, through a scurf of bitten grass and scattered cabbages which would have made one feel one were in Artois had one's ears not been popping.

But at the pass (which, of course, was no pass in the geographical sense but only a road-sign at the summit) there came one of those razor-edged changes which arrive only in mountain country. The mist cleared as swiftly as a chemical solution, and below lay all the saucer of Aveyron.

One's first impression is that this is beyond dispute a southern department. The roofs of the little houses clinging to the hills above the roads are ribbed and Italianate: bead curtains cover café-doors: there are peach orchards: the local transport is orientated towards Béziers and Montpellier and Nimes rather than Clermont. There is even a soft and sunlit feel to the moat of valleys, though the heartland is *dur et pénible* enough.

*

There are a few picturesque tourist villages in the green belt beyond Decazeville, such as Salles-la-Source and Marcillac-Vallon. But once one is over the ridges and in the valleys of the south-western rim, Aveyron becomes dominated by its county capital as few departments are. This ascendancy is partly because the *préfecture* stands very close to the centre of the gravity of Aveyron, and partly through contrast with the surrounding emptiness. But I cannot explain how Rodez, the ancient capital of the Rouergue, became today's most important centre of the whole uplands. It *is* on a major road, the 88: it *does* hold a bridgehead, standing where the Aveyron becomes a river. But all this applies to a dozen other towns with more promising sites within fifty miles. Yet the fact remains that Rodez has a statistical distinction which is as striking as it is unremarked.

For Rodez has a population of some 20,000 and an altitude of over 2,000 feet—the last 400 being gained from the river-bed. It is hence the highest place of its size in France—or, if you prefer, the largest at its height. Le Puy challenges it; but no town in the Alps or the Pyrenees can do so, and all Europe has few cities so lofty and so important together. This is not a mere freak, I think, but part of Rodez's soul. Here is a place which grew great, without any outstanding industries or natural resources and simply because the High Auvergne had to have a city, however inaccessible (significantly, Rodez stands on a branch-line), which would be respected from side to side of France. In Rodez one is as conscious of the plateau-ness of the plateau as anywhere.

The outstanding memorial to the days when count and bishop vied in richness in the twin cities which were Rodez (and so squeezed out Alphonso to beget Villefranche) is the semi-fortified cathedral of Notre-Dame, given two stars if only because it is the largest and finest bit of gothic in an area not much given to medieval glories. Certainly the first sight of the lanterned church is overpowering: with its sixteenth-century red sandstone tower nearly 300 feet high it tears at the eyes—particularly at sunset—as do few greater churches. The view from the fertile western valleys or the barren crests to the east is indeed comparable only to that of some of the towering cathedrals of Europe—of St Albans from the plains or Durham from the railway, of Chartres from the Beauce, of Barcelona or Rouen when dropping down from the hills above them, or most of all (as Mrs Edwards noted) of Ely from the fens.

A little disenchantment lies in wait, for externally Rodez cathedral is an odd blend of starkness and inappropriate, even frivolous, renaissance ornament. Today, too, the belfry supports a crowning silliness in the shape of one of those many-mouthed sirens which

Illustrations 1, 40

howl noonday over the rural cities of France. But the whole building
has considerable presence and a unique form: it lies north and south,
so that the usual architectural and liturgical terms become meaningless, and is indeed two churches set back-to-back—the cathedral of
the *ville* or episcopate and the parish church of the *bourg*. The initial
impression of the noble and spacious interior is of simplicity to the
point of coldness; but late-gothic and renaissance carvings in wood
and stone are plentiful and good, if rather lost in the lofty basilican
spaces.

For the rest, Rodez is a patchwork-city. There is a norman church
of note, called St Amans, which was surprisingly-faithfully restored
in the eighteenth century. There are memories of a celebrated
murder-case, the remains of an old episcopal palace, a museum and
so many high schools that one has the sense of being in a university
city. There are some pleasant squares with fine renaissance mansions
of a comfortable size, viewpoints round the ramparts, big-town
amenities, and some rather grim manufacturing outskirts too. And,
of course, there are the usual gastronomic claims deriving from the
little Cabecou goat cheeses and white wine to the north, the pâtes
and pâtés to the east, and a lot more to the south.

Out of all this Rodez has developed a feel of her own. As the
French say of a woman who makes the most of her limited charms,
elle se porte bien.

*

All the rest of the Rouergue part of Aveyron lies essentially in two
group of towns. One is twenty miles north of Rodez along the Lot—
the river which some consider as marking the south-western edge of
the true Auvergne—and the other fifty miles south-west of it along
the Tarn. The key to the former, standing where the 121 from St
Flour comes down from the dizzy cornices, is Espalion.

This rose-red city prides itself on being a gastronomic centre: certainly its hotels are pleasant enough, and the tourists which it assiduously attracts are not likely to be disappointed in its charms. The
old hump-backed bridge (which no longer takes much traffic, since
the main road is cut right through the town on a higher level): the
timbered tanneries with their balconies along the river: the noisy
weirs and above all the renaissance palace: these blend into one of the

most charming waterfronts which anybody knows, and substantiate the claim that the Auvergne's Lot valley is as mellow as the valley of the Dordogne in Quercy.

Behind them there are some attractive streets and squares, and the old church—now disaffected in favour of a rather splendid Victorian one—has its sad interest. But the place for ecclesiologists is Espalion's suburb of Perse. There, out in the meadows beyond the brick-works, is a pink eleventh-century church distinguished by its tympanum and dedicated to the beheaded St Hilarion: it is of amazing charm and (like so many hidden churches) in an amazing state of preservation. The cypress-shaded funereal art of the graveyard, too, is worthy of some note, as is the neighbouring village of St Côme—a very satisfying spot a few miles upstream which is as utterly medieval, fortified and generally curious as a town can be.

*

The twin city to Espalion is to be found only a few miles down the Lot and the 120 road. Its tumble of red-slated houses and its ancient bridge are reminiscent of Espalion itself though it has only one individual building of real interest—now a convent but once the castle-seat of one of the greatest families of the plateau. Soldiers and statesmen, including the owners of the château of Val; bishops and builders including the bishop-builder of the lantern of Rodez; these flowed from little Estaing on the Lot for four centuries. And it may be that, despite its mild picturesqueness and rather tourist-slanted procession of St Fleuret in early July, Estaing resembles Lapalisse in being more notable as a name than as a place.

The third of this cluster is further removed. One must, indeed, pass through the gorges of the Lot—gravelly, but full-watered for this land—as far as its confluence with the Truyère and move north as well as west, back to another map sheet, to find it. When one does, it is particularly confusing to discover that it too has trim and mellow old houses, a rare thirteenth-century bridge, and a name which begins with an *E*— Entraygues, the place *entre eaux*.

Here there is not *one* building of distinction, even the castle being rather dim; but Entraygues should not be dismissed as the plain sister of the Lot valley. History and tourism have passed it by, and it is a very unexpected place indeed to find a small uranium mine. But it is the least spoiled, the most completely medieval, of the three 'E's. Also, men make good wine here—or at least they do so nearby.

North of Entraygues the Truyère mounts back savagely, turn upon turn, into the Châtaigneraie. Westward the Lot flows down, very steep and lonely and lovely, past Viellevie to Grandvabre and the turning for Conques. There is indeed only one other town—if you discount Bertholène, which has a ruined castle but is otherwise little more than a disused railway junction—which belongs to this belt of Aveyron. That is Bozouls.

The fame of Bozouls is its *trou*; and there are not many towns in the world famous for their holes. But Bozouls' is an abysmal crack in the limestone plain which is not merely spectacular in itself but conveys an eerie feeling to which a sense of medieval theology contributes more than a knowledge of geology—a feeling that the plateau is supported, as the world swims, less by mechanical factors than through the will of God. For suddenly from those smooth heights one looks down on a trivial stream as Dante looked down on the ice-pit at the foot of hell. The average depth of the southern chasms is 1,500 feet; but once they all lay *below* sea level, for the limestone plains of south-central France are relics of a vast inundation of the sea which occurred about 200 million years ago and flooded the gaps between the granite hills of the Auvergne and Cevennes—themselves more than twice as old—with what is now called the gulf of the Causses. Fifty million years ago, after the land had been gently uplifted and the shells of the sea-creatures become accreted limestone, the plain—like all central France—was cracked by the pressures of the uprising Alps and Pyrenees. And it was these cracks which became such gorges as that of Bouzols. One is more conscious here than anywhere else I know which looks up *or* down of the sense of height above sea level.

The township hangs on both sides of its horseshoe canyon: it is mostly a crumbling, tumbling confusion, but the romanesque church is notable for more than its site on a cliff's-edge, like that of an eroded east-coast village. It is fitting that here I met a sorcerer. He was advertised on the posters as a conjuror who had made a furore in Paris by turning himself into a dog; but he sat unobserved, in the corner of the pub where he was due to appear that evening, and in the haunted heat of a midday siesta he muttered what sounded very like a Black Mass.

*

An eagle flying forty miles south from Bozouls would skim over the lonely township of Pont de Salars on the 111 east of Rodez. It would cross a bleak and haunted wilderness—sometimes called the Lévezou, for the names are outlandish here—which is about 3,000 feet up and studded by dolmens and by shallow romantic lakes, reservoirs and hydro-electric accumulators like the vast Paraloup. It would see the Tarn as a narrow strip of grey or silver as the seasons changed. And if then it stilled its wings it would land not far from St Affrique.

St Affrique . . . The name shatters, summoning up all the darknesses of the Massif. Here surely (though the church is late gothic) there should be the darkest of all dark Virgins, brought back long ago by some crusader from Barbary.

It is not so, however. The colour of St Affrique is not black but red—the red of the easternmost point of the predominating rock of Aveyron. If it has any affinity with Africa it is only in its terraced look of Mediterranean heat and light. But it is in its own right a high, wide and handsome township of over 7,000 souls, sweetly set on the rolling plain which is here about to climb into a sterner continuation to the east and to ebb down to the valleys of the south. Those looking for silence and space in a wide green-grey world of cropped turf and limestone and sky might choose worse centres than St Affrique; and it is not only the fact that—though it has lost the dead-end railway which once fed it—it has surprisingly good bus services which makes it a place where I am always glad to find myself.

*

There are three dependencies on St Affrique, all along the Béziers railway which here bows west into an alien land and crosses the heights of the plateau. The northern one is called St Rome-de-Cernon, and the southern one Tournemire, and both are dominated by a sense of sound husbandry—of a decent living being scraped from this infertile land through co-operative enterprise. It is perhaps odd that in the heart of the Massif, where the French peasant tends

216

to be at his bloody-mindedest, men should have laid aside their shot-guns to get things done; but it is so, and it is sane marketing as much as quality which has given the middle of these three villages a world-wide fame.

Ask a group of gastronomes to point to Roquefort on the map and they would probably be even more disconcerted than by Dunlop (which, improbably enough, is a suburb of Glasgow). But it is here, in a little grey town just over 2,000 feet up on an edge of a country called the Cambalou, that each year 10,000 tons of ewe-cheese (culled from nearly a million sheep grazing an area which sometimes ex-tends from Spain to Corsica) come down to mature in their dark and over-fragrant cellars. Apart from a lush hotel which seems to cook everything with cheese, in fact, there is little in the steep streets of Roquefort except *caves co-opératives*. The most visited catacombs are naturally those labyrinthed out of the limestone cliffs which Pliny wondered at, in acres as low-vaulted and odorous as a malting-floor; and these recall all the traditional oddities of Roquefort-making—the brown-cloaked shepherds of old with their beehive-shaped huts mounted on carts where they could sleep secure from wolves, for instance. But the straightforward concrete cellars are quantitatively more important, if less romantic.

*

I am writing this last page in another upland of limestone caves and noble cheese. But I think it is more than that coincidence which makes me reluctant, here in an inn of the Mendip hills, to leave the little land of St Affrique. Its windy spaces—bare and lonely but never savage, a vastly enlarged version of our western downs—linger in the mind's eye as vividly as any part of the Massif. Here under the lash of an English late October I unreasonably remember the terrace of a crossroad café, as enclosed by vines as an Afghan hound's eyes with hair, where the spiders dropped *plop* into my wine. And the old lines (which, of course, put the rivers out of their geographical order) again come to mind.

'Qui croise lou Lot, lou Tarn et l'Aveyron
N'est pas ségur de torner en sa maison.'

The whole of the Rouergue, Aveyron, call it what you like, has

217

Illustration 42

been kind to me; and now that I look at the map which I have drawn to represent two lonely thirds of it, I wonder what may lie in those whitenesses away to its unexplored south. Even climatically the warmth but not the wetness of the western valleys has followed me to Roquefort, more than halfway to the medial watershed, as it has *not* followed in Cantal. And there is more of Aveyron yet. . . .

But it is higher, sterner, *different*. It is the white land, rather than the red, on to which one has already trespassed. It is one beginning to the land of the Causses.

The Desert at your Door

O f all the zones of the high plateau none has a stronger individuality and a sharper form than the Causse country. Most of it falls in the department of Lozère: all of it falls on Michelin sheet 80. Its rough outline is again an ellipse—though this time a very broad one—with its major axis only just off the meridian. Round most of its edges there are other identifiable areas and familiar rivers; and if by its nature the area has no central capital it is ringed by clear-cut frontier towns. Finally, it is sliced by one tremendous crevice known to every tourist.

Yes, one thinks, the Causses will make a tidy chapter: they have made, after all, a tidy few books. But coming on them from the north there is the usual Auvergnat *hors-d'oeuvre*, the something-in-the-way. Here it is called the Montagnes d'Aubrac.

*

The Aubracs are the southernmost, the last and the most eroded of all the volcanic hills of the Auvergne, standing a little south even of the Carladez. They are also amongst the least-known (and least-populated) of all its regions. Latitudinally they stand—like so many Auvergnat border-lands—about a join of the maps, and also about the great parallel which runs from Figeac to Montelimar. In longitude they are flanked on the west by Laguiole (a little cutlers' and cheese-making town, just south of the 121's entry into Aveyron, which has a high sixteenth-century church, likes to be called *la capitale de la montagne*, and in any case is pronounced 'Layol') and the Viadène, and to the east by the 9 road, the Béziers railway, and Aumont under the Margeride. Far to the north, the headwaters of the Truyère course round in a great bend encompassing all their

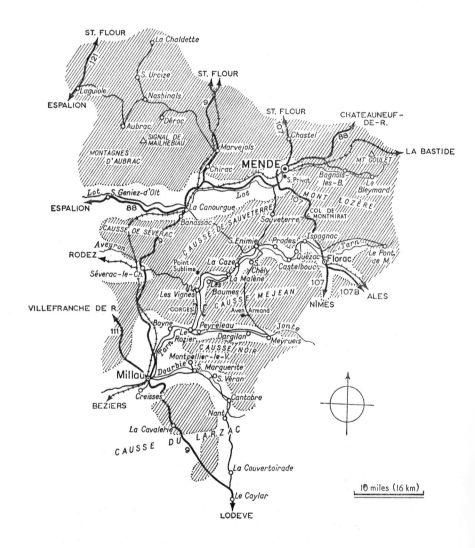

rolling semi-periphery: the Lot guards the steeper southern flank which falls sharply down from nearly 5,000 feet at the peak to the floor at a mere 1,500 feet.

Culturally, as geologically, the Aubracs belong in Cantal, though in fact only a tongue of that department thrusts down to the triple point with the other two cardinal departments of the southern Massif, Aveyron and Lozère. Here too the lava is occasionally crystallized into *orgues* but exists mainly as a skin giving a topsoil fertility to the granite: here too—despite a local pride in strawberries and fruit tarts—is essentially cattle land, and with its 50,000 beasts (20,000 of which have tuberculosis) mainly beef-cattle land, too, if on a diminishing scale. The streams run red from the proud village abattoir and the air sounds with condemned lowings which await the rattle of the captive bolt and the poleaxe's thud. It is doubtless all very hygienic, very humane and better organized than in Britain. But the Auvergne is not a happy land for those who do not share the strictly unsentimental French approach to edible life.

There *is* a village called Aubrac, 4,250 feet up in Aveyron and close to the crest of the Signal de Mailhebiau, which in all seriousness holds itself out as a tourist resort on the strength of its *spécialités de la région*, which are skim milk and potatoes. Jaded Parisians are stupid enough to think it rather chi-chi, so the place still has a station —thirty miles away—bearing its name though it can support a post-office only in the summer: it also has a few scattered remains of the age when it housed an order of monks who tended the holy wells and succoured such pilgrims to Compostela or Rocamadour as found themselves in these desolate lands. Today Nasbinals—a few miles away in Lozère and the commercial as opposed to the tourist centre—is slightly more important, especially at the beginning and end of the seasonal marches of the aestivating cattle. Like Aubrac it has a norman church (and rather an unusual one too) and like many towns in the area it was a stronghold of the freebooters. But it is hardly the place it was when a nineteenth-century faith-healer or osteopath gave it its own little hour of fame. The modern faith-healing centre is la Chaldette, *eaux tièdes*. In addition to the fishing-spots which are surprisingly numerous in the Aubracs, there are two final tourist attractions—the grotto and waterfall of Déroc, and St Urcize in Cantal whose village church with its rich treasure and furniture is a small but true romanesque marvel, a buried treasure whose chevet is the High Auvergne's sole answer to the glories of the north. But even these places are not easy to find, for few roads run through the hills.

Despite their admitted lack of variety or striking features (*ils ne sont pas sans grandeur, ni sans monotonie*, says the guide-book dryly, and they certainly do ramble on) and their air of being shut off from the neighbouring ranges, the Aubracs might afford splendid country for walkers following ancient cattle-routes and steering by the blazons and drystone walls and granite cairns. I have not tried this myself, however.

*

To the south-west these mountains of moon-silvered mists fall into Aveyron at St Geniez-d'Olt. Fifteen miles or so east and upstream of Espalion, this weaver's township and strawberry-market (twenty tons a day of them in season) straggling the river has the peculiar charm of all the Lot towns, with its old houses, its church and augustinian chapel, its pilgrimage and its monument to the wife of a pioneering PLM railwayman which gets into the guide-books. I like St Geniez, with its curiously lost feeling. But Marvejols, to the south-east (or Lozère) side of this artificial boundary, is more distinguished in itself as well as being a place which returns one to the axis of road and rail on their southward way from St Flour to Béziers across the Causses. Its feeling begins with the 3,000-foot tower of pink rock at the town's back gate.

Marvejols is the most perfectly fortified yet still-lived-in town of the Auvergne, of which it was formerly a great redoubt (and, at one time, a protestant stronghold). Three or four of its ancient gates—one of them splendid—remain, and the little place is tightly-packed within its walls with only the cattle-market spreading down to the river and ringed with drovers' taverns. There is a good hotel, where you will lie snug from the winds which beat about and there savour the town's sense of embattlement; but even if you only pass above Marvejols on the railway you will see from the curled ellipse below you that this is an uncommon place.

Despite the slowness of the aforesaid main line, which with the advantage of electricity averages about nine m.p.h., you will eventually cover five more miles south, past Chirac where in a gay moment Merle slit the throats of thirty priests, to the Lot bridge. And there, at a crossroads of the 9 and 88 roads and at a rail junction too, is the old frontier of Auvergne and Languedoc, the change from metamorphosed land to pristine limestone. This, though the place has barely a name, is one of the crucial crossroads of the plateau; for for a few miles its most important north-south, and one of its most important east-west, roads combine beside its great lateral river. And even the train picks up a little speed as if deluded that the worst is behind.

There are small things of individuality and note scattered all about. But the most important town lies to the right, to the east, twenty miles upstream. It is Mende, the *préfecture* of Lozère.

*

Lozère is named after a misty, watershed, porphyry mountain and not a river—after the highest non-volcanic mountain in all the heartland. It is one of the most artificial departments of the whole Massif even though it has a historical equivalent in the Gévaudan, the land of the Gabalis, of which too Mende was the capital. Its northern third is a heathland patchwork of the Aubracs, the Margeride and their associated ranges: westward are the bare Causses: to the east the huge single mound *called* Mont Lozère leads over to a far greener land. I am not sure, however, why it was once regarded with as much horror as the Morvan up in Burgundy, though it is certainly a confusing region where the white wines taste of unexpected things like orange or aniseed, where men begin to speak in thick Italian accents and most of my notes get lost. Certainly the Lot divides it almost arithmetically from side to side; and neatly in the middle of this its first reach, where all the Lozères meet, is the county town.

I have earlier written with less than passion about several of the small, dim *préfectures* of the plateau. Mende, with a population of about 6,000, is as small and dim as any; but it is a thoroughly pleasant, leisured and amiable place, which has quite forgotten that for eighteen months it was Merle's headquarters. Below the station, where the autorails potter to and fro between the Béziers and the Nimes arteries on the penultimate railway of its type to be built in

223

Illustration 43

France, you will find an inn with a little terrace on the Lot not far from the old bridge which has resisted so many of its floods. Even if you cannot afford some of the most genuine of the High Auvergne's gastronomic specialities, you can at least drink there, and let the sound of water mingle with the taste of wine, before you cross that steep-arched bridge and climb up amid houses with un-expectedly dutch roofs and the remains of fortifications to the one sight of Mende, its much-suffering cathedral.

Baring-Gould dismissed this place—built at the orders of Urban V, a former bishop of Mende—with contempt. But I am rather fond of it. It was almost completely rebuilt in the last of all gothic after the sack of the huguenots, and errs on the side of bleakness rather than of the expected over-elaboration apart from those flamboyant and asymmetrical towers which Mrs Edwards compared to two roses on one stem, the bloom and the stunted. Nobody could call its furnish-ings dull, for they are of excellent renaissance woodwork, Aubusson tapestries, the crypt of the local Saint Privat, a black Virgin, and fine modern glass too. Under Merle's axe what was in the seventeenth century the largest clock in Christendom disappeared, however, as well as more precious things. It is hard to see what was so particularly popish about this, but Merle was as mad as Thomas Cromwell.

There is one other thing of note about Mende—if you forget an old tower, the usual museum with some quite interesting bronze-age remains, and the village of Chastel on the 107 where Baring-Gould saw some remarkable neolithic stuff to which the modern guide-books pay no attention. This is the legend of the Beast of the Gévaudan—a dog-like monster much resembling an ass yet shaped like a pig, a beast the size of a bullock with paws like a bear, a breast like a horse, a back like a leopard yet eyes like a calf's. It wore sabots: it ate alive dozens of children and young and old women: it was stalked by 125 parishes, hunted by a company of dragoons and anathematized by the bishop of Mende: its ravages were reported from St Flour to la Bastide. Over three years of hysteria, it achieved a Europe-wide notoriety. Ten thousand *chasseurs* hunted it: the king intervened: but when at last the shooting of the beast ended the matter it was found to be quite a small wolf.

What is of particular note here is not only the strange pinewood

The nightmare loneliness of the Causse Méjean (*above*) leads over to Roquefort, where the cheeses are made (*below*).

43

44

Northern guardians of the Causses—Marvejols of the gateways (*right*) and Mende (*left*).

universality of wolf-legends and the irrationality of lycophobia, but the date 1767. By this year the steam engine was fully practical and Mongolfier had gone up in a balloon.

*

But time moves slowly in the Gévaudan, a land which never knew the norman discipline and which was throughout the twelfth century ruled from Barcelona. It no longer strikes the traveller as 'wild ... uncultivated and but recently deforested from fear of wolves' as it did RLS, but it is hard to distinguish the officially dead villages up amid the broom from those which are just snoring. One sight of the neighbourhood, however, is the chapel of the third-century martyr St Privat himself, up above the town and marked by one of the huge crucifixes which crown these ragged and wooded hills. Then upstream comes Bagnols-les-Bains—rather tautologously-named, rather absurd for all its roman pretensions and bits of legend, but with the only *téléphérique* of these parts up to its 3,000-foot peak; and above that again is le Bleymard, where there is nothing but a memory of Stevenson drinking mulled wine with the men who surveyed the railway. These towns lie on a minor road off the 88. The branch line itself climbs to a crest of this tangled watershed of the two mountains called Lozère and Goulet. Men told Stevenson that from there you could see the Mediterranean, and he did not believe them either; but certainly these heights give rise to three great rivers and feed a fourth, and the railway passes within a few miles of the sources of both the Lot and the Allier before it runs down beside the latter to la Bastide and the Nimes line.

These are about thirty miles east of Mende. West of it one returns to the crossroads south of Marvejols, and then passes on a few more miles to la Canourgue.

*

This place is of some note in itself, for it has a distinguished market-place inside and a special bit of landscape-curiosity outside. Banassac, the site of a mint for the merovingians and of a still more ancient pottery-trade, is also a place worth reflecting on whilst in this region. But just as noteworthy is its situation on the map. For here is another crossroad, where the 88 turns west again and leaves

Lozère beside the Lot on its way through St Geniez to Espalion, while the 9 continues south. The highroad has a steep knot of hairpin bends to climb as it does so, but the mound is not of great topographical significance and the railway skirts round it to join up again at Séverac-le-Château.

Probably even today not one English francophile in a hundred has heard of Séverac-le-Château in Aveyron. But it has five separate claims to fame.

The first is as a rail junction: for just as a few miles north a cross-country branch has left the Béziers line eastward for Mende and the Nîmes line, so here a longer one leaves westward for Rodez and the links to Toulouse *via* Capdenac. For this reason you see 'Séverac' on the plates of an express in the Gare d'Austerlitz: the night train out of Paris, for instance, most of which wound up in the small hours of Puy-de-Dôme, ends here as one *couchette* and two day-cars as the sun is beginning to blister its paint and the need for breakfast is becoming intolerable. For a train which has faced the central mound of the massif, the scaling of the Causses is the last straw. For the Wagons-Lits company, anyway, Christ stopped at Clermont.

Never since they gave up routing the Barcelona expresses this way has there been any pretence at running a *direct* on the Béziers line. For either Rodez or Béziers itself you entrust yourself to an unashamed local, and hence most of those who *do* know Séverac will know it only from its station. But even thence one can see the abandoned slag-tips in the hollow which mark Séverac as a worked-out mining town, an odd thing to find in these parts. And behind them, on an isolated mound shaped like a straw hat, the medieval town itself climbs up—spacious and old and charming, half-forgotten and itself half-forgetting the glory and gaiety it knew in the age of Cyrano de Bergerac—to that unusual yellow-grey gothic castle which names it, which fell into ruins only after eighteenth-century improvements, and which was the scene of an heroic *maquis* battle in 1944.

The fourth distinction of Séverac is that just south of it, from an undercliff of rock, springs the Aveyron, whose source hence *just* lies in the land of its name: the headwaters of this river are very unregarded, and very lovely. And the last is that Séverac guards the westernmost point—as Mende guards the northernmost—of the Causse country.

The 88 and 9 roads, in fact, between them define the north-western flank of this table-land. But what—at last—*what* are the Causses themselves?

*

If one believed everything one read (including chapter-titles) they would be just a monotonous limestone desert. Limestone they certainly are, on that surface where once marine creatures worked, though the cliffs disclose the underlying lias, sandstone, schist and ultimate granite: their very name means *caux*, chalk, lime. This is a land of dolomite unrelieved, sponge-permeable and so cement-white that one wonders (since sunlight cannot bleach rock) why similar strata in Britain look by comparison like the 'before' part of a detergent advertisement. But despite the fact that even in 1900 terror ruled these uplands, 'desert' is, on the whole, putting it too strongly.

For today there is not one Causse, even if—as one geological theory has it—they all derived from one in the Sauveterre region. There are five or six major Causses, and a dozen more minor ones, covering over a quarter of a million acres though supporting only three or four thousand peasants. They are divided by significant valleys (which may have begun as warm ocean-currents where coral could not build and were later deepened by glaciers) and are often quite different in aspect. Only the heartland of the two or three largest is utterly abandoned except for military manœuvres; and some of the outliers—such as the Causse de Séverac itself, which one has already crossed from the north—are no more barren or strikingly wild than (say) the Roquefort region a little to the south-west: things can get much worse in the east and the far south. But there *is* a prevailing spirit to the true Causses, where the rivers are born underground, where only the thinnest of brown and scraggy grass covers, only dwarf-cypresses, cork-oak, juniper and blackthorn sheltering in the hollows divide, only mossy tundra and lavender and herbs and thistle-patches carpet, those pebbly crests which arch between every outcrop —arid save for the *lavogne* dew-ponds and the tiny *sotchs* of arable land growing potatoes or buckwheat where a pothole has fallen in.

That barrenness is to a degree man-made, for greedy deforestation has reduced the precipitation rate to below that which the permeable rock can absorb, and has bled the soil too. Look down the glacier-sharpened cliffs which drop 500 or 1,000 feet below the plateau: the valleys are *wadis* now, dampened only by intermittent springs, but the *seigneurs* of the renaissance were more scientifically-minded than the vandals of the revolution and once these canyons carried true rivers.

But if there are few pretty flowers bar scabious and pimpernel on the Causses where winter endures for eight months, the creatures which fly above and stalk across them almost make up for the loss. I am no entomologist; but I have swept a hand through the brittle, crackling scrub above Mende and found in my palm things as strangely-shaped as a man ever put on an aqualung to see, as gaudily-striped as a jockeys' fancy-dress ball. And, finally, these uplands can smell spicy-sweet from enough herbs to fill a kitchen shelf.

The central Causses are not quite a desert. But they lack the historied feeling of the Causse de Gramat away to the west. They are the most blasted of heaths, the most wuthering of heights, the coldest of comfortless lands. Some dolmens there are; but I know of no comparable country which shows so little evidence of roman or celtic habitation, such scant witness (except on its extreme southern edge) of the living of man from the beginning of the world until a few short centuries ago. Certainly it was not until 1879, when Martel began his energetic publicity, that anyone not a Caussenard voluntarily approached these stonefields which are rather curiously called by the locals *glèbes*.

*

You must travel a little further south from Séverac, leaving to your left the Causse de Sauveterre with its village-capitol, before you find anything startling, however. And before it comes you meet first a major river—the Tarn—and then an important cross-country road—the 111—and then a great city—Millau.

A great city? Not by international, or perhaps even national, standards. Not in size; for though with 20,000 inhabitants Millau is bigger than many a *préfecture* it has the misfortune to stand in the department dwarfed by Rodez and must there take second place. Not in history; for not even the most hopeful guide-books

can say much more than this was a *cité des gants* with its traditional trade founded on the skins of the fleshless Caussenard sheep.
Not in industries; for with the revocation of the Edict of Nantes the
fleshers' skill went north and though today Millau still produces half
the gloves of all France the factories make almost as much money
from showing tourists round as in actually manufacturing these ex-
crescences. Not in art; for once you have unearthed a few crumbling
renaissance squares and houses and pottered round the usual museum
of pottery Millau's only monument is a ruined belfry from which—
so beetling is the cliff of the Causses—there is no view at all; and not
in scenery, for the place is hemmed-in and only a tributary canyon
gets a guide-book mention. But there is an *allegro* quality here which
sets Millau apart from every other township of the Massif save a
handful only—Clermont of course, le Puy, Rodez itself, and a few
others like Aurillac and St Etienne around the edges. Mrs Edwards
complained that it was a 'noisy, roistering, singing, lounging place'—
as if those southern qualities were not to be welcomed in sleepy
Aveyron.

This activity derives almost entirely from the city's situation. It
stands on the great north-south artery; and though most road and
rail traffic has by now given up the direct Béziers route as a bad job
that still counts for something. It happens to be conveniently sited as
a centre for a number of tourist attractions, so that it supports hotels
where a Belgian or a Swiss could sleep and which an Englishman
can only sigh over—hotels boasting as entertaining a choice of
menus as you will find for seventy miles. And the very bareness of
the region has made of it a garrison town—which is a plus rather
than a minus factor in France, where by tradition the girls follow
the boys. Catterick and Aldershot are places to be got out of as
quick as a whistle down Glasshouse Street: but in any town which
follows the discipline of the Army of the Republic, dark eyes com-
pete in glitter with the pin-table machines.

It is at first sight curious that the *poilu*—almost the rawest, lowest-
paid, most ill-dressed conscript in the western world, the goon-jawed
sullen boy who makes G I Joe look like a guards officer and who
needs to be told at the railway station: 'Provost marshal's office here
—*militaires*, adjust your dress'—should attract the most glamorous
camp-followers. But not all those bracingly attractive girls making

their *passeos* under the trees of Millau's graceful, semicircular square
have immoral intent, I am afraid. Some are just expressing the fact
that their town has real Mediterranean roofs and buses which after
a day's ride will take you to Narbonne: that the worst is past: that
over this city which stirs my blood rather than my heart a south
wind is blowing lemon-scent through the planes: that men *care*
about food, even though all they can offer to scent the pyre of French
cuisine is a *chèvres* called *pélardons,* a fowl-mess drenched in saffron
called *alicot,* and a horribly sweet cake called *fouasse*: that, at last,
Millau is nearer to Béziers than to Clermont—and, by being so, is
nearer to Marseilles than to Villeneuve-en-Pas-du-Tout.

*

But south of the city there are still steeps to come, of course: terrible
steeps. A tabloid example of them is to be found at Creisses, a well-
named suburb only a mile west of Millau where the church grows
out of rock, a stream cascades under the streets, and everything
smells so of the desert heights that it is a surprise to find its castle a
sophisticated folly. The real thing awaits on the 9 itself—the templars'
and hospitallers' road, the road to Compostela—which just south
of Millau makes a tremendous arrow-head bend which screams out
of the map, *argent a chevron gules,* to scale the largest of all the
Causses, the 200-square-mile Causse du Larzac.

This southernmost of these plateaux—which formerly gave to
the whole range its name meaning 'waterless'—is certainly not the
least bleak or the least typical for all its accessibility. It is a Bodmin
to the Exmoors and Dartmoors of the central Causses, which the
highway crosses for perhaps twenty-five miles at an altitude of nearly
3,000 feet with few other landmarks than military encampments
round la Cavalerie, the crossroad which leads eastward to Nant
('the garden of Aveyron', they call this splendid and remote place
which Mrs Edwards found a *'proprette,* gay, delightful townling'
where the Causses and Cévennes touch; for from the seventh century
to the seventeenth the monks of Nant fought against Saracens,
heretics, protestants and nature to build an amazing network of irri-
gation channels as well as church after church), the bump over the
abandoned railway which once led up from Roquefort, and at last,
as the land grows greener, the formerly-walled town of le Caylar.

Le Caylar is famed for its little eighteenth-century church up amid the rocks, just as its magnificently picturesque neighbour la Couvert-oirade is famed for those intact thirteenth-century ramparts which the templars built and the hospitallers ornamented. But more than that it is an indisputable frontier-town of all the highlands, and reflects in another turntable-country the situation of the Chaise-Dieu itself. For below le Caylar the main road plunges 1,750 feet in ten miles. And le Caylar itself is in Hérault . . . *Hérault*.

So one has now passed down all the western edge of the Causses —and even trespassed on to them. To define the eastern or Lozère side implies a long return, not quite to Mende but at least to the point a few miles south of it where the 107 road peels south-westward from the Lot valley, skirts the grim landslide-landscape of the Causse de Sauveterre, and brings you—after twenty steering-wheel-gripping miles over the 3,500-foot Col de Montmirat—to the Tarn again. There, on the river of Millau but near to its source on the latitude of Séverac, stands Florac.

*

The only town of Lozère except Mende with more than a thousand inhabitants (and even *it* barely makes the four figures), Florac is the *sous-préfecture*. But it has not a trace of urban feeling. A small and dusty place (though no longer 'very dirty', as Baring-Gould found it), centred on one long square of pollarded planes, this is a very quiet town indeed. It is, in fact, little more than an upland fruit-market where an aged generation predominates—a heart-town of the plateau so sleepy that ordinary tourist activities like leaving a suitcase some-where or ordering a cup of coffee at 8.30 at night become herculean tasks.

The ecclesiastical situation is interesting, with the protestant *église réformée* psalm-chanting in the centre of the place and the romanists (having abandoned their gothic templars' chapel) exiled to a very nasty building on the hillside which tries to be classical and in fact looks rather pagan. There *is* something attractive in Florac the *fleur des eaux*—a little river which escapes from under the Causses and flows through a cascade of pools where the municipality protects the trout. But it is a forgotten, backwater spot which seems to have sunk deeper in sleep since Stevenson's time and has not even capitalized on the nearby natural curiosity of one of those boulder-cities of the Causse.

Florac, in fact, would be a very forgettable place were it not for a certain indefinable oddness (there's something *fishy* about it, as well as the trout) and its situation. And this last is particularly impressive if one comes to the place at sunset from the east and sees the cliff's-edge behind it rising in one black wall to the flat table-land of the Causse Méjean against a green or golden sky.

The 107 itself continues south from Florac. A more important road—rather oddly numbered 107b—leaves south-westward, and beside this runs the narrow-gauge railway (one of the only three ever built in the southern Massif, all of which survive) which gives the town its most reliable, as well as its most remarkable, connection with the outer world. And north-east the narrowing Tarn doubles back past le Pont de Montvert.

Do not pass through this place too soon, little though it has to show. For it is a potent frontier. East and west of it lie great but different hills: southward the land is a single shelf which belonged historically to the Languedoc and bears its brand to this day. Stevenson noted, and a man may still note, the first beautiful women and the first quick-witted men south of le Puy at le Pont de Montvert —and in one day's ride the change from a passive to an active concept of the sabbath. North even of Millau, the village stands at the extreme tip of the most ineradicable frontier of christendom.

But christendom was once a bitterly divided place; and though the thing started in the Dauphiné and Champagne it was among this 'undecipherable labyrinth' of hills that the last and bitterest act of the wars of religion was played out under Louis XIV at the close of the seventeenth century—so late in time, indeed, that the first Cevenol factories of the industrial revolution were still fortified against raids as if they were medieval churches. The protestants—called chemisards or camisards—were a superstitious and credulous enough crowd, witch-burners and firers of grains of corn from their muskets, believers in babes and epileptics; but they had the excuse of a particularly savage roman and Sanflorentine persecution along their marches. They were beastly, treacherous and mercenary people who betrayed their colleagues, roasted catholic infants over slow fires, had no faith but hatred and a vague dedication to the Holy

232

Ghost, and blooded their own children in the human gore of the 'philistines'; but they were ingenious people at living off the land, and as brave as men come as they shouted their fallible charm— '*Tartara*—from Lozère to the sea, let Israel come.'

Their tall and toothless leader, Séguier the Mower, Séguier of the Holy Spirit (who, asked his domicile by a magistrate, replied 'late of the desert, shortly of paradise') was as mad and bloody and hysterical as a man can be; but he was a bearded romantic soul, and almost a cavalier by Merle's mean standards. And his host was competent and organized, trusting in William III as in an archangel since ignorant of the fact that he had his own spiritual shenanigans to cope with three seas away. London sympathisers even promised to send a fleet to the camisards' aid—which was not quite as quixotic as it at first sounds, for you are only two days' march from the sea at le Pont and the easy-going Languedoc would probably have let a task force pass. It *could* have happened. But could the six departments have become the Six Counties, Alès Belfast, and orange a holy colour in the high Cevennes?

The little massacres, the tortures and blood-lettings of brave, passionate, deluded men—and even more of the innocent—had a frenzy which rivalled that of a New England witch-hunt or (as Stevenson noted, passing that way only two lifetimes later) of a Scots religious raid. The full history has been related often and well, and hence there seems no point in repeating it here—especially as nothing came of the whole unedifying matter which redounds to either the glory of God or the dignity of man. The battles of the Cevennes ended, like most battles of faith, in weary compromise; and when the camisards' last and bloodiest commander lay dying as governor of Jersey he confessed that there was not much behind it all save a hunger for English beef and ale. Perhaps the gallantry of the *maquis* of the Cevennes is more worthy of commemoration, for all its small effect on history, than these ancient and obscene atrocities. But the clash of faiths has done more to shape the land. And in le Pont de Montvert —as all the way from Florac across the frontier into Gard and halfway to the sea—the *Old Hundredth* still sounds as loud as the *Salve Regina.*

*

233

For all the historic interest of this arbor of cultures there is a sense at Florac of things escaping like the crashing waters of the southern rim of the plateau—escaping from that great *mesa* of the Causse Méjean which presses down from the west, fifteen miles wide, twenty long and an even 4,000 feet above the sea. Only by-roads run round its south-eastern flank, curving back through tiny but striking villages to Nant again (whose name *is* simply the celtic for 'valley', as you will find it in Brittany and Wales), under the small Causse Noir, and so at last to the 9 highroad.

These lines define the Causses. But what of the Causses themselves, the area between all these boundary-corridors? For the tourist there is only one answer. The Causses are the heights which are cracked by the Tarn gorges.

For fifty miles from Florac south-west to Millau a road snakes back between the Causses. It is a minor road, a narrow yellow road; but in summer it might be a trunk from London to the south coast as the coaches brush terrifyingly past. For this is not a route for the nervous. A friend of mine was conducted down the gorge in an English charabanc *en route* for Lourdes, the wrong side of the road for a right-hand-drive vehicle and with an inexperienced driver. He scraped the rock at a bend, braked hard, got out to inspect the damage—and found his front offside wheel two inches from the precipice edge. His pious passengers then knelt to give thanks that their pilgrimage was organized by the Friends of St Christopher . . .

The eighteenth century would have found the place horrid. But in fact only a hundred years ago the area was unrecognized by French geographers and an English tourist in Avignon, asking for the Causses received the perplexed reply 'l'Ecosse . . . ?' In the late nineteenth it became romantic and worth a diligence: 'sublime and quaint', 'great beauty and savagery' were some of the descriptions of that era. In the twentieth, since Martel made countless million francs for France by establishing an Auvergnat tourist industry, it is a *must* for the unvertiginous. The Gorges du Tarn christen a standard guide for the whole southern plateau. It is as simple as that.

*

I think that the fame is justified. There are many ravines, defiles, individual features of the type which the Victorian explorer-tourists

234

Illustration 36

loved to call canyons, and all the rest, more impressive from one or two viewpoints. But only beside the Tarn does the splendour last for two hours, as the road follows the right or north bank of the river—climbing and falling with the cornices, tunnelled-out for scenic as well as for engineering reasons, but never changing sides as the river winds on without accepting one visible tributary—though fed by forty buried ones.

And all along its valley (V-shaped in the clay, vertical-walled in the limestone) are strung those tourist villages where you can hire a canoe at an exorbitant rate or stare up at the floodlit set-pieces. From the Florac end these run; Ispagnac in its fruit-fertile basin (which likes to be called the garden of Lozère), where Merle lowered his cannon, with forty oxen taking the strain, in an attempt to seize the valley; Quézac with its ass-back bridge and pretty pilgrimage church up in the hills; Ste Enimie, the capital of the valley (and now not at all the cesspit which appalled Baring-Gould) which boasts its one sophisticated building in the shape of a ruined seventeenth-century monastery; little Italianate la Caze whose château (now a *luxe* hotel) was once inhabited by eight sisters all so beautiful that no suitor who got to the place could decide which to woo; la Malène, where the aforesaid Merle failed to get the aforesaid cannon out again, and which was so assaulted at the revolution that you still see on the cliffs the smoke-marks of its 'black hole'; Point Sublime, with the finest view of all; les Vignes where they grow the vines and le Rozier, the gracious village where the valley opens, where they turn them into a surprisingly good brew; Peyreleau whose fame is that its marquis worked after the revolution as a London chef while the local peasants sacked his manor for the treasure which his own ancestors had looted; and at last, over into Aveyron, Boyne.

These are the better-famed spots. But there are other notable villages in the valley or just off it like St Chély with its church and *orgues*, or Prades where Merle at last accepted defeat. There are the cave-dwellings and rocks like les Baumes with its amphitheatre round the hermitage where St Ilerius and Ste Enimie (herself a lovely princess stricken by leprosy if she tried to leave the gorge) chased the devil disguised as a mouse and smashed him with the mountain-fall dismissed as a mere earthquake by Gregory of Tours; the isolated castles like strange Castelbouc with its erotic legend, and all the abandoned sites of saints and brigands. The guide-book in your shaking hand will tell you where to find all these—and will tell you for the length of just how many stars you should look at them. They recommend picnic spots as well.

But when the eyes begin to dazzle with the ever-changing contortions of limestone and dolomite 1,500 feet or more above, with the contrasting contours and the clashing streaks of mineral colours, lie down by the water in a broad *planiol* carpeted with blue pimpernels and maidenhair fern, or by a rustling rapid, and rest your vision on the coolness which runs there. There is the kingfisher or peacock blue-green of the river itself (for *that*, after all, is what the gorges are all about), and the changing colour of deciduous trees against dark conifers. Somewhere a cat will be sunning itself, a peasant cultivating his few poor vines or almond-trees, an old woman drawing water. Somehow, even in the valley of the Tarn, peace persists.

*

The attraction of this small area, furthermore, is not restricted to the places which lie within a few kilometres of the main watercourse; for two of its tributary valleys are of note. One is that of the Jonte, where the grottoes of Dargilan open from the hillside: at the combe-head here, close to the end of the department and the beginning of the Cevennes, is Meyrueis with its octagonal protestant chapel and lovely castle nearby. The other gorge is the Dourbie's; and *there* the places to note are the startling village of Cantobre (*quelle œuvre!*), St Véran, and Ste Marguerite. But most people found in this area— another one of turntables and triple points—will be travelling over fiendish roads in search of Montpellier-le-Vieux.

Up in the Causse Noir east of Millau, this is the most famous of those fantastic dispositions of Doré-like dolomitic stones called *chaos ruiniformes*, two square miles described in the handouts as 'whimsical' though the peasants who gave the place its name had more reverence, believing this in truth to be a fossilized city of giants. Mrs Edwards found it 'eerie and awesome', but admired its upland flowers. She also feared that within a generation or two it would boast that proudest fruit of progress, a steam tram. But this wild and haunting landscape is still very remote. And its farmhouse-café still leaves much to be desired.

Aven Armand

The most famous site of all, however, is Aven Armand. *Aven*—cognate with 'abyss'—means 'pothole'; and you will find the term, amongst others harder to translate, all across the whiteness of the southern plateau where the map leaves room for it. Limestone country everywhere in the world is riddled underfoot with linked caverns—dating geologically from the secondary jurassic period—where water has flowed or is still flowing: it eats away the stone and drips through crevices to lower chambers where its minerals crystallize into hanging or standing accretions which change their form down the millennia with the shifting of the earth and become stained with iron and encrusted with lichens. But the Massif and its western foothills are particularly rich in them, particularly those of the pothole type which swallowed many an unwary shepherd on a misty night or served as suicide-instruments for Caussenards sick of life but unable to find enough water to drown a rat, let alone a man: a solid (or, if you prefer, a hollow) crescent of them extends from the Rhone two-thirds of the way to the Atlantic. And out of the countless 'avens' on the map some dozen—mostly in the Dordogne undercliff, but with two or three highland specimens—have been systematically explored.

Their sponsors would say *scientifically* explored; but it is very disputable if there is any scientific reason at all to grub below the Causses. In the western foothills, where the caves open from hillsides, you may find a Lascaux and have in wonder to rewrite the history of mankind; but no explored cave of the high plateau was ever inhabited, nor is there any new principle of geology which they can illuminate. Their attraction is to men's pure curiosity—to learn what lies over the hill or, in this case, what is blocked-off by that boulder in a chamber 300 feet high and 300 feet more below the earth.

But speleology is an expensive hobby: it can demand draglines and dynamite to follow your nose. Smartly, the French authorities subsidized their subterranean enthusiasts, who replied by furnishing a brand-new tourist attraction in the part of France which most needed one. *Les recherches continuent*, with a fervour reminiscent of a Texan digging for oil, and any season now some lonely pothole in the limestone desert may blossom with cafés, souvenir stalls and car-parks. Meanwhile, Aven Armand—with a single hall as large as Notre-Dame—is one of its few three-star specimens.

237

How can one evaluate such things? Much though all buried things excite me, I am revolted by the conducted party, the 5s ticket, the crocodile shuffling up and down cement stairs, the compulsory group photograph taken by flashlight, the corny jokes in those majestic halls of translucent, curtained stone and the guide who, despite his behests, I contrive to forget. I remember prowling illicitly through the Hell Fire Caves of Wycombe before they were opened, and the grottoes of County Galway where an old woman gives you a torch and a 'Sure, you finds your own way.' But, in fairnesss, the Auvergne provides this kind of cave too for the adventurous. And the majesty of a place like Aven Armand—which *does* demand floodlights and access stairs—is to Wookey Hole like a Drury Lane musical to a provincial panto.

Theatrical, contrived, artificial as they may be, one at least of these many-chambered grottoes should be seen. It will afford a unique spatial experience even if the man cannot grasp its time-scale. It will assault the eye with forms which it is hard to remember were always lifeless, even if it leaves the imagination unmoved. And if after it all your vote goes to nature unadorned, the great Causses still spread above your head—spread where the wind sings through the small grasses, a peasant goes gathering snails, and the streams begin which fill two seas.

Travels without a Donkey

We all know about the Cevennes, a region which has recently become so familiar to the British that the accent is usually dropped. They must be where Stevenson travelled. They must be where the Réseau de Vivarais used to run a train called *La Flèche des Cévennes* and the SNCF now runs the vista-domed *Cévenol*. They must be where the map says CÉVENNES.

In fact all these definitions are thoroughly misleading, and according to one authority you can use the word anywhere on the south-eastern edge of the plateau from St Etienne across the Velay and Causses and almost to the Pyrenees. But before one opens map sheet 80—on which all the true Cevennes, like all the true Causses, lie—there is once again a little approach-belt trespassing on No 76. It lies along and to the south of the 102 road; and this branches off the 88 south of Le Puy, swings round at Pradelles north of Langogne, and then heads straightly south-west for fifty miles across the waist of Ardèche. It was part of the Roman highway from Clermont to Nimes, and even today has an aura different from that of any other road I know.

*

As soon as it enters Ardèche at about 4,000 feet you will be invited to visit the Auberge de Peyrebeilhe, and I suppose you had better do so. A low-eaved hillside building of stone, for which 'rude' is about the best word, is almost the only hostelry in France with any legend or historic association—for it was here, *circa* 1800, that a series of memorable, Sweeny-Todd-like murders-for-trade were executed until their perpetrator was himself guillotined outside. Baring-Gould tells the unedifying story excellently, noting such details as that Haussmann (then *sous-préfet* of Yssingeaux) was almost murdered here—

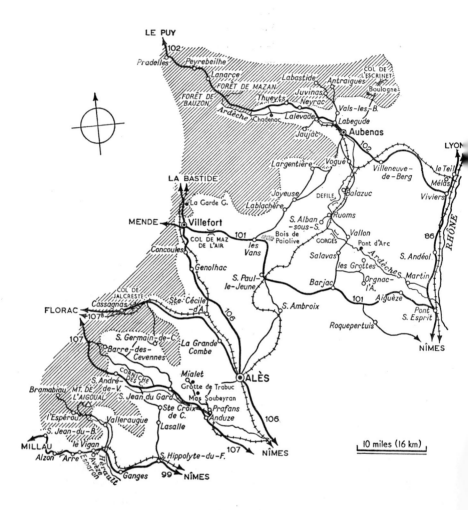

45

Two townships of Ardèche—Vogué (*above*) and les Vans (*below*) with
its typical protestant church.

46

47

The green Cevennes (*above*) contrast with the bleached submarine
landscape of the Bois de Paiolive (*below*).

48

an event which, had it materialized, would have left France a prettier land—and such generalities as the pusillanimity of French peasants and magistrates, which have not changed much in fifty years.

There is not the tiniest bloodstain to see there today as a result of more than sixty murders, though they will take your money and fill your imagination. Furthermore the place is not an inn in the sense that the *Ostrich* at Colnbrook is, for it is easier to buy a tawdry trinket than a drink today. But its like still serve as taverns hereabouts, and recall the days when travelling the plateau (and above all entering a warm parlour out of snowdrifts) was a more uncertain experience than now, when the *Auberge* is thrown in as a makeweight on the Le Puy tourist circuits.

The road heads on, surprisingly direct considering the contours and at times indeed giving the effect of a Roman wall on the march, through the village of Lanarce and a number of others pinned tightly against it. There are many streams too, of which one is the Ardèche itself rising halfway down the department which it names: the Loire is just over the left-hand shoulder, south of its source. It is a tangled country all about, this of the forests of Mazan and Bauzon, and one which I would like to walk or ride at leisure based on some inn in Thueyts. For the map promises castles like Chadenac, abbeys, and curiosities such as the local Giant's Causeway. But only a pony (or Shanks's) would get you about, for there are no side-roads or even tracks off the fifteen or so descending miles of the highway.

No roads . . . But, as the map and the country assume a deeper green beside the young Ardèche, superb scenery opens on either side. Serrated ridges, fingering up between the chestnut-valleys of the tributaries to the south, change their texture but preserve their form as the sun wheels round from the Rhone to the Cevennes or sets in the Margeride. The road never quite takes one's breath away; but it is never dull or ignoble.

Silliness enters in at about 1,000 feet: the silliness of spas.

*

Lalevade: Vals-les-Bains: Aubenas: these stand tightly contiguous where the Ardèche becomes a real river. They are touristy, hypochondriacal towns with a joint resident population of nearly 15,000 (which is phenomenal for Ardèche) such as one has not met since Puy-de-

Dôme. They even have their own satellites, like prettily-named volcanic Jaujac up a pretty valley, Labegude, and Neyrac. Lalevade is easily dismissed: it is the highest, most straggling of the chain, the railhead for which the ill-fated le Monastier line was heading, but nothing more: even industries assiduously planted in the nineteenth century never took roots hereabouts. Vals (dismissed by Baring-Gould as an ugly worm in a hole) is a typical spa, catering for a range of infirmities of the digestive system: beyond its hotels and hydros are the less profitable heights, tributary valleys, and places called Labastide, Juvinas and Antraigues (the site of a procession to a very dubious saint) which are somehow recommended. But Aubenas is a real town with two curious churches, the remains of a castle which was once a prize in Mediterranean sea war, and a sense of being *something*, if only a centre of silk spinning.

Perhaps this is because, on its lower level, it is another guardian of the steeps. From its terraces you can look south along the departing Ardèche or east towards the noble Col de l'Escrinet 2,500 feet up above Privas, the rambling, half-forgotten castle called Boulogne, Villeneuve-de-Berg and the church of Mélas. You can reflect on the odd coincidences which link this small but spectacular corner with Puy-de-Dôme, not merely in its random volcanic soil with the concomitants of spas and other oddities, but with the Ventadours of (remember?) Ussel. And maybe you will see the Rhone at le Teil.

Le Teil however, features only on the railway timetables as a junction through which certain trans-Rhone local trains are routed. Viviers just below it is not only notable in itself with its towered, romanesque church (which was once the cathedral of a see which *may* have named the Vivarais) and its *sympathique* old quarter below the castle on the craggy yellow hill, but repeats on a still greater scale the effect of Serrières and Lavoûte and Tournon. I am surprised that Baring-Gould dismissed it as 'the deadest of dead cities', for it does not get into the *Guide Provence* for nothing.

But here, on the 80 map, the Rhone has ceased to be a valley and become a plain, with the most fertile land on the right bank now. St Andéol, next south, is virtually a Mediterranean town with a southern church; and even its shoulder-satellites like the two St Martins at the last steep reach of the Ardèche, barely belong with this book.

That river meets the Rhone: the department ends with it above Italianate Pont St Esprit on the 86, a gateway of the *routiers* into the highlands: and inland the Cevennes await, sibilant with bats.

*

But just *where* they await is—as I have suggested—a subject which we could all argue about for a book or two. Stevenson himself claimed that all his route lay loosely in the roman Cebennae, but had to admit that only its last part belonged in those hills as they were locally understood—in the 'Cévennes with an emphasis, the Cévennes of the Cévennes'. On my reckoning his 120 miles' tramp fell into three equal parts of which the first was spent in Velay, the second in the Causses country, and only the last third in the hills of his title.

Even so, a glance at the 80 map shows that these Cebennae are really there. They are, indeed, vividly there, a waving vastness of emerald between white deserts with almost as sharp a frontier as if they were a country coloured for contrast in a political atlas. And neither this symbolism nor the local name of the '*Cévennes vertes*' is misleading. Their underlying geology is the limestone and schist of all south-eastern France, but these hills slope to the Mediterranean sun and are clad with walnut and holm-oak and juniper and above all the noble Spanish chestnut—the bread-tree of the Cevennes—on the heights: they are also sweet with orchards so low down on the valley floors that their apple-crops must be drawn up on aerial ropeways.

There is a cultural homogeneity here too. Two centuries ago the Cevennes were the most passionately protestant part of France, with their uncountable crests and valleys providing hide-outs for the psalm-chanting fanatics of Séguier and his fellow-leaders. In Stevenson's time the reformed still outnumbered the unreformed church by five or ten to one, with a number of odd results. (One was that the region exported a flow of young ladies uncontaminated by Rome as governesses to Victorian England, so that today's Cevenols are almost as aware of our existence as are the Normans.) Modern indifference has brought something of a returning, Vaticanwards swing, but you will still find, scattered through these villages, not merely the temples of the *église réformée* but the meeting-houses of such curious enthusiasts as Jehovah's Witnesses and Moravians. And your country bus may well be invaded by a very different army from that of the pillaging Camisards—Salvationists, crusading only with sounding brass.

A more modern characteristic of the Cevennes is that in valley after valley coal and industry have broken in between the heights reafforested by the pioneering Fabre. At times—again on map and land together—the green is replaced by black. But this change has at least accentuated three traditional characteristics of the area. It was always one of the most populous parts of the plateau: now, with its industries, it can count three or four times as many heads to the hectare as surrounding lands. It was always one of their most sophisticated parts: now gastronomy has broken in, with all the top-level silliness of trying to make regional something which is universal but with a bracing effect on day-to-day meals too. It was always one of their most Latin parts: now Italians seeking work bring a new demand for *pasta* and liver-sausage to the shops. At the taverns where men change buses (and there are plenty of buses here, it *is* a Mediterranean land) I have helped these exiles to order their wine, an experience which always gives the Saxon a splendidly inflated sense of his linguistic ability.

One more thing distinguishes the region. It is a traditional resort of honeymoon—and pre-honeymoon—couples. This is something to do with the mushrooms, which for erotic purposes count as etchings. Come the fungus season, the Paris funnies carry whole pages of cartoons which make it clear that more than *cueillure* goes on amid the chestnuts.

With all these features the green Cevennes should be easy enough to outline, even though the name is certainly known to far more people than have set foot there. But in fact they are a wild muddle of middling-high *serres* of hills and valleys with not one clear river or watershed or political frontier or even contour to act as a guide-rope through their knotted sylvan slopes. After long nights of staring I think I shall delimit the Cevennes as a cigar dropped slantwise on the map, burning into ash at its southern end but with its band left on. I doubt if this definition will help anyone. But at least it makes the point that the Cevennes have two halves.

*

Down the west side of their northern part drops the railway from la Bastide. There is no valley here to guide it (and the narrow 106 road) through on the last lap towards Nimes, though the border of Lozère and Ardèche roughly parallels it until a tongue comes up from the Mediterranean department of Gard. It is simply a chain of cuttings, a necklace of high tunnels with just a glimpse of the tower of the stronghold of la Garde Guérin until some kind of foothold is gained at Villefort.

The names ring. Villefort looks just a pleasant, quiet place with good hotels to beguile anyone driving south along this serpentine way. It will tell you about its old bridge down in the deep gorges, and its local, spectacular valley. But it was not always thus: it is not called a stronghold of the Cevennes for nothing.

There is a tourist village a few miles further on, Concoules, 3,000 feet up but the first town in Gard and looking like it with its oleander trees. There is another real town as far again south at Génolhac: prettily contoured, surrounded by dark ridges of pine and with several rather romantic castles of the Camisards in easy reach, a man might find this a good place to linger in.

Nobody, perhaps, would want to linger in the last town of this corridor, la Grande Combe. Almost a lowland town, it stands on the great carboniferous crescent which curls round the undercliff of the plateau from Limoges to Grenoble. The gas-mains spanning the descending roads, the pit-head gear, the silver skips of ropeways soaring up to slag-tips amid the pines, the Manchester voices—need one leave Ebbw Vale to find this? Perhaps so. Miners drink wine under trailing vines in the station court here. The centre of the town is clean and seemly. And it may be that a long stay would discover some lively secret in the Great Combe unknown to the green valleys above.

*

Slanting into la Grande Combe over yellow roads comes the other edge of the northern Cevennes—the edge which begins, perhaps forty miles north as the road runs but little more than half that in a bee-line, at Largentière in Ardèche. Spacious, with old houses, a good gothic church and a remarkable clock, Largentière is worth more note. I am rather glad it has not received it: it is an unspoiled spot.

South of it, Joyeuse—like Allègre—long haunted me with its

name. I knew, of course, that it would not be very joyful when I
eventually found it; but there is certainly nothing wrong with it or
its castle. A good dry spot, it seems to have been the provenance of a
leading catholic admiral; for—like Allègre again—it was a ducal
stronghold which christened a great family. Les Vans is even better.
Trim and pleasant and lost, with a humble inn worthy of more
note and a dizzy track over the pass of Maz de l'Air leading back to
Villefort, it smells of bonfires and has an abandoned tramway station. It is a place after my own heart, is les Vans; for not even the
usual two-star valley brings many people to this side of the Cevennes.

St Paul-le-Jeune has a hotel. Then, in Gard, St Ambroix brings
you back to the coal valleys.

*

It brings you back, too, to that cigar-band of the range. And if in
the east this is industrialized, the west which lies beyond the railway
and the border of Lozère is as lonely a zone as you will find.

RLS entered the Cevennes along it. But the 107b road was not
built then; and the narrow-gauge line from Florac (which will, I
suppose, soon be abandoned, for all its staggering viaducts and
recently-improved service and fine approach to the wild hillside junction of Ste Cécile-d'Andorge) was not even dreamed of. The Col de
Jalcreste, dividing the Atlantic from the Mediterranean, was just
another watershed between trickles so trivial and numerous that men
could not be bothered to think up individual names for them and
simply christened them a Tarn*on*, a Gard*on*, and so forth. And
Cassagnas, now a main-road village, was still amazed at its first
wheeled traffic, still remembering the days when its only catholic
inhabitant was an unfrocked priest living in sin.

Stevenson passed, below gate-holding Barre-des-Cévennes where
the inland sea flickers into sight as it did for the romans on their
highway, to St Germain-de-Calberte; and there he marvelled at the
fact that it took seventeen days to take a census of this scattered cantonment of a few hundred houses, and remembered the legend
(which may well be a lie, since told by the other side) of the priest
who exhorted his tiny flock to be as resolute as the catholic leader who
had just been stabbed to death with 250 wounds, one from each re-
former, until in mid-sermon the news came that the protestants were

246

Illustration 46

at the door and all concerned fled to the safer lowlands. Baring-Gould, after him, noted the caverns where the camisards scraped saltpetre from the walls to make their gunpowder. But at last both for the last forty years has been spelt Alès but is still pronounced Alais.

*

Alès is about 1,000 feet up. It has nearly 40,000 inhabitants and a cathedral not quite as contemptible as it is usually cited as being. It is one of the cardinal towns guarding the plateau, as its great walls witness. It marks the end of all the troubles of the Nimes railway, 100 miles and 100 tunnels and 50 viaducts south of Brioude. Its historical distinction is that it was here in 1629 that the main wars of religion ended in an exhausted tolerance. Its job used to be silk ribbons and silver mining and is now general ironmongery. Out of it branch the roads and railways of the plains. Apart from this it is tidy, seemly—and about as dull a thing as can be stamped out of stone. But still, Alès *does* hold this great band; and whilst the Cevennes above it lie on a north-south axis the other limb of the cigar (which is, perhaps, a little bent) runs nearer east and west.

Along the northern crest of this westward surge, which marks the break between Lozère and another promontory of Gard, runs a hill-top track some 2,500 feet up which they call the Corniche des Cévennes and which may be a pre-roman highway: another Gardon river and a secondary road pass through a chain of resorts here after a memorable entry at Anduze, which still has the air of the great protestant stronghold which it was in the early seventeenth century.

This is a green and pretty town which challenged Alès in importance before Alès discovered coal and Anduze had to make do with sausages. It is also one which I wish I knew far better. I have passed often through its street of round towers and on upstream through the portal of the Cevennes—a Scylla and Charybdis of great rocks which guard it, limestone rocks with their strata bared like the diagrams of syncline and anticline in a geology text-book. It has always struck me, for all that it stands a bare 500 feet above the sea, as one of the most dramatic gateways of the plateau. But I have never climbed above Anduze to investigate its two extraordinary curiosities.

First there is a forest of giant bamboos (borrowed whenever the

247

Illustration 49

French cinema wants to go on location in the tropics) at a village called Prafrance; and then, further north, a *musée du désert*. Whatever have either bamboos or deserts to do with the chestnut-green Cevennes, one asks at first. But in fact here, some ten miles from Anduze, is a savage enough land and one which sheltered many protestants in the second phase of the wars of religion—men such as Roland, last of the camisards, who is especially commemorated here at the Mas Soubeyran with its curious holy place of dissent dedicated to the 'martyrs of the desert'.

St Jean-du-Gard, up past the castle which looks down on this cyclopean gate, is more ordinary. Its narrow dusty streets seem quite busy and its girls are pretty; but even RLS, selling Modestine here before making haste to Alès and all the world of banks and *postes restantes* and main-line stations (for even the loneliest voyage must come back to such things), found nothing to record of this place under the hills. There is an old bridge, and the railhead of an almost disused railway, but not much else, here as you climb into those most eastern Cevennes where there were wolves a mere half century back—harmless beasts, exterminated for superstitious reasons, which would now be a tourist-bait. In their absence, you may be attracted by the Grotto of Trabuc near Mialet. Large, but not very exciting visually, this was a prehistoric and camisard refuge. It has recently been re-opened thanks to the efforts of the coal-miners of Alès—not, one would have thought, the most likely men to choose a hobby in a world hidden from the sun.

The routes here on the north side of the southern Cevennes are numerous. Ste Croix-de-Caderle, l'Espérou, Lasalle, and that impossibly high Valleraugue of the 4,000 steps on the tumbling young Hérault river—all provide their facilities for silkworm-spotting, ski-ing, mushroom-picking and allied pleasures. But my own favourite is St André-de-Valborgne, high up in sunless gorges and pinched along a road which owes more to gelignite than geology. Here steps climb through narrow arches into a photographers' dream of slanting, smoky light, and horses stand tethered to 'No Parking' boards beside the 107 road.

From any of these resorts you may climb by motor-road to the crow's nest of all the Cevennes, the weather observatory more than 5,000 feet up on the replanted granite massif called Mt Aigoual—

248

Illustration 47

a name derived from *aqua*, for it is a great mist-gatherer and water-shed. This looks east to the Alps, west over the source of the Hérault river and the village of Bramabiau with its buried river, to the bridge of St Jean-du-Bruel at a green and fertile edge of Aveyron and to the white Causses beyond. It also looks, they say, at last upon the Pyrenees, and so extends a view spreading from Switzerland to Spain.

But the lower edge of this lurching thrust of Gard, where three climates battle in the skies and shred them to mares-tails, has its own attractions. Ganges, perhaps, has only some very minor gorges and the memory of an 'orrible murder to offer. But it is a prosperous-looking place ('bright with good inns', said Baring-Gould tersely), and the centre of the French nylon-spinning which is succeeding the moribund sericulture which was not long ago the life-blood of the Cevennes and which offered the great Pasteur one of the most brilliant and dramatic of his Holmesian deductions with the microscope.

One of those strange international coincidences to be found here by anyone who knows South Wales particularly intrigues me, as I write this page in the county of (almost) my name. For if Ganges is the French Pontypool, le Vigan is its Abergavenny—the sub-country town of a frontier land where sheep wander half-wild through the streets and where white heights lead down to dense green valleys scored by heavy and light industries, to a littoral plain, and thence to an enclosed sea.

It is a big, comfortable, well-situated but sad and unregarded place. 'You want a *room*?' they ask in the hotels of le Vigan. 'But we weren't expecting you.' Across the chestnut-shaded square and the buried holy spring of Isis, *portes-cochères* open on hay-littered coaching yards and the water runs down to a norman bridge; and here is the most perfect example I know in the whole of provincial France of an Edwardian brasserie. As *typique*, if not as cosy, as a London mews pub, it is all marble and gilt caryatids, dusty and ill-lit because few beckon the last, old, white-coated waiter who stands confronting the neon and juke boxes of rival establishments—as if sericulture had been more than a short-lived Victorian attempt to capitalize on this tragic land, as if still hearing the voices of the mill-girls. Even those are hardly gay, though; for le Vigan's glory ended when it had given two heroes to the *chasseurs d'Auvergne*, and its prosperity died with the age of silk or even of coaching. It has cleaned itself up since

Mrs Edwards' time, but it has certainly not fulfilled her prophecy that it would become a metropolis.

Once again, I commend it to those who love passé, period towns living between two worlds. Is there a French Betjeman to essay them before some new plastics works drags them by their greying hairs into the twentieth century?

*

Le Vigan has still a local rail service to Alès, which is nearly fifty miles east as the line runs. But symbolically the tracks which were not yet laid when Mrs Edwards travelled the region in the 'eighties are now abandoned west of it, where the old Midi company once took over from the PLM to run on, through Avèze and Esparon and the dyeworks village of Arre and a 2,500-foot pass to Alzon, and so through again to Aveyron, the southern Causses, and at last Roquefort far away on the Béziers line. And though the green hills slope northward and eastward from here right round to Alès and the Gard they are low and gentle things with no more of those doubled and redoubled lane-passes, knotted like the bindweed underfoot, which characterize the high Cevennes. To find highlands again one must return almost to the Ardèche spas and explore the land which stretches between them and the departmental boundary, between Joyeuse and the Rhone.

This outlying country of the Cevennes is the last of all the regions of the south-eastern plateau. It is as strange, and to my mind as noble, a region as any.

*

Inland of le Teil, near a castled and historic Ardèche-side town with the elegant name of Vogué, a branch railway peels off the spur to Lalevade and enters upon one of the strangest journeys in France. The train—probably a railcar followed by one cast-off coach with blistered paint and its blinds permanently down—grinds over light and rusted rails with a Spanish disregard for speed and punctuality—one which may not behove the SNCF but which does befit this seared Iberian land which lies either side of the department-naming river. The line narrowly misses the two sights of the valley, which are a wildly-situated village called Balazuc and the so-called

250

Illustration 45

Ruoms defile—a long, spectacular gallery blasted to take the by-road above the brown and green stream. But it *does* hit Ruoms itself, the capital of this limestone land which geologically belongs with the Causses even though the Cevennes have thrust themselves between.

It is a small town, Ruoms; but you see its name upon café-blinds even up to Clermont. For Ruoms, as well as having the remains of its walls and a rough romanesque church, is the plateau's one brewery-town. Even without the advertisements you could hardly miss this fact, for the brewery stands as proudly above the Ardèche as if that river were the Liffey or the Lahn; and up from the white cliffs of this southern stream rises an array of mock-fortified towers which would not disgrace Burton, Copenhagen or Dublin itself. To northern eyes it is a sight as refreshing—and as improbable—as would be a pint tankard of draught bitter. But it is no mirage; and after this evidence that French beer is produced by some process remotely resembling fermentation I am even ready to persuade my-self that Ruoms brew is a shade less synthetic, a shade more sincere and substantial, than its rivals.

From a place called St Alban-sous-Sampzon under a perpendicu-lar rock the railway runs south into nowhere: its destination, if one can use so positive a word, is Alès. The Ardèche bends eastward on its own strange course. But westward, up towards the edge of the Cevennes, lies something stranger still.

*

I have a recurrent dream of descending—usually by an ancient hy-draulic lift which turns into something like a narrow-gauge railway train—through basement after basement of a great office block, to emerge in an open landscape miles underground yet roofed by some-thing older and more terrible than the sky. I first walked through this land with my eyes open when I walked through the Bois de Païolive, only a little out of comfortable Les Vans town. It is a *paysage ruiniforme*, but wilder than that of Montpellier-le-Vieux. Baring-Gould amazingly considered it inferior to similar things in Germany, but admitted it all the same to be 'very fantastic and stimulating to the imagination.' For myself, I find the fascination of this wood of Païolive difficult to describe.

For it differs from the surrounding landscape of southern Ardèche by only as much as a waking man differs from a sleeping one or a sleeping one from a corpse: it lies beyond a frontier of being. There is a bare and bleached limestone plateau above the deep chasm where a stream cuts through soil-less rocks and water seeps below the potholes. There are lichened saplings which will never grow from childhood and stunted conifers, box-scrub and a few mulberry trees which have drilled through the rock securely enough to shade a man. Underfoot there are herbs, spicy rather than cool-fragrant when crushed, passionate orchids, violets, and most notably a blue-green kind of spurge with a cactus-look of desert succulence which is called *euphorbia characias*. (This is the only time I intrude Linnaeanism into this book; but the thing is unknown in Britain and so typical of the limestone deserts that I sent some to Exhibition Road for identification.) Finally, there are minuscular creatures—insects and quasi-insects bizarre in colour and form and movement, wee industrious beasties boring through the vegetation, red crickets which explode like rockets from your path, dumbell-shaped things which seem like Fairlie locomotives to have four legs and two eyes going each way, and lizards, the blessed lizards, in their marvellous multifariousness.

But all these flora and fauna could be found above Ruoms or even in the Causses; and yet the Bois de Païolive (whose form, in cold fact, is due to the uneven solubilities of dolomite) is marked on every tourist-map. I like to believe that it was some nightmare-ridden northerner who put it there about a century ago; for only a stranger can understand it, and the fascination and terror of its animate rock and caverns are not of the southern blood. *Envisagez-vous*, then, a wasteland two or three miles either way, 1,500 feet above the sea yet feeling deeper below it. Envisage the sky where earth should be, the living things like fossils, the dead stones like human hands or thigh-bones, baked yet underwater (those are pebbles which were his eyes...) or the whole wide world in the afterflash of the atom age with life toothily surviving. Put into this petrified forest—which is nothing of the sort—a few dwarfed human figures seeking the advertised, abandoned hermitage with the aid of a dye-line *plan-guide* sold in the town hall of les Vans—a document so misleading that it could not have been drawn up solely by human hands since east is west *but not always*. That is the Païolive wood.

*

Illustration 48

The place has two legends. One concerns the kings of Païolive who lived here until the revolution. The other begins a little later, when to support any kind of king was to be an outlaw and when royalists hid themselves in the potholes here: they were smoked-out by sulphur and shot down like foxes, except for those who discovered that one could breathe through a musket-barrel thrust through a crevice. Ponder on these, as you cool your eyes on the rivulet which slips below this cataclysm and runs down to the Ardèche as the Ardèche runs down to the Rhone.

This Ardèche is itself a trivial river for France. It is a trickle to the Aveyron or the Truyère or the Viaur even, it is only the stain a dog makes against a tree to the Gironde streams of Lot and Tarn or to the Allier, it is a dewdrop to the Rhone or the Loire. Yet it christens a department, and rightly so. For in its less-than-100-miles from below Lanarce to Pont St Esprit as basalt gives way to lias and then to dolomite, the Ardèche rehearses every phase of a great river.

Here for instance, in its much-described polychrome gorges, it does all that the Tarn does in four times the length. The most celebrated sight is the 200-foot long—and 200-foot high—natural bridge of the Pont d'Arc, which has played its parts in history from the Romans on. But beyond there are many rocks riddled like gruyère cheese by water-action, many caverns and *goules*, and whispering green grottoes so numerous that the motto of the Ardèche seems 'every man his own grotto'. It is not surprising that Baring-Gould described this as the most extraordinary river in Europe. No road follows the canyon of the Ardèche below its castled guardian towns of Salavas and Merle's stronghold of Vallon (an unexpected place, this latter, wherein to find a distinguished *hôtel-de-ville* with distinguished tapestries, and perhaps an even more unexpected one to have been the site of a forgery combining the best of Ossian and the latest girl-prodigy). Even a canoe or punt, unless guided by a professional used to the shallows and rapids, can rarely in the year keep afloat for more than a reach at a time as you work down to the gorge's end at the abandoned village of Aiguèze. With indefatigable ingenuity, the French tourist trade has now pressed DUKW's into service to give you a view of all these splendours so remote that in medieval times they were leper-land. But it costs about £2 the trip.

*

On the plateau to the south of the river stands les Crottes—one of those massacred villages, those little Oradours, with which the maquis-lands of the massif (and Ardèche was renowned for its guerrillas even in the Franco-Prussian war) are proudly scarred. Beyond that is Orgnac-l'Aven, recently discovered but one of the greater buried splendours in Europe and the peer of Aven Armand: it is a good place to recall the Victorian speleologists who explored all such things by magnesium light and rope ladders, or swung like spiders at the end of 500 feet of rope. And beyond again the rocks of Roquepertuis stand above the sources of many streams and below the boundary of Gard.

The landscape here has changed, changed for the last time. Beyond Barjac great windowless farmhouses and black cypresses grow from the sun-hot rocks: there are the dolmens and menhirs and villages of ancient habitation: the churches are flat-roofed and sometimes crowned by iron lanterns. The look is Provençal: the province is the Languedoc: the Vivarais is most certainly behind now.

But still the familiar images remain, of the spurious life and the real. A honeymoon couple are exploring the hollows, a diligent tourist is evaluating Vallon's tapestry, a speleologist backed by the Ministry is chipping through to another calcite hall of remunerative forms and tints. At the same time a peasant is bent over his scrubby potato-patch with a wooden hoe, the ox and the ass are yoked to their cart, the sheep nibble what nourishment there is off the land. And all below lies the plain with its ancient cities, its Roman ports, its young strong lively latin men. Down there they are taking trains, making machinery, building ships, blending wine. Up here, the aperitif hour will come at six—and the bus next Thursday.

The Last Round Up

The sea—the same sea as I now write these words beside, half-way to Africa—is within sight and almost sound. It was dubious, imagined rather than seen for all that the *tables d'orientation* said, on the cathedral tower of Rodez or the finial of the Mont Lozère. But one does not, on the southern edge of the Causses or the Cevennes, need to climb and gaze in the eye of the terrible noon sun to know that it is there.

The Mediterranean littoral swings round in an unbroken line from the Pyrenees to the Alps; and for all of its length which bears any relation to the Massif Central—from beyond Narbonne, that is, to the Grand Rhone—it belongs to the Languedoc. Once, of course, 'Languedoc' implied the whole half of France south of the Loire, the land where men said '*Oc*' instead of '*Oui*'; and even when the provinces had crystallized into their pre-revolution form it was still the largest of them all. Today it sprawls across six departments: do not believe the guide-books when they try to steal Nimes and the Camargue for the better-known land of Provence.

It is also an extremely homogeneous province, a Latin corridor of olive and aloe and fig and almond which links Italy and Spain like a fast train which happens to pass through France on the way. Between its strange salty shores and the mountain hinterland it is almost a single vineyard—a burning gravel plain scored by straight plane-lined roads, dry watercourses, aqueducts and rusty light railways used once or twice a year for shifting wine. The country, perhaps, has an abandoned look with its roofless farms and its fallen arches. But it is always thus in a Mediterranean land, and the towns *are* Mediterranean with their neon and late nights, their splendid women and their shiny men who, even when bent over their fields look younger,

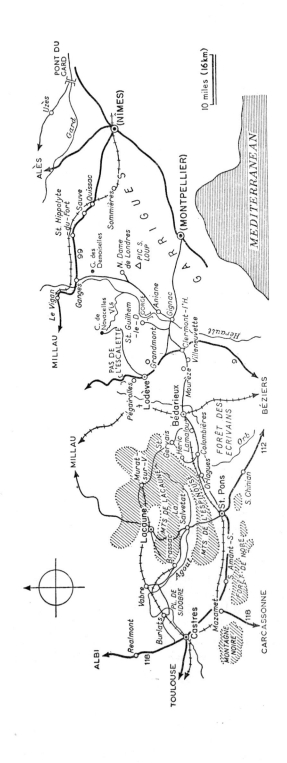

10 miles (16km)

MEDITERRANEAN

PONT DU GARD

Uzès

Gard

ALÈS

(NÎMES)

St. Hippolyte-du-Fort

Sauve

Quissac

Sommières

(MONTPELLIER)

G A R R I G U E S

99

G. des Demoiselles

Ganges

N. Dame de Londres

△ PIC S. LOUP

MILLAU

Le Vigan

C. de Novacelles

St. Guilhem-le-D

V¹⁵

GORGE

Aniane

Gignac

Clermont-l'H.

Villeneuvette

Hérault

PAS DE L'ESCALETTE

Grandmont

MILLAU

Pégairolles

Lodève

9

BÉZIERS

Bédarieux

Mourèze

FORÊT DES ÉCRIVAINS

Murat-sur-V.

Héric

Lamalou

Orlagues-Colombières

Orb

MTS DE L'ACAUNE

Gervais

112

Lacaune

La Salvetat

St. Pons

S. Chinian

Brassac

MTS DE L'ESPINOUSE

MILLAU

Agout

S. Amant-S.

118

CARCASSONNE

Vabre

PL. DE SIDOBRE

FORÊT DE NORÉ

Realmont

Burlats

Castres

Mazamet

MONTAGNE NOIRE

ALBI

118

TOULOUSE

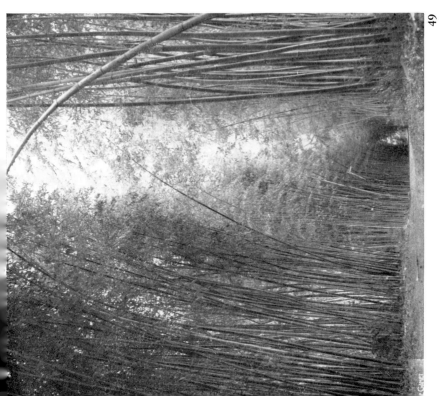

49

50

The curiosities of the southern Cevennes include a bamboo forest (*left*) and the Irish-looking abbatical church of St Guilhem-le-Désert (*right*).

53

Three gateways of the south-east—La Voulte-sur-Rhône (*left, above*), Uzès (*left, below*) and the Pont du Gard (*above*).

51

52

livelier and stronger than Auvergnat peasants and who, in any kind
of uniform, become the smartest-looking cops and bus-conductors in
Europe. It is an individual land, too, which has in its time peacefully
accommodated many races (even Etruscans and Saracens), where
everything has a different name (a *fête* becomes a *faire*, *boule* becomes *petanque*) and where new sports enter. They play *pelote*,
offering prizes still computed in louis d'or: in smoky taverns smelling of ham the bull-fight posters are not a tourist stunt but a part
of vernacular life: Sunday is a day of exhilaration, not slumber.

In this scorched, stained arc which curves from Tarn through
Hérault into Gard you can take a train journey from west to east a
whole day long with almost no change in the feel of the land, no
sense that there is more in the world than the plateau on one hand,
the sea and Africa on the other, and between them this strip dedicated to the desert and the vine. But remember that the shoreline
here is a mysterious mingling of salt and sand, mere and marram-
grass, which makes nonsense of the concept of a 'classic' landscape.
The break between the mountain men and the men of the plains is
no less confusing, and no less fascinating.

*

It is not a matter of distance from the sea, though the swing of this
hemline of the Massif roughly follows the curve of the Lion Gulf.
And it is not a matter of contours, for there are 1,000-foot mounds
only five miles from the coast which belong wholly to the Languedoc
and there is the country behind Alès which is only a few hundred
feet up yet purely Cevenol. Culture rather than geography is what
we are looking for; and so active was the culture which began in
Rome, and which can be read from the railway time-tables today, that
it drove—and drives—not merely up the Rhone almost to Lyons but
over the heights in tongues which touch Millau and almost Rodez.
(One could, for instance, erect a *borne* at every kilometre of the N9
showing its spiritual distance from Béziers.) And one must sometimes seek as far north again to find cities which look to the Loire
rather than the Mediterranean, to Clermont rather than Montpellier.

One has come down from all these heights, these farthest outliers
whose inhabitants still descend like hop-pickers to live in wretched
conditions during the *vendange* or the summer fishing-season, who

are still despised as clottish peasants by their Latin employers, and who still weep for home. But for those fascinated by the changing habits of men—and above all by the presence of this most crucial frontier of all Christendom—the last pleasure awaits.

This is the pleasure of tracing, all across the Languedoc, the tide-lines of high and low water, the overlapping of Latin and Auvergnat man. In the centre and the east the frontiers are rarely more than a few miles apart and sometimes almost coalesce into a single line. But at the western end there is a structural feature which swells this last corridor of the plateau into the shape of a tadpole. Its head is the mountains of Lacaune.

*

The Lacaunes, and their associates such as the Montagne Noire and the forest of Nore, touch the heights of Aveyron and the southernmost Causses; and though you find them on the 83 map sheet they are continuous with all that limestone. Despite this they are quite different in look from, say, the land of St Affrique. Their contours are soft and rounded except on their southern precipices; and treeless as they are their texture is softer than that of the Causses. Their grandeur is perhaps best appreciated from the littoral itself, whence no neighbouring hills obstruct them. Above a typical sun-scorched and Bordeaux-blue wine-town of Hérault like St Chinian, these hills of gneiss and schist and granite and porphyry and mica rise as bare and noble and cool as the downs behind Brighton.

The Lacaunes meet two earlier chapters of this book on their north, and on the west edge gradually down and away until they lose themselves in the Revel gap towards Toulouse. But the happiest entry to them is from the town of Castres, about 600 feet up and standing on the river which runs westward for the full length of the Lacaunes.

Castres is a unique place and far, far more southern in feel than its situation on the latitude of Toulouse prepares one for. One would not be wholly surprised to turn a corner of its peeling lime-washed streets and find a *casbah*. Such of its charms as belong to the Mediterranean plains do not, perhaps, belong here, and I prefer to forget that it was in Castres in 1668 that an illiterate girl claimed to have seen an angel who forbade her to attend Mass, spoke in tongues, and

released all the beastliness of the Camisards. But the town has another thing which links it most colourfully with the great hills. That
is the third of the just-surviving narrow-gauge railways of the massif.

You can meet this in the streets of Castres itself. You can travel a
few first easy miles on it through the green meadows of the Agout.
But after the twelfth-century church of Burlats, where the river
swings away in great ox-bows, the little railway faces the high
shoulder of the comparatively-wooded Plateau de Sidobre.

This is an earthquake landscape of tumbled stones. *Rocs* and
rochers and *chaos* star the map, some with the usual names challeng-
ing you to identify them with homely objects: there are *cirques* and
sauts and *grottes* and *gourps*: and there are a few things which mark
where men have not merely gaped but worshipped or fought—a
menhir or two, witnessing that astonishing civilization which left
identical monuments from the Orkneys to Ceylon, or an isolated
castle. The Sidobre plateau is not a place for trippers, for it is perhaps
ten times the size of the Bois de Païolive and the secondary roads,
like the railway, do no more than skirt its flanks. But there can be
few better places in France for those who like rough walks vaguely
leading somewhere. From very limited experience, I recommend a
compass, hobnail boots and maybe wellingtons too: the place is
notably tougher than Dartmoor.

*

At the end of the plateau, near a town called Vabre, the line divides
at what is amongst the most dizzily-situated junctions in the world
though it is only about 1,500 feet up. A brief spur follows the Agout
southward to Brassac, one of the numerous places in the Lacaunes
(la Salvetat over in Hérault is another) with touristic and even thera-
peutical pretensions. Northward a far longer track drives on, gain-
ing some foothold from a terrifying little tributary, up through a
land of Tennysonian crags jade-stained by lichens and waters swirling wildly in fuming pools, to Lacaune itself.

One says 'itself' because the place names the range; and to do
Lacaune justice it is a bigger village than Aubrac and has a *luxe*ish
hotel. But that does not mean that it is very big—or very active. It
has indeed little to show for itself except a few rocks about a crumbling fourteenth-century fountain, slate roofs contrasting with the

tiles of the lower valley and—since over 2,500 feet up—a very drowsy mountain flavour.

Even this is not quite the end of the metric railway. Beside the tinkling trout-stream, through birchwoods which I once described as among the strangest places in the world to find *any* kind of railway, it struggles still onward and upward to the village of Murat-sur-Vèbre, some thirty miles east of Castres but more hours away than the *Indicateur Chaix* confesses. But there it does end, in a place whose only claim to fame is that a lot of chauffeurs come from it. It was obviously heading for a through-route on over the watershed—over the boulder-strewn peak of the Lacaunes which supports the triple point of Aveyron, Tarn and Hérault, over and down to St Gervais in the forest-country on their east where the streams flow to that strange brief river the Orb, and so to the Mediterranean. But it never dared the pass; and to find this other slope one must return to Castres and take a more conventional railway out of it.

*

The SNCF branch and the 118 (and there are no other *routes nationales* to note here) from Albi and the north have come down to Castres by way of Réalmont. Now, at the big modern town of Mazamet, the route bends eastward through St Amans-Soult to seek an end-on pair of valleys which cut some ten miles south of the Agout but still through uplands. One would have to go ten miles south again to find the ultimate edge of the Massif, for it bulges to its southernmost point in forests which may look a little like the Landes, which may fall into the Pyrenean department of Aude, which may stare down on Carcassonne but which can still (and it is a surprising statistic) touch a contour of 3,500 feet.

This is, then, a true lateral valley of the plateau; and though the railway has few tunnels and the 112 branch road few hairpins, the pass which divides Tarn from Hérault between Labastide (*another* one) and St Pons is still 1,600 feet up and boasts a grotto important enough to have a price on its head. St Pons itself, too, is a most attractive big village: once a cathedral city, it would be comparable to Dorchester (Oxon) if the Wittenham clumps took some vitamin pills. But in all this belt—which sheltered rather eccentric hermits within living memory—there is somehow an incentive not to linger.

High and bare and sterile the mountains rise to the left: to the south they are still there though infused by the sense of an expiring upthrust. And between them the line moves on round this northern curve of Hérault and under the part of the Lacaunes which are called the Monts de l'Espinouse—on to Olargues and its ancient bridge, on to the small gorges which feed the Orb, on past Héric and Colombières and a forest which I ought to have explored since it is called the Forêt des Ecrivains, on to the residential watering-place of the area, Lamalou, whose claims to cure St Vitus' Dance once rated a through-train from Paris, and so at last a final node at Bédarieux.

Bédarieux is a dense, half-industrial place which never seems to have recovered from a strike of avaricious miners sixty years ago. It also partakes a little of the spa, as do many of the towns of this deeply-sheltered, luxuriant and populous flank where it seems that a whole civilization is pressing back against the Causses. But it is a station of much more importance in the English sense; for it is here that, through a tangle of unrelated-looking and tunnel-carved tracks, the arterial railway comes plunging down, at last within a pant of Béziers, Montpellier, journey's end.

Remember, though, that the line did make a swing away from the 9 road to avoid the Causses. It chose Roquefort rather than Le Caylar; and so to meet the highway one must move on again, closing a curtain across the Lacaunes, to rest in Lodève.

*

I know few better places in France to rest in. For Lodève, *sous-préfecture* of Hérault and quietly prosperous from the wool-trade of the sheep who at spring and autumn work their *transhumance* along the *drexilles* between the littoral and the hills, has just the feeling I like in a town. Not too noisy, not too dim, it is typical of this red-limestone hemline, and resembles or excels le Vigan as well as having (for it too is an abandoned railhead) affinities with Privas. You *can* find life here—Mediterranean, Ligurian life in the cafés, barbers' shops and busy bus-parks with their loud-speakers—but the hotels are large and old-fashioned and rather deserted, quite different from anything one would expect on the great 9 road. You will hear more foreign than French spoken in them, too. It is as if transport needed the extra impetus of coming from Calais or Brussels rather than Paris to carry it all the way down the long 450 miles.

Lodève has a fine fourteenth-century church—an ex-cathedral, like so many hereabouts, dedicated to one of the most amiable figures of that curiously civilized part of European history, the French ninth century, St Fulcram. Despite Fabre and the accidentally odd proportions of the place, I find this pure northern gothic. There is another good church or abbey at Grandmont near by, where also you will find a classic dolmen. But to me this town—in many ways reminiscent of Galway—is remembered by the sound of its river, the cool waters which come down from the hills and swirl and chatter above its weir or below its ancient bridge, and all the history of its hundred bishops.

Stand here as dusk comes down, luminous and Latin, darkly alive with men as well as with bats and swallows. Perhaps two hours' walk away a black ridge bristling with menhirs rises against Polaris: it is the last line of the Causses, but the same as you will see from Florac where now they are all asleep. The lights which you can just discern beyond the pretty village of Pégairolles are the lights of le Caylar, only ten miles north but a thousand feet higher. And between lies the weathered, dolomite horseshoe of the Pas de l'Escalette which less than sixty years ago travellers had to climb by ladder, and which is still as great an entry as the whole massif can show.

The historic village and the *cirque* of fabulous rocks of Mourèze, the noble troubadours' town of Clermont-l'Hérault to the south, and the seventeenth-century model town of Villeneuvette with its army serge monopoly, barely belong here; for at Lodève these figures-of-eight southernmost hills have narrowed to a corridor, a line, perhaps even a point. The ranges which to its east balance the Aubracs are little smaller in area, but except round the Pic St Loup near Notre-Dame-de-Londres they rarely climb even to 1,500 feet. They are densely wooded, with a population including a species of oak once cultivated hereabouts because it fed the red-dye-making kermes insect; but they are nameless, a mere collection of Bois *de* this-or-that, spreading for the thirty or forty miles from Lodève east and a little north to Alès.

There are one or two towns of note on the northern edge of this belt, such as St Hippolyte-du-Fort with its confused ecclesiological history, Sauve, Quissac and Sommières, all on the devious railway line which comes down from le Vigan; and there are the last remnants of two local crops—the nettlewood tree which grows agricultural implements 'on the hoof', and the herbs of the chalk-white desert country called the *garrigues*. But elsewhere this is a belt less populous even than the Lacaunes, one whose greenness on the map is broken only by a scattering of villages, a ruined frontier castle or two, and the three tourist sights which are all which lure strangers into the area.

There is the Cirque de Navacelles, a spectacular enough but perhaps over-famed bend where water cuts 1,000 feet below the blindingly limestone-white plateau. There is St Guilhem-le-Désert which, though far south and only a few hundred feet above the sea, is set in wild picturesqueness amid these woodlands. It surprises by the latter part of its name; the former part derives from a snub-nosed but noble character who as aristocrat, troubadour, carolingian cavalier and monk alike epitomized all that was noblest in the ninth century. But here the woods thin to the bareness of the Causses from which the Hérault and its mysterious, shrunken, half-buried Vis tributary have come, born middle-aged and doomed soon to die; and St Guilhem is a fascinating spot. It is essentially a tiny but dramatic village with an abbatical church—which still enshrines the relic of the True Cross which William received from St Zachanaus—deep down in the lonely meadows of the Hérault and with numerous other gorges and waterfalls and ruined towers about it: the church itself is rude, romantic, half-ruined and (again) Irish-looking. Here one feels that the Hérault, as it leaves the last of the hills and runs down to Aniane and Gignac, must be heading for the westernmost Atlantic rather than the middle sea.

There remains the Grotte des Demoiselles, back on the northern edge. The most famous of all the numerous cave-sequences which open out of this turmoil of escarpments, it is indeed the peer in fame of Armand or Orgnac—and far older, since opened in 1780 or nearly a century before Martel established the industry. I do not think this is the place to describe the maidens' cave at any length; but I would like to record that one visits its illuminated splendours with the help of a little electric railway, a fact which has hitherto escaped those of us who thought we knew all the odd railways of France.

*

263

Illustration 50

Beyond the grottoes, at this latitude, the hills fall for the very last time into the plain of Languedoc which streams past Nimes to the Rhone. If there is a final lingering taste of Auvergnat things to be found amid the vine and the olive, the dust and the Mediterranean mistral, it is not there but north-eastward, beyond St Hippolyte-du-Fort, in the dim basin of the Gard and Gardons about Alès. And even there, perhaps, it all comes down to the single city of Uzès.

I would like to claim Uzès for this book; for though my first experience of it as I came down through a snowstorm of many winters past was less than happy, I have since come to hold it as one of the golden dozen such towns in France and—if only for those arcades more typical of southern Aveyron or of Ardèche than of Gard— almost the equal of Villefranche-de-Rouergue. The interior of the castle which was once the seat of the premier dukes of France (and hence linked to many Auvergnat sites) is a pointless Victorian sell: but its skyline is overwhelming, all black and green and gold with tiles which could come from Beaune, forms which recall Mantua, and yet—perhaps—some last Auvergnat hint even though it stands on an isolated and dramatic crest, little more than 600 feet up, south even of Alès and separated from the last of the Cevennes by a pebbly basin more reminiscent of the Craus of Provence than of either the plateau or the Languedoc.

I cannot call Uzès an Auvergnat city, whatever its historical links: it is an outrider, not yoked to the team. Still less can I trespass down the valley to the Pont du Gard, which is nearer in time and space and spirit to Marseilles or even Genoa than to Montluçon. And yet, and yet ... when a man comes upon this titanic arch from long sojourns in Latin lands it is possible to see even it not merely as engineering or archaeology or architecture, but as a symbol too. Is it itself, perhaps, only the last and grandest of all the lodge-gates to the fastness of France?

Illustrations 52, 53

Envoi

It is over five years now since my publishers and I conceived this book; and at first it seemed a simple enough project. After all (I thought) I had crossed the Massif many times and knew its solitudes and its few but memorable cities, its small old towns and its host of tiny tourist villages of which all that can be said *has* been said once one has recorded their names, its peaks and its rivers. My mind's eye then fused all that I knew into a single impression like that in a medieval manuscript. There was a walled town which might have been Murol or St Flour, standing on cliffs above a foam-flecked river and with all about it a single lonely landscape of purple and gold, sunlight and storm-light, rounded for the most part but broken here and there by grey or blue-black rocks.

Like many medieval visions this was symbolically right. But in literal detail it was very, very misleading.

For five years *have* passed—five seasons of the *montade* and *dévalade* of cows and Virgins, five springs of sunlight and autumns of snow, five tourist summers of headlamps skimming past the white marker-posts of hairpin bends and the redcap *bornes* along the *routes nationales*, and five winters of ski-slithers and peasant isolation. I have crossed these heights, have watched them from below as an astronomer watches the seasons change on the face of Venus, and have even been flown high over them, through a whole lustrum of water flowing quietly away to the ancient bridges of Aquitaine and of

> 'Red Rhones in flood (which) thunder down
> Past many a tower'd and tiery town.'

Always, it seemed, my land could with sufficient acquaintance be grasped as a whole and cut down to size. But always it expanded and fragmented, until my vision became a refracting glass of a hundred landscapes and a thousand towns.

This, then, has not been a swift or easy book to assemble. At one stage, indeed, it threatened to divide into two by a kind of amoebic fission, and we even considered tearing the map in half somewhere south of Clermont. But the mechanical problems of writer and publisher are, after all, their *own* problems. And this long delay in composition would not be worth referring to were it not that in the interim France and the Auvergne have changed.

The signs of what is most positive about these changes are almost misleadingly conspicuous—the garages which improve in ratio as the hotels decline, the fluorescent light lying livid on mass-produced clothing and tinned food, the commercialization of everything of use or beauty which can be commercialized. It is easy to blame the coming of the civilization which these things represent on to a penetration from America. But a new culture does not arise unless an old one is dying.

Today France does many things—running trains to time, building steel mills, exploring atoms and space—as well as any comparable nation. She does some things, like executing hydro-electric projects, better than any other nation I know. But these techniques—however admirable, important and exciting in their own way—are habitation-less ones; and one can only *love* a land for its differences. There is no harm in drinking Coca-Cola—if you do not forget how to drink Chambertin. There is no harm in building a Chastang—if you remember how to build a Chartres.

Does France recall these ancient arts? My answer must be that I see little enough sign of it. Can she recover them? My answer must be that I doubt it. Perhaps the good wine of France has been over-praised too long: now, unmistakably, the taste of water is striking through.

So at the end the light fades on this book. Yet much abides, and not least amid the deep spaces of the Auvergne. The cities remain, sleeping below the centuries of history which lie on them like coverlets. The small and great rivers remain, and all the bare or purple heights between. The last of the old and independent men remain. France remains—or her ghost does.

Index

The author would like it to be known—if only to his publisher and his wife —that the classified index which follows has been compiled (like the book itself) on a system.

In the first place, it is a purely topographical index which omits any reference to personalities or to the general topics of Chapter I. Within those limitations, the first section lists all the departments referred to in the book— out of their logical order, perhaps–so as to establish the contractions which are used later.

The second section attempts to separate the *inhabited places* of the Massif —whether great cities or a couple of huts sheltering under a castle—from the pure curiosities. In this section, particularly, I have had to make my own ortho- graphical rules, for the French are no more consistent than any other nation about the spelling of place-names and certain Auvergnat ones border on the barbaric. I have in general followed the usage of the Michelin maps (rather than guides) in this, except where it seemed to conflict with local usage.

In collating, I have followed what I take to be standard practice in dis- regarding the definite article except where it is conjoined to the name—e.g. 'Babory, le', but 'Labastide'; in listing the saints (first male and then female) in a separate sub-section, and otherwise in following strict alphabetical order irrespective of hyphens or separated words.

The third section is a hotchpotch of what the schoolbooks call principal geographical *features*—at first sub-classified, but concluding with a miscel- lany of sights and artefacts. In this I have assumed that it is 'Armand (Aven)' rather than 'Aven Armand' which will be sought. The index concludes with a section on divisions other than departments.

Throughout this book, my guiding principle has been that text, maps and index should agree as to content—though for various technical, aesthetic, economic or personal reasons I have agreed that the maps should be incon- sistent as regards the capitalization of le's and la's and that certain place- names like Cevennes, Nimes, Rhone and Lyons should be anglicized in one place and left in their French form in another. But everything that is *of*, rather than *marginal to*, the Massif should be found in all three places.

Finally, I have generally given only single references to places and fea- tures which are mentioned in the text several times: these are usually to the first mention, unless this is casual and a much more important one follows. An exception to this rule is made for rivers and roads, which by their nature flow through several chapters.

All these explanations make a fairly lengthy introduction to an index. But then, with nearly a thousand entries, it is a fairly lengthy index.

Index

Index

Index

Index

Index

III FEATURES

A ROADS

B RIVERS

Index

Index

Index

IV POLITICAL

For Departments, see start of Index

279